Peer-to-Peer
Leadership
Transforming Student Culture

Gregory Metz
University of Cincinnati

Joseph B. Cuseo
Emeritus, Marymount College

Aaron Thompson
Eastern Kentucky University

W9-ADG-993

Kendall Hunt

Book Team

Chairman and Chief Executive Officer   Mark C. Falb
President and Chief Operating Officer   Chad M. Chandlee
Vice President, Higher Education   David L. Tart
Director of Publishing Partnerships   Paul B. Carty
Senior Developmental Editor   Lynnette M. Rogers
Vice President, Operations   Timothy J. Beitzel
Assistant Vice President, Production Services   Christine E. O'Brien
Senior Production Editor   Charmayne McMurray
Permissions Editor   Caroline Kieler
Cover Designer   Janelle Cannavo

Cover image © Shutterstock, Inc.

www.kendallhunt.com
Send all inquiries to:
4050 Westmark Drive
Dubuque, IA 52004-1840

Printed in the United States of America
10 9 8 7 6 5 4 3 2 1

Brief Contents

Table of Contents

Contents

Chapter 11: Civic Leadership: Making Change at Local, National, and Global Levels 295

If you're reading this book, you are, or soon will be, a peer leader. Congratulations! Your efforts will enrich the quality of the college experience for the students you lead and the quality of education provided by your college or university. Don't underestimate the impact of your role. As you will see in the very first chapter of this book, research resoundingly shows that peer leaders exert positive influence in many ways, roles, and situations. You have the potential to improve your campus, your community, and your world "from the ground up."

Plan and Purpose of This Book

Effective leadership involves a varied, multidisciplinary knowledge base and a wide assortment of skills. Nobody could or should expect you to master them in a day, a week, a year, or even a lifetime. The best you can do is to (1) become knowledgeable about what constitutes effective leadership, (2) use that knowledge to develop an intentional leadership plan, (3) put that plan into action, (4) seek feedback regularly on how well you're doing, and (5) use that feedback to continually grow as a leader.

This book is designed to help you become the best peer leader you can possibly be by touching all the bases of effective leadership and equipping you with the most powerful leadership principles. The book helps you get it right from the start by providing you with a strategic plan that's built on a solid foundation of leadership research. If you haven't been a leader in the past, this book will help you become one in the future; if you've had previous leadership experience, this book will make you an even more effective leader.

One of the most powerful principles of effective leadership is *mindfulness*. When we are mindful, we're aware of what we're doing while we're doing it and know whether we're doing it effectively. Self-awareness is the critical first step toward self-improvement and successful performance of any role we play in life, including the role of leader. As a peer leader, if you get in the habit of watching yourself as a leader and maintain awareness of whether you're doing leadership well (e.g., if you're applying the key principles identified in this book), you have taken a giant step toward becoming an effective leader.

Specific, action-oriented strategies grounded in the college experience make up the heart of this book. You will find that these practical strategies are not presented to you in the form of a laundry list of leadership tips. Instead, the recommended strategies are accompanied by a research-based rationale for *why* they are effective, and they are organized into broader *principles* that tie the strategies together into a meaningful plan. It's not only important to know *what* to do as an effective leader, but also *why* you should do it. If you understand the research and reasoning behind a suggested strategy, you're more likely to learn it on a deeper level and apply it in a wider variety of leadership roles and situations. We believe that you're ready and able to meet the challenge of deep learning with respect to

> *The man who knows how will always have a job. The man who also knows why will always be his boss.*
>
> —Ralph Waldo Emerson, influential 19th-century American essayist, poet, and champion of personal freedom

leadership, and that you will find it more intellectually stimulating than simply amassing a long list of leadership tips or completing a series of leadership exercises and activities.

Since the strategies recommended in this book are research-based, you will see references cited throughout all the chapters and will find a sizable reference section at the end of the book. The references cited represent a balanced blend of older classic studies and more recent cutting-edge findings from a wide variety of fields. This range of research underscores the fact that the subject of leadership, like any other subject in the college curriculum, is a scholarly field that is supported by a solid body of knowledge that spans many decades.

Author's Experience I have been associated with peer leaders and mentors throughout my professional career, and most recently have had the privilege of coordinating an extensive peer-led Learning Communities program at the University of Cincinnati. I have learned from each peer leader and each leader of peer leaders. I have been inspired and informed by a number of books on peer leadership, but have not found one that brings together the mentoring, team-building, academic support, and connecting roles that effective peer leaders perform. So, along with my colleagues, I humbly but excitedly accepted this challenge of putting together a resource to help peer leaders and mentors thrive in their varied and challenging roles. Writing this book has provided me with an opportunity to share what I have learned from my professional experiences with peer leaders, from my professional colleagues, and from the many peer leaders I've worked with over the course of my career.

— *Greg Metz*

Preview of Content

Chapter 1
The Purpose and Power of Peer Leadership

In this introductory chapter, you will identify what leadership means and why peer leadership matters. It lays out the variety of areas, roles, and positions in which peers can serve as leaders in higher education. The chapter pulls together numerous studies indicating that students who receive mentoring and guidance from peer leaders are more likely to continue in college, complete their college degrees, and get the most of their college experience. Research also shows that when peer leaders help other students, they also help their campus achieve its educational mission, and they help themselves by acquiring skills that promote their personal and professional success beyond college.

Chapter 2
The Essence of Leadership: Foundational Principles, Practices, and Personal Attributes

This chapter identifies the myths and realities of effective leadership, and provides an overview of the core characteristics of effective leaders. The chapter equips you with powerful principles of effective leadership that are the foundation for all strategies and practices presented throughout the book, and which are applicable in virtually all leadership positions and situations.

Chapter 3

The College Experience: Applying Student Development Research and Theory to Promote Student Success

The college experience, particularly the first year of college, can be a life-changing transition for students during which they experience immense learning and personal growth. Unfortunately, the initial passage to college is also the time when students experience the greatest challenges, the most stress, the most academic difficulties, and the highest dropout rate. The highs and lows of college underscore the importance of peer support and positive peer influence for student success. This chapter will help you gain a deeper understanding of the college experience in general and the first-year experience in particular, the causes of student success and failure, and the most effective practices for helping students remain in college, attain their college degrees, and get the most out of their college experience.

Chapter 4

Social and Emotional Intelligence: The Foundation of Effective Leadership

Relating to and communicating with others is an important life skill and an important form of "social intelligence." Similarly, "emotional intelligence"—the ability to identify and manage our emotions when dealing with others, and to be aware of how our emotions influence our thoughts and actions—is essential to effective leadership. This chapter supplies effective strategies for communicating, interacting, and creating meaningful relationships with students that enable you to be an effective student-support and student-referral agent.

Chapter 5

Setting Goals, Managing Time, and Maintaining Motivation

Helping students succeed begins with helping them identify their goals and the means (succession of steps) they need to take to reach their goals. Studies show that when students set specific goals, they're more likely to be successful than when they simply tell themselves that they're going to try hard or do their best. This chapter contains practical leadership strategies for helping students set goals, manage the time and tasks required to reach their goals, and maintain their motivation until their goals are reached.

Chapter 6

Becoming a Learning Coach: Helping Students Learn Deeply and Think Critically

This chapter is designed to help you help students become more committed, dedicated, and effective learners. It empowers you to be a "learning coach" by providing you with specific, research-based strategies that you can share and model for students to improve their performance on all academic tasks required in college, such as note taking, reading, studying, and test taking. The chapter's ultimate objective is to help you foster meaningful, long-lasting learning in your peers that moves them beyond memorizing and regurgitating factual information toward deeper learning and higher levels of critical and creative thinking.

Chapter 7

Holistic Leadership: Leading and Developing the Whole Person

Students cannot reach their full potential and achieve peak levels of personal performance without attending to all key elements that comprise the "self": mind, body, and spirit. Successful learning and personal development depend on students maintaining wellness and being mindful of what they put into their bodies (healthy food), what they keep out of them (unhealthy substances), and how well they restore them (sleep). Success also hinges on how well students handle emotional stressors (e.g., anxiety and depression) that can interfere with their academic performance and their ability to persist to completion of their goals. This chapter supplies you with leadership strategies for helping students cope with the stress of college life, maintain balance in their lives, and develop themselves as "whole" human beings.

Chapter 8

Leading Groups: Understanding Group Dynamics and Facilitating Teamwork

Leadership often involves having a positive impact on groups of people rather than individuals. High-impact leaders understand how groups function and how groups can be transformed from collections of individuals into spirited teams. This chapter prepares you for leading groups by supplying you with strategies for building a group vision and maintaining group commitment to that vision. It also equips you with practical skills for motivating and managing groups, making presentations to groups, facilitating group discussions, and reaching group decisions.

Chapter 9

Leadership for Diversity: Appreciating and Harnessing the Power of Human Differences

This chapter explains what *diversity* truly means and explains how it can deepen students' learning, elevate their critical and creative thinking, and enrich their personal and professional lives. Simply stated, we learn more from people who differ from us than we do from people similar to us. The chapter provides ideas for breaking down barriers and biases that block students from developing rewarding relationships with members of diverse groups, and supplies you with strategies for fostering collaboration and mentoring among students from different cultural backgrounds.

Chapter 10

Organizational Leadership: Making Change at a College-Wide Level

Leadership can go from influencing individuals or small groups to influencing entire organizations. Leading in this larger arena requires knowledge of how organizational systems operate and how you can "work the system" to make it work for you and your leadership cause. This chapter identifies organizational leadership strategies that you can use to promote positive change in student organizations you lead or on your campus as a whole through effective use of positional power, committee work, assessment data, and persuasion strategies.

Chapter 11
Civic Leadership: Making Change at Local, National, and Global Levels

Peer leadership can extend beyond the campus community to promote positive change on a wider scale that includes the local community (neighborhood), the nation, and the world. These wider forms of civic leadership are examined in this chapter and specific leadership strategies are provided for promoting students' civic engagement through community service, voting in local and national elections, and political involvement in worthy societal and global causes.

Appendix
Leadership Self-Assessment

Effective leaders engage in an ongoing process of taking stock of where they are and identifying what they need to know and do to get better. The self-assessment questions contained in the Appendix are designed to support you in this process of continuous leadership improvement.

Epilogue
Leadership: A Matter of Character

When all is said and done, strong leadership stems from something larger than acquiring knowledge about and applying effective leadership strategies. It emerges from an inner core of positive qualities (virtues) that define a person of character. The Epilogue defines *character* and demonstrates how effective and ethical leadership is built on a foundation of five key character traits: wisdom, integrity, drive, discipline, and determination.

Sequencing of Chapters

The book's chapters are arranged in an order that asks and answers the following sequence of questions:

1. Why is peer leadership important?
2. What are the attributes, skills, and practices of effective leaders?
3. How do I become an effective leader in different leadership situations on campus and beyond?

The early chapters are intended to reinforce your decision to become a peer leader and help you discover what leadership roles and positions best fit your leadership interests and talents. These initial chapters are intended to supply you with a blueprint or mental map for developing leadership self-awareness and leadership role-awareness. The middle chapters are designed to prepare you for the practical, day-to-day realities and responsibilities of peer leadership in college. The final chapters focus on leadership in a larger context and how you can apply what you learned in the book to leadership roles beyond campus.

Process and Style of Presentation

How information is delivered (the process) is as important as *what* information is delivered (the content). When writing this book, we made an intentional attempt to infuse the content with the following effective-learning processes.

Reflections

At the *start* of each chapter, a question is posed to activate your thoughts and feelings about the chapter topic. This pre-reading exercise is designed to "warm up" or "tune up" your brain, preparing it to connect the ideas you're about to encounter in the chapter with the ideas you already have in your head. It's an instructional strategy that implements one of the most powerful principles of human learning: we learn most effectively by connecting what we're about to learn with what we have previously learned or experienced.

Throughout each chapter, questions are interspersed that allow you time to pause and reflect on the material you've just read. These timely pauses are designed to keep you mentally active throughout the reading process. They serve to break up and break down "attention drift" that typically takes place when the brain continually receives and processes information for an extended period of time—as it does while reading.

These reflections also deepen your understanding of the material you read because they prompt you to *write* in response to what you're reading. Writing encourages thoughtful reflection, deepens learning, and stimulates a higher level of thinking than simply underlining or highlighting sentences.

Multiple Modes of Information Input

Within each chapter, information is delivered through a variety of formats that include diagrams, pictures, images, advice from current and former peer leaders, words of wisdom from famous and successful people, and personal stories drawn from the authors' experiences. Delivering information through multiple formats allows you to process that information through multiple sensory modalities (input channels), which enables it to be stored in multiple places in your brain. This deepens learning and strengthens memory by recording multiple memory traces (tracks) in your brain.

Boxed Material

At different points in the text, you'll find boxes containing summaries of key concepts and strategies. These boxed summaries are designed to pull together all the major ideas relating to the same concept and get them in the same place on the page so they get in the same place in your brain.

Sidebar Quotes

Quotes from famous and influential people appear in the side margins that relate to and reinforce ideas discussed in the chapter. You'll find quotes from accomplished individuals who have lived in different historical periods and who have been successful leaders in a wide variety of fields, including politics, philosophy, religion, science, business, music, art, and athletics. The wide-ranging time frames, cultures, and fields of leadership represented by the people quoted demonstrate how the wisdom of their words is timeless and universal. You can learn a lot from the firsthand experiences and actual words of real people. It's our hope that the words of these highly successful and respected leaders will inspire you to aspire to similar levels of achievement.

Tales from the Trenches

Throughout the book, you'll find insights from students and advice from peer leaders at different stages of the college experience as well as recent college graduates. Studies show that students can learn a great deal from their peers, especially from students who've "been there and done that." As a peer leader, you can learn much from the success stories and stumbling blocks of other peer leaders and from the students they've led.

Authors' Experiences

In each chapter, you will find personal stories drawn from the authors' experiences. We have learned many lessons from our years of work with peer leaders, as college instructors, as student advisors, and as former college students ourselves. We share these experiences with you for the purpose of personalizing the book and with the hope that you'll learn from them—even if it's learning not to make the same mistakes we made!

Concept Maps

The book contains a number of concept (idea) maps that visually organize ideas into diagrams, images, and figures. When you see key concepts in a visual-spatial format, you're more likely to retain them because two different memory traces are recorded in your brain: verbal (words) and visual (images).

Internet Resources

At the end of each chapter, you'll find websites for additional information relating to the chapter's major ideas. Our hope is that the material presented for each chapter topic will stimulate your interest and motivation to learn more about the topic. If it does, you can use the online resources cited at the end of the chapter to access additional information relating to the major ideas covered within the chapter.

Exercises

At the end of each chapter are leadership exercises designed to help you think more deeply about the material covered in the chapter and to apply it to your leadership role on campus. Acquiring knowledge is just the first step to effective performance; it needs to be followed by translating that knowledge into action through application.

> One must learn by doing. For though you think you know, you have no certainty until you try.
> —Sophocles, ancient Greek philosopher

Self-Assessment Questions

In the Appendix, there are leadership self-assessment questions relating to each chapter of the book. This is not a test! It is a tool designed to stimulate self-examination and self-development. You can answer these self-assessment questions at any time during your leadership experience to assess where you are now, and you can assess how you've changed or improved by answering these questions before and after you've had more leadership training and experience.

> The unexamined life is not worth living.
> —Socrates, legendary Greek philosopher

This is more than just a textbook to help peer leaders help other students. By learning and modeling the strategies contained in this book, you will not only contribute to the success of others, but to your own success as well.

It is our hope that the ideas presented in this book, and the manner in which the ideas are presented, will motivate and empower you to make the most of your peer leadership experience. If you continually strive to apply the ideas in this book, you should continue to thrive as a leader in college and beyond.

Sincerely,

Greg Metz, Joe Cuseo, & Aaron Thompson

Acknowledgments

I am grateful for great friends, great colleagues, great professional networks, a great wife and daughter, and the hundreds of incredible peer educators I have worked with over the years at the University of Cincinnati. I thank you, Paul Carty of Kendall Hunt, for having the vision for this book, seeking my participation, and being persistent and patient during its ebbs and flows. I thank you, Pam Person, for your imagination, ingenuity, and artfulness in cultivating UC's First-Year Experience and Learning Communities Program, placing your faith in me to lead the peer educator program, and heartily supporting my involvement in this book and similar efforts. You are a colleague and friend. Thank you to co-authors Joe Cuseo and Aaron Thompson—amazingly engaged educators, difference makers, and fine human beings. I thank my wife Sharon and daughter Lauren for your understanding as I toiled many a weekend with drafts of these manuscripts. You are my lights. Most of all, thank you to hundreds and hundreds of peer educators that I have worked directly with at the University of Cincinnati and thousands of others that I have yet to meet. Your care for, concern for, and commitment to fellow students is truly laudable and remarkable. You make a profound difference each day in students' lives. We must transform learning and teaching in higher education. You have the power and potential to play integral roles. I hope this is just the beginning.

Greg Metz

Peers have made a major difference in my life, starting with two of my best childhood friends (Brian and Michael McMahon), who welcomed me into their neighborhood and led me to value the person I was, rather than trying to persuade or pressure me to be someone that I wasn't. I also owe a lot to my unofficial peer mentor in graduate school, Jim Cooper, who took interest in me as a whole human being and took as much pride in my accomplishments as he did in his own. Lastly, I'd like to thank the peer leaders who did so much for my son while he was in college, helping to transform him from a self-conscious, cancer-stricken high school student into a peer leader in his own right; they changed his life.

Joe Cuseo

There are many peers in my life that have had powerful influences on my professional and personal development: those peers who protected me from the bullies, those who helped guide me through some rough waters in high school, college, and graduate school, and those coworkers and friends who "had my back" and got me back on track as an adult when I sometimes got off track. I want to thank all of them for being my friends, mentors, and leaders.

Aaron Thompson

About the Authors

Greg Metz is the Assistant Director of the University of Cincinnati First-Year Experience and Learning Communities Program. Greg oversees UC's extensive Learning Community Peer Educator Program. The program trains and supports 80 to 100 peer educators each year and typically serves more than 1,500 first-year students each year. For over 20 years, Greg has taught extensively at the undergraduate and graduate levels as well as in high school, coordinated college opportunity programs, worked in K–12 school change efforts, designed and taught first year seminars, and has been a faculty member for the Peer Educator Institute of the National Resource Center for First-Year Experience and Students in Transition. Greg is a wholehearted music aficionado and basketball fanatic. Greg still plays hoops and will for as long as he can.

Joe Cuseo holds a doctoral degree in educational psychology and assessment from the University of Iowa. He is a professor emeritus of psychology at Marymount College (California), where for more than 25 years he directed the first-year seminar, a college success course required of all new students. He was also a 14-time recipient of the Faculty Member of the Year Award, a student-driven award based on effective teaching and academic advising. He's been a recent recipient of the Outstanding First-Year Student Advocate Award from the National Resource Center for the First-Year Experience and Students in Transition, as well as the American College Personnel Association (ACPA) Diamond Honoree Award for contributions made to student development and the student affairs profession.

Joe has delivered numerous campus workshops and conference presentations across the United States, as well as Canada, Europe, China, and Australia. He's authored multiple articles, monographs, and books on student learning, student retention, and student success. Currently, Joe serves as an educational advisor and consultant for AVID, a nonprofit organization whose mission is to promote the college readiness and success of underserved student populations.

Aaron Thompson, Ph.D., is the senior vice president for academic affairs at the Kentucky Council on Postsecondary Education and a professor of sociology in the Department of Educational Leadership and Policy Studies at Eastern Kentucky University. Thompson has a Ph.D. in sociology in the areas of organizational behavior and race and gender relations. Thompson has researched, taught, and/or consulted in the areas of assessment, diversity, leadership, ethics, research methodology and social statistics, multicultural families, race and ethnic relations, student success, first-year students, retention, and organizational design. He is nationally recognized in the areas of educational attainment, academic success, and cultural competence.

Dr. Thompson has worked in a variety of capacities within two-year and four-year institutions. He got his start in college teaching within a community college. His latest co-authored books are *Infusing Diversity and Cultural Competence into Teacher Education; Diversity and the College Experience; Thriving in the Community College and Beyond: Research-Based Strategies for Academic Success and Personal Development; Humanity, Diversity, & the Liberal Arts: The Foundation of a College Education; Focus on Success;* and *Black Men and Divorce.* His upcoming book is entitled *The Sociological Outlook.* He has more than 30 publications and numerous research and peer-reviewed presentations. Thompson has traveled over the U.S. and internationally, giving more than 700 workshops, seminars, and invited lectures in the areas of race and gender diversity, living an unbiased life, overcoming obstacles to gain success, creating a school environment for academic success, cultural competence, workplace interaction, organizational goal setting, building relationships, the first-year seminar, and a variety of other topics. He has been or is a consultant to educational institutions, corporations, nonprofit organizations, police departments, and other governmental agencies.

The Purpose and Power of Peer Leadership

What Is Leadership?

Although there are different models, theories, and styles of leadership, all forms of effective leadership have one thing in common: they promote *positive change* (HERI, 1996; Komives, Lucas, & McMahon, 2007; Kouzes & Posner, 2008). Thus, a leader is a *change agent* who exerts positive influence on (1) individuals, such as helping fellow students reach their personal potential and achieve their personal goals, or (2) groups, communities, and organizations, such as a college or university (Conner, 1992; Kouzes & Posner, 1988; Veechio, 1997).

> *The work of leaders is change. And all change requires that leaders seek ways to make things better.*
>
> —Kouzes & Posner, *The Student Leadership Challenge*

The Range and Scope of Leadership

As illustrated in **Box 1.1** below, leadership takes place at different points along a spectrum or continuum, ranging from the micro (changing an individual) to the macro (changing society).

Box 1.1

The Leadership Spectrum: Micro to Macro

Macro

Society—civic leadership or political change at a larger societal level (e.g., student service in the local or regional community, or at the national level).

Organization—promoting change in an organization's policies, programs, practices or procedures (e.g., as a student government officer or club president).

Group—promoting change or empowering others in small- or large-group settings (e.g., as an orientation group leader or peer co-instructor for a first-year seminar course).

Individual—promoting positive change in other individuals, one person at a time (e.g., helping students individually as a peer tutor or peer counselor).

Micro

Reflection 1.2

In which of the micro-to-macro leadership *contexts or situations* described in Box 1.1 do you think you have the most interest or potential as a peer leader? Why?

Why Peer Leadership Matters in the 21st Century

A college degree has always been a stepping stone to personal development, career advancement, and access to leadership positions in society. However, in today's knowledge-driven, globally interdependent world, a college education is more essential than at any other time in history. The expectation now is that all young people should continue their formal education after high school in order to be effective in today's workforce and accommodate the current economic challenges facing the nation (College Board, 2008b; McCabe, 2000). Our "knowledge-based economy" now requires six out of every ten jobs to be filled by someone who has completed at least some type of postsecondary education (Carnevale & Desrochers, 2003). In this unforgiving labor market, college students must complete in order to compete; if they withdraw from college without completing a credential or degree, their prospects for finding gainful employment will be seriously jeopardized (Collins, 2009). Moreover, among those students who withdraw from college, three out of ten will depart with loan debt (Johnson et al., 2009). Thus, students who do not complete college pay a double penalty: they incur immediate debt and at the same time they forfeit subsequent income (and other benefits) associated with attainment of a postsecondary credential.

Some students show up on campus already equipped with the personal, academic, and civic attributes needed for success in today's world. However, for many students, there are gaps between their day-to-day habits and the habits they need to develop in order to succeed in the 21st century. Other students may come to college with productive habits, but may still lack personal direction. As a peer leader, you can play a pivotal role in helping students persist to complete their degrees and make the most out of their college experience. Ultimately, students are responsible for their own actions. However, you can help students appreciate and accommodate to the challenges, adjustments, and choices they must make in order to succeed in college and beyond. Furthermore, when you contribute positively to the development of your peers, you also develop the leadership qualities and personal skills that contribute to your own development.

Beyond helping students on an individual level, as a peer leader, you can be a key catalyst for creating positive change on your campus. Good communities are built "from the ground up" and student leaders can serve as architects and artisans who help shape and design better college communities. By collaborating with faculty, advisors, student development professionals, and campus administrators, you can change the lives of other students, strengthen your campus community, and begin to make the world a better place.

Author's Perspective I believe in the power and impact of networks. I believe that peers are vital for inspiring and helping each other to weave those networks. Peers lead, emulate, and motivate one another. If campuses make the commitment to develop, mobilize, and honor the power and potential of peer leadership, the sky's the limit.

— *Greg Metz*

The Importance of Social Capital

Humans are inextricably connected with each other, especially to those in their immediate social environment. We construct our own destinies, but we do so in the context of our relationships. Those relationships have a profound impact on our personal development and can make a huge difference in determining the outcomes of our lives. Just as investors invest economic capital in businesses for financial growth, we can invest in each other, creating "social capital" for personal growth.

> *Social capital refers to the collective value of all social networks [who people know] and the inclinations that arise from these networks to do things for each other. Social capital creates value for the people who are connected.*
> —Harvard Kennedy School

Social capital may be viewed as "sociological superglue" (Putnam, 2000); it binds people together in social networks. To a significant extent, each of us owes a good deal of our personal success to our social-capital networks. The people who have encouraged us, guided us, stayed with us through thick and thin, and kept us on course have contributed substantially to our past accomplishments and influence our future aspirations. New students, in particular, are likely to have strong needs for "belongingness" and social capital; they are looking for support and direction from peers who have already made the college transition successfully.

> *When spider webs unite, they can tie up a lion.*
> —Ethiopian proverb

As a peer leader, you can provide fellow students with social capital by:

- Sharing your understanding of the rules of the road and how to navigate their social environment;
- Directing them to opportunities and resources;
- Helping them acquire and refine skills needed to succeed in college;
- Supporting them during setbacks and crises; and
- Helping them create social support networks.

As a peer leader, you have an extraordinary opportunity to influence others because your peers are in the midst of making a life-changing transition in an unfamiliar social environment, which grants them considerably more personal freedom of choice and requires more decision-making responsibilities than they've ever had before. When people find themselves in unfamiliar social situations, particularly those that are less structured and demand more personal choices and decisions than they're accustomed to, they often look to others for cues and direction about how to act. During times of social confusion and upheaval, people hunger for a leader (Parks, 2008); they often look for support and direction from others whom they see as successful and similar to themselves (Bandura, 1997)—someone like you. Your peers are watching you; your leadership matters.

Author's Experience I've experienced the power of positive peer influence twice in my life. First, when I was a new graduate student and having doubts about whether I could "cut it" at the graduate level, a student two years older than me took me under his wing, advised me, and instilled

> *I think they're really searching for someone to kind of follow, someone to see as an example, more than we think.*
> —Peer leader, quoted in Harmon (2006)

in me the confidence I needed to survive my first year. He also helped me find a graduate program that best matched my interests, abilities, and values.

The second time I witnessed the power of positive peer influence came as a parent of a teenage boy who spent his high school years fighting a severe form of cancer and suffering severe side effects of chemotherapy (baldness, anorexia, stroke, and loss of social self-confidence). He entered college with extreme self-doubt and trepidation. During his first term on campus, peers in a leadership fraternity (Delta Tau International) persuaded him to join their organization and it changed his life. He was transformed from a scared, self-conscious freshman into an optimistic, altruistic, and gregarious student leader himself, serving as an orientation-week leader for three years and vice president of student government during his senior year.

Thus, peers have played a major role in shaping my life and the life of my only son. I've never forgotten or underappreciated the role of peers and will forever be grateful for their positive influence. One of my motives for co-authoring this book is to express my gratitude to peer leaders and mentors everywhere.

— *Joe Cuseo*

Reflection 1.3

Has a peer made a difference in your life? In what way(s) did that person contribute positively to your personal development or personal success?

What Is a Peer Leader?

The growing use of peers as student support agents has produced a growing number of terms used to describe who they are and what they do. They have been referred to as "peer mentors" (Rice & Brown, 1990) and "peer educators" (Ender & Newton, 2000). The term *peer leaders* is used primarily in this book because it's a comprehensive and inclusive term that we think best captures the wide range of peer support roles that students have assumed on campuses across the nation.

Peer leadership also accurately captures a common goal in college and university mission statements: to develop future leaders (Astin & Astin, 2000; Zimmerman-Oster & Burkhardt, 1999). In fact, the primary goal of the first American colleges was not to prepare students for specific careers or vocational roles, but to develop character traits and personal skills necessary for filling leadership positions in colonial society (Conley, 2005). Many scholars argue that there is an emerging leadership crisis in our society and America needs to renew its historic commitment to preparing future leaders (Ehrlich, 1999; Korten, 1998; Lappe & DuBois, 1994).

> *Education at Harvard should liberate students to explore, to create, to challenge, and to lead.*
> —Mission of Harvard College
>
> *Helping students develop the integrity and strength of character that prepares them for leadership may be one of the most challenging and important goals of higher education.*
> —Patricia King, "Character and Civic Education: What Does It Take?"

Peer Mentoring

While we use *peer leader* as the primary term in this book, *peer mentoring* is becoming an increasing popular term on college campuses. We consider it to be a special and important form of peer leadership that warrants further discussion in this opening chapter.

Mentoring has been defined in a wide variety of ways (D'Abate, 2009). One comprehensive review of the literature on mentoring revealed that there were over 50 definitions of the term (Crisp & Cruz, 2007). However, one common thread that weaves through all the multiple meanings of *mentoring* is that it involves a close interpersonal relationship. The origin of the term *mentor* can be traced to Homer's *Odyssey*—an epic poem in which King Odysseus was away from home for many years fighting in the Trojan War and left his son to his most trusted friend and advisor, a gentleman by the name of Mentor. Thus, the meaning of *mentoring* is rooted in the idea of a close, ongoing, one-to-one relationship between an experienced leader (mentor) and a less experienced person (mentee or protégé).

In one of the earliest formal definitions of *mentoring* to appear in the peer leadership literature, Lester and Johnson (1981) define it as a "one-to-one learning relationship between an older person and a younger person that is based on extended dialogue between them. [It is] a way of individualizing a student's education" (p. 50). Peer mentoring may be viewed as a more intensive, personalized form of peer leadership that occurs over an extended period of time.

The best mentors don't wait for personal relationships to happen by chance: they make them happen intentionally by being social catalysts who initiate, facilitate, and cultivate relationships with others.

> *Mentorships first and foremost are relationships.*
> —W. Brad Johnson, *The Elements of Mentoring*

Author's Experience Over the past few years, I have spoken personally to hundreds of student leaders and read thousands of reflections on their work. Over and over again, leaders report that the establishment of relationships through which the leader was first and foremost a "peer" and only then a source of expertise was fundamental to effective leadership.

— *Greg Metz*

> *Some people make things happen. Some people watch things happen. Others wonder what has happened.*
> —Gaelic proverb

When peers are mentors, the boundaries between mentor and friend can often become delicate and blurred. Although you may have lots of experience and wisdom to impart to the students you lead, you are first and foremost a peer and trusted friend. That being said, it's important to help students realize that you're a friend of a different type—someone who is also interested in helping them achieve their academic and personal goals, who has experience and wisdom to share that will help them reach their goals, and who models behavior they should aspire to and emulate. Establishing this special type of balanced relationship with your students will enable you to be a special type of friend and a very effective mentor.

> *Mentors don't stop with words . . . they furnish a living example.*
> —Tim Elmore

Tale FROM THE Trenches

The most significant change I have dealt with was the transition from my students viewing me as a teacher/stranger to my students viewing me as a mentor/friend. I found a comfortable way to handle myself so that my students felt secure enough to come to me with personal problems, while they continued to view me as a mentor and someone to look up to.

—PEER LEADER

> *Mentoring . . . friendship with a vision.*
> —Evan Griffin, Professor of Communication, University of Cincinnati

Reflection 1.4

Have you had someone in your life whom you would consider to be a mentor?

If you have, what did that person do with and for you?

The Power of Peer Leadership

> *The student's peer group is the single most potent source of influence on growth and development during the undergraduate years.*
>
> —Alexander Astin, *What Matters in College?*

Contrary to how peers are often portrayed in the popular media, they are much more than competitors and sources of negative "peer pressure." More often, they are sources of positive social influence by serving as collaborators, teammates, role models, and leaders. When inexperienced college students become connected with role models, they are supplied with a source of peer power that's repeatedly been found to propel them to higher levels of academic performance and personal development (Cuseo, 2010).

Peer leadership is particularly powerful because it's a form of social support that students are likely to perceive as more approachable and less threatening than that provided by older professionals and authority figures (Gross & McMullen, 1983; Rice & Brown, 1990). Since peer leaders are at a slightly more advanced stage of development than those they are leading, students can more readily identify with them and relate to them (Bandura, 1986; Ender & Newton, 2002; Vygotsky, 1978). Research indicates that students desire and prefer to receive personal support from students who are one to three years older than they are, rather than from students of the same age, administrators, or faculty (Rice & Brown, 1990). In addition, peer support can take place in multiple situations that go beyond classrooms and campus offices, and can be received on a more ongoing basis than "officially scheduled" support provided by faculty and professional staff.

Author's Experience I was a first generation college student and did not know of anyone who I could discuss the paths to follow to graduation. What I had learned from my family and friends from high school was that if I could find a group of peers who seemed to understand the lay of the land, I would be able to use their knowledge to assist me. Thus, my first semester in college was spent identifying the students who made good grades and joined organizations designed to be beneficial to their positive behaviors in college. Those connections helped me to make others (e.g., college faculty and staff). Because of the individual leadership I took to identify those peers and because of their leadership abilities and willingness to share their knowledge with me, college became a fun and interesting place to learn and not a foreign land where I did not speak the language.

— *Aaron Thompson*

Positive Outcomes Associated with Peer Leadership

A long historical trail of research points to the power of peers for promoting the development and success of college students (Astin, 1993; Feldman & Newcomb, 1997; Pascarella & Terenzini, 2005). Peer leaders, in particular, can contribute to students' success by promoting their: (1) retention (persistence to graduation), (2) learning and academic performance, (3) social and emotional development, and (4) career success.

Increasing Student Retention (Persistence to Graduation)

Research consistently demonstrates that student persistence to graduation is enhanced by peer interaction and support (Astin, 1993; Pascarella & Terenzini, 2005). In a major study of student retention, it was found that peers exerted more influence on student persistence than all other social agents on campus, including faculty (Bean, 1985). Campus research reports indicate that students who are supported by peer mentors are more likely to remain in college at higher rates than students who do not receive such support (Schwitzer & Thomas, 1998; Black & Voelker, 2008). Simply stated, when students become connected with peers, they come to see themselves as integral members of a campus community, which increases the likelihood they'll continue to stay in that community until they complete their college degree (Tinto, 1987, 1993; Braxton, Sullivan, & Johnson, 1997).

Promoting Student Learning and Academic Achievement

Peers can exert powerful impact on student learning and academic performance. For instance, studies consistently show that when students teach (tutor) other students, both the peer teacher and peer learner make significant gains in learning (Whitman, 1988). Peers who tutor other students also experience significant gains in self-concept and are likely to achieve higher scores on graduate school admissions tests (Astin, 1993).

In a national study of almost 500,000 students at colleges and universities of all types, it was found that when peers interact with each other while learning, they achieve higher levels of academic performance and are more likely to persist to degree completion. Furthermore, the learning benefits achieved through peer interaction are not restricted to formal, academic settings; college graduates report that their most significant learning experiences occurred *outside the classroom* and were heavily influenced by their peers (Marchese, 1990; Murphy, 1989*)*.

Effective leadership involves the integration and application of knowledge from multiple subject areas and academic disciplines (D'Abate, 2009). You will find that your peer leadership experiences will stimulate your ability to draw upon diverse bodies of knowledge, such as philosophy, psychology, sociology, history, political science, and business, and to utilize a broad base of *general education* skills, such as critical and creative thinking, social and emotional intelligence, self-awareness, and learning how to learn.

Supporting Students' Social and Emotional Development

Peers also play an important role in promoting the development of students' social and emotional skills (Cross, 1985; Feldman & Newcomb, 1969; Goleman, Boyatzis, & McKee, 2002). Research suggests that peer mentors are able to provide students with greater social and emotional support than older mentors (Barrow & Hetherington, 1981; Grant-Vallone & Ensher, 2000). Furthermore, students who serve as peer mentors also experience gains in social and emotional development, such as improved social skills, self-confidence, self-esteem, sense of purpose, and personal identity (Astin & Kent, 1983; Harmon, 2006; Schuh & Laverty, 1983). It has also been found that student involvement in peer leadership and mentoring activities is associated with increased social concern and development of altruistic values (Pascarella, Ethington, & Smart, 1988).

Teaching is the highest form of understanding.

—Aristotle, Ancient Greek philosopher and a founding father of Western philosophy

The best answer to the question of what is the most effective method of teaching is that it depends on the goal, the student, the content and the teachers. But the next best answer is students teaching other students.

—Wilbert McKeachie, *Teaching and Learning in the College Classroom*

Leadership and learning are indispensable to each other.

—John F. Kennedy, 35th president of the United States

I know that being a peer leader will greatly benefit me when I begin my career. What I am even more sure of is what will come at the end of the day: self-pride, respect, knowledge, and contentment. I have made a difference.

—Peer leader, quoted in Hamid & VanHook (2001)

Promoting Career Success

Alumni consistently report that their participation in campus leadership roles had a significant impact on their development of career-relevant leadership skills (Pascarella & Terenzini, 1991; Peter D. Hart Research Associates, 2006). These reports from college alumni are reinforced by job-performance evaluations from employers, which indicate that previous involvement in student leadership positions in college is the best predictor of college graduates' performance in managerial positions on the job (American Telephone & Telegraph, 1984; Howard, 1986). In a multi-campus study that tracked students throughout their college experience, it was discovered that student-student interaction had the strongest effect on students' leadership development; in other words, students who interacted most frequently with peers during college were most likely to have acquired leadership qualities and qualifications by the time they graduated from college (Astin, 1993). Studies also show that students who participate as peer leaders show significant gains in civic engagement and character development (Bennis, 1989; Komives & Wagner, 2009).

In addition to all of these findings, research pointing to the power of peer leadership and mentoring on a number of different campuses indicates that peer leaders have a positive impact on students in a variety of other areas, including (1) academic advising (Carns, Carns, & Wright, 1993), (2) health and wellness (Burke, 1989; Lenihan & Kirkm, 1990), (3) facilitating interpersonal relationships (Waldo, 1989), and (4) promoting intercultural interaction (Berg & Wright-Buckley, 1988; Keup, 2010).

Taken together, the sum of these research findings points strongly to the conclusion that as a peer leader, you are well positioned to create a "win-win-win" scenario for three different parties:

1. Your *peers*—who benefit from your leadership.
2. Your *campus*—you help build a culture of student success on campus "from the ground up."
3. *Yourself*—you develop leadership skills that will contribute to your success in college and in your life beyond college. When you help other students become more self-aware, define their goals, learn strategically, and develop as whole persons, you do the same for yourself.

The bottom line: As a peer leader you have the potential to promote positive change in other students, in yourself, and in the college or university where your leadership takes place. That's a trifecta that can't be beat!

Reflection 1.5

Look back at the positive outcomes of peer leadership. Which outcomes (if any) were you not aware of, or thought could be strongly influenced by peer leaders?

Arenas of Peer Leadership in College

Peers serve as leaders in a wide variety of specific contexts and situations on college campuses; the ways in which you can demonstrate leadership in college are almost limitless. However, most formal peer leadership positions on college campuses may be grouped into the following three general categories:

> *Not only was I able to use the [peer leadership] experience as a resume builder, but it actually became the center of my discussion in an interview. My interviewer spent 20 minutes during a one-hour interview discussing the responsibilities of being a peer leader. He was impressed that I was chosen for such a program.*
>
> —Peer leader, quoted in Hamid & VanHook (2001)

> *I enjoy it when my former students return [and] express to me the impact I have had on their lives. This [is] one of the best jobs I ever had.*
>
> *I wanted to become what so many others had been for me. This experience has given me an incredible opportunity to learn more about my school and myself while helping others.*
>
> *While working on the program, I learned how to be a dedicated and diligent leader and have acquired new skills that will stay with me long after my college experience has ended.*
>
> —Peer leaders, quoted in Hamid & VanHook (2001)

> *In the final analysis, you will be the primary beneficiary of your helping interactions. Helping others grow is, in itself, a personal growth-promoting activity.*
>
> —Ender & Newton, *Students Helping Students*

1. **Academic leadership.** Peers can perform a variety of academic leadership functions on campus, including (1) leading study groups and group projects, (2) serving as peer tutors in the Learning and Academic Support Center on campus, or (3) serving as co-teaching facilitators in college courses (e.g., first-year seminars). You can provide academic leadership in any of these roles without necessarily being intellectually gifted or brilliant, simply by being knowledgeable, being available as a learning resource to peers who seek your support, and modeling effective learning strategies. For instance, you can model intellectual curiosity and academic motivation by being highly attentive in class and contributing insightful questions or informed comments during class discussions.

2. **Social and emotional leadership.** Peers can provide social and emotional leadership by making others feel welcome, reaching out to shy or bashful students, and simply listening empathically to students or being available to them in times of need.

3. **Organizational and civic leadership.** Peers can also demonstrate leadership on a wider scale by organizing and motivating groups of people to pursue worthy social and political causes. This type of leadership includes such activities as initiating clubs and directing student organizations, effectively delegating tasks and responsibilities, maintaining group cohesiveness and cooperation, and keeping groups on track and making progress toward a common goal.

> *I wanted to be here because somebody was there for me.*
>
> —Peer mentor, quoted in Harmon (2006)

Formal Peer Leadership Positions in Colleges and Universities

Use of peers to support and promote student development began in America's colonial period when peers were used exclusively as tutors (Winston & Ender, 1988). Since then, the formal roles played by peer leaders have steadily grown. By the 1950s, peer leaders were providing leadership in new student orientation programs and residence halls (Powell, 1959). By the 1980s, peer leadership expanded to other positions, including judiciary programs, student activities, advising, counseling, study skills, and crisis intervention (Ender, 1984).

During the 1990s, the scope of peer leadership expanded dramatically (Dugan & Komives, 2007); one national survey revealed that more than 85% of all colleges and universities reported that they had students employed in peer leadership positions (Carns, Carns, & Wright, 1993). This growing trend continued into the 21st century, as evidenced by the growing number of national conferences on peer leadership (College Summit, 2011; Institute on Peer Educators, 2010) and by the expanding number of positions on college campuses. You are joining a major movement that's spreading rapidly across the United States and around the world (Keup, 2012).

Some of the more common positions occupied by peer leaders are listed in **Box 1.2** below. The wide range of positions on this list demonstrates the variety and versatility of peer leaders in higher education. The list is long, but it's not exhaustive. Students undoubtedly occupy other leadership positions in higher education that don't appear on this list.

Reflection 1.6

As you read the list of leadership positions in Box 1.2, place checkmarks next to those you think best fit your personal strengths, talents, and interests.

Box 1.2

Peer Leadership Positions in Higher Education

1. **Student leaders of campus clubs and organizations** provide leadership for student government, special interest groups, fraternities, sororities, etc.
2. **Student ambassadors** work with college admissions offices to represent the college, recruit new students, and facilitate campus visits from prospective students and their families.
3. **Peer orientation week leaders** welcome new students to campus and facilitate their transition to the college experience and college life.
4. **Peer resident advisors (a.k.a. community assistants)** provide advice, support, and guidance to students living in campus residences.
5. **Peer mentors** serve as role models and success coaches for new students.
6. **Peer tutors** provide learning assistance to students on an individual and group basis in learning centers and centers for academic success.
7. **Supplemental instruction (SI) leaders** provide learning assistance for students enrolled in difficult courses (e.g., courses with high rates of Ds, Fs, or Ws) by leading supplementary group study sessions that are regularly scheduled outside of class time.
8. **Peer leaders for learning communities** meet regularly to support students who enroll in two or more courses together (a learning community), helping these students connect with each other, their course instructors, and learning support professionals.
9. **Peer co-instructors/co-facilitators for first-year seminars** work with instructors of first-year experience courses, providing a student perspective on course topics, serving as a liaison between instructor and students, and promoting student involvement in class and on campus.
10. **Peer academic advisors** help students select and register for courses.
11. **Peer counselors** provide paraprofessional support for students seeking assistance on social or emotional issues and mental health.
12. **Peer wellness counselors** assist students on matters relating to physical health and well-being.
13. **Peer ministers** support students' spiritual development and organize faith-based experiences.
14. **Peer community service leaders** facilitate volunteerism and service to the community by organizing, publicizing, and encouraging student involvement in community-based experiences.
15. **Team captains** provide leadership for teammates participating in college and university athletic programs.

The Importance of Self-Awareness for Effective Leadership

Leadership development is fundamentally self-development, and it begins with an exploration of your inner territory.

—Kouzes & Posner, *The Student Leadership Challenge*

Do what you value, value what you do.

—Sidney Simon, author, *Values Clarification* and *In Search of Values*

A cardinal characteristic that all effective leaders have in common is self-knowledge and awareness of self (Bennis, 1989; Wagner, 2006). Leadership first requires introspection and discovering of one's own leadership identity—you must first know who you are before you can become the type of leader you want to be.

Self-awareness is the awareness of your personal *values*. You're more likely to promote positive change in others when you have deep knowledge of your values and your actions are deeply rooted in those values (Higher Education Research Institute, 1996).

Know Thyself
© Kendall Hunt

Self-awareness is essential for effective leadership.

When you take on leadership roles that align with your personal values, you're more likely to develop the drive, passion, and commitment to become the best leader you can be. It's noteworthy that *value* derives from two root words: (1) *valor*, to be strong, and (2) *valence*, to be strongly attracted to. Thus, when you do what you value, you're likely to do it with greater effort, energy, and intensity.

Specific Peer Leadership Roles and Functions

When peer leadership positions are analyzed at a more micro level, we find that embedded within these formal positions is a host of specific, informal, but highly influential functions, such as those summarized in **Box 1.3** below. The long list of functions found in the box serves as testimony to the wide variety of ways in which peer leaders can contribute to students' academic and personal success.

Reflection 1.7

As you read through the alphabetized list of leadership roles described in Box 1.3, circle those that you feel most closely match your talents and underline those that you think would require the most preparation and practice on your part.

Box 1.3

Specific Roles and Functions Performed by Peer Leaders

Coach provides guidance and feedback for improving personal performance.

Communicator delivers messages in a clear, concise, and convincing manner.

Community builder promotes cohesion and a sense of belonging among people on campus or in the local community.

Confidante is a non-judgmental listener whom students can confide in, and feel comfortable about sharing their personal values, beliefs, concerns, and issues.

Educator teaches students to "learn the ropes" and learn how to learn; serves as a knowledgeable source of accurate and timely information for students about the curriculum, co-curriculum, college policies, and administrative procedures.

Facilitator stimulates interaction, discussion, collaboration, and teamwork among group members.

Guide helps students stay on course, navigate the system, and circumvent potential obstacles or stumbling blocks to success that commonly occur at particular stages of the college experience.

Institutional catalyst mobilizes the campus to make positive changes in practices, procedures, and policies.

Meaning maker helps students make sense of (find meaning in) the college experience, and enables them to see the connections between their present academic experience and their future life plans.

Motivator challenges students to set personal goals and inspires them to reach their goals.

Organizer plans and designs group functions, projects, and activities.

Problem solver helps students recognize and resolve academic and personal problems.

Referral agent is a connector who refers students to the right resources in a sensitive and timely manner.

Role model is an example setter whom students can identify with, emulate, and aspire to be like—academically and personally.

Troubleshooter helps students solve problems and resolve issues that cross departmental borders or "fall between the cracks" of the institution's formal policies, rules, or procedures.

Reflection 1.8

Looking back at the leadership functions cited in Box 1.3, which ones do you think represent the best match or fit with your personal abilities and talents? Why?

Summary and Conclusion

All forms of effective leadership have one thing in common: they promote *positive change*. A leader is a *change agent* who exerts positive influence on (1) individuals, such as helping fellow students reach their personal potential and achieve their personal goals, or (2) groups, communities, and organizations, such as a college or university. Leadership can take place at different points along a spectrum or continuum, ranging from the micro (changing an individual) to the macro (changing society).

Peer leadership in college has always mattered, but it matters even more in the 21st century. In today's knowledge-driven, globally interdependent world, a college education is more essential than at any other time in history. Some students may show up on campus already equipped with the personal, academic, and civic attributes needed for success in today's world. However, for many students, there are gaps between their day-to-day habits and the habits they need to develop in order to be successful in today's world. As a peer leader, you can play a pivotal role in helping students persist to complete their degrees and make the most of their college experience.

A long historical trail of research points to the power of peers for promoting the development and success of college students. Peer leaders have been found to contribute to students' success by promoting (1) retention (persistence to graduation), (2) learning and academic performance, (3) social and emotional development, and (4) career success. Peer leadership is particularly powerful because it's a form of social support that students are likely to perceive as more approachable and less threatening than that provided by older professionals and authority figures. Since peer leaders are at a slightly more advanced stage of development than those they are leading, students can more readily identify with them and relate to them. In addition, peer support can take place in multiple situations that go beyond classrooms and campus offices, and can be received on a more ongoing basis than "officially scheduled" support provided by faculty and professional staff.

Just as investors invest economic capital in businesses for financial growth, we can invest in each other, creating "social capital" for personal growth. Social capital binds people together in social networks. New students, in particular, are likely to have strong needs for "belongingness" and social capital; they are looking for support and direction from peers who have already made the college transition successfully. One of your key roles as a peer leader is to help students build social capital, because new students are in the midst of making a life-changing transition in an unfamiliar social environment, which grants them considerably more personal freedom of choice and requires more decision-making responsibilities than they've ever had before. When people find themselves in unfamiliar social situations, particularly those that are less structured and demand more personal choices and decisions than they're accustomed to, they often look to others for cues and direction about how to act. They look for support and direction from others whom they see as successful and similar to themselves—others like you.

Beyond helping students on an individual level, as a peer leader, you can be a key catalyst for creating positive change on your campus. Good communities are built "from the ground up" and student leaders can serve as architects and artisans who help shape and design better college communities. By collaborating with faculty, advisors, student development professionals, and campus administrators, you can change the lives of other students, strengthen your campus community, and begin to make the world a better place.

During the 1990s, the scope of peer leadership expanded dramatically. This growing trend continued into the 21st century, as evidenced by the growing number of national conferences on peer leadership and by the expanding number of positions on college campuses. You are joining a major movement that's spreading rapidly across the United States and around the world.

Peers now serve as leaders in a wide variety of specific contexts and situations on college campuses, most of which may be grouped into three general categories:

1. **Academic leadership.** Peers can perform a variety of academic leadership functions on campus, including (1) leading study groups and group projects, (2) serving as peer tutors in the Learning and Academic Support Center on campus, or (3) serving as co-teaching facilitators in college courses (e.g., first-year seminars).

2. **Social and emotional leadership.** Peers can provide social and emotional leadership by making others feel welcome, reaching out to shy or bashful students, and simply listening empathically to students or being available to them in times of need.

3. **Organizational and civic leadership.** Peers can also demonstrate leadership on a wider scale by organizing and motivating groups of people to pursue worthy social and political causes. This type of leadership includes such activities as initiating clubs and directing student organizations, effectively delegating tasks and responsibilities, maintaining group cohesiveness and cooperation, and keeping groups on track and making progress toward a common goal.

When you're aware of your values and when you take on leadership positions that align with your personal values, you're more likely to develop the drive, passion, and commitment to become the best leader you can be.

Internet Resources

For additional information related to the ideas discussed in this chapter, we recommend the following websites:

What Is the Role of a Peer Leader? What Is a Peer Leader?
http://www.sru.edu/academics/enrollment/academicservices/Documents/
FYRST%20Seminar%20Peer%20Leader.pdf

Peer Leader Program, University of Cincinnati
www.uc.edu/fye/learning_communities/peer_leader_program.html

National Mentoring Month
www.nationalmentoringmonth.org

The Mentoring Group
www.mentoringgroup.com

Exercise 1.1 *Journal Reflections*

Note: We recommend that you start a leadership journal by recording and saving your responses (either electronically or in a composition book) to the following reflection questions and the other questions included at the back of the remaining chapters of this book. This practice promotes self-awareness and personal growth as a peer leader; it can also help lay the foundation for development of a leadership portfolio that you can present to potential employers or include as part of your admission application to graduate and professional schools.

1. Do other students currently see you as a leader? Why?

2. In what specific situations have you found yourself behaving as a leader?
   a. What did you learn about yourself as a leader in this situation?

   b. What did you do most effectively?

3. In what situations do you think you have the most leadership potential?

4. Whom would you like to lead/mentor, and what positive changes or outcomes would you like to produce as a result of your leadership/mentoring?

5. What personal skills or attributes would you like to acquire or strengthen as a result of your experience as a peer leader?

6. If you had the opportunity to observe or interview a peer leader or professional holding a leadership position that interests you, what position would that person hold?

7. Think about the leadership position that you're considering, preparing for, or currently occupy.
   a. Why are you pursuing or working in this particular position? (What led you to your interest in this position?)

   b. Would you say that your interest in leadership is motivated primarily by *intrinsic* factors (i.e., factors *inside* you, such as your personal abilities, interests, needs, and values)? Or, would you say that your interest is driven more heavily by *extrinsic* factors (i.e., factors *outside* you, such as impressing your family and friends, building your resume, or earning extra money)?

Exercise 1.2 *Gaining Self-Awareness of Interests, Talents, and Values*

1. No one is in a better position to know who you are and what you want to be than *you*. One effective way to get to know yourself more deeply is through self-questioning. You can begin to deepen your self-awareness by asking yourself questions that can stimulate your thinking about your inner qualities and priorities. Effective self-questioning can launch you on an inward quest or journey to self-discovery and self-insight, which is the critical first step to effective leadership. You can launch your quest toward self-awareness by asking yourself thought-provoking questions relating to your personal:

   a. Interests—what you *like* to do,

   b. Abilities—what you're *good* at doing, and

   c. Values—what you believe is *worth* doing.

The following questions will sharpen your self-awareness with respect to your interests, abilities, and values. As you read each question, briefly note what thought(s) come to mind about yourself.

Personal Interests

1. What tends to grab your attention and hold it for long periods of time?

2. What sorts of things are you naturally curious about or tend to intrigue you?

3. What do you really enjoy doing and do as often as you possibly can?

4. What do you look forward to or get excited about?

5. What are your favorite hobbies or pastimes?

6. When you're with your friends, what do you like to talk about or spend time doing together?

7. What has been your most stimulating or enjoyable learning experience?

8. If you've had previous work or volunteer experience, what jobs or tasks did you find most interesting or stimulating?

9. When time seems to "fly by" for you, what are you usually doing?

10. What do you like to read about?

11. When you open a newspaper or log onto the Internet, what do you tend to read first?

12. When you find yourself daydreaming or fantasizing about your future, what do you most often imagine yourself doing?

From your responses to the above questions, identify a leadership role or position that's most compatible with your personal interests. In the space below, note the role or position and the interests that are compatible with it.

Personal Talents and Abilities

1. What seems to come easily or naturally to you?

2. What would you say is your greatest talent or personal gift?

3. What are your most advanced or well-developed skills?

4. What seems to come naturally or easily to you that others have to work harder to do?

5. What would you say has been your greatest personal accomplishment or achievement in life thus far?

6. What about yourself are you most proud of, or what do you take most pride in doing?

7. When others come to you for advice or assistance, what is it usually for?

8. What would your best friend(s) say is your best quality, trait, or characteristic?

9. What have you done that gave you a strong feeling of being successful?

10. If you've received awards or other forms of recognition, what have you received them for?

11. On what types of learning tasks or activities have you experienced the most success?

12. In what types of courses do you tend to earn the highest grades?

> *Never desert your line of talent.*
> *Be what nature intended you for*
> *and you will succeed.*
>
> —Sydney Smith, 18th-century English
> writer and defender of the oppressed

From your responses to the above questions, identify a leadership role or position that's most compatible with your personal talents or abilities. In the space below, note the role or position and the abilities that are compatible with it.

Personal Values

1. What matters most to you?

2. If you were to single out one thing you really stand for or believe in, what would it be?

3. What would you say are your highest priorities in life?

4. What makes you feel good about what you're doing when you're doing it?

5. If there were one thing in the world you could change, improve, or make a difference in, what would it be?

6. When you have extra spending money, what do you usually spend it on?

7. When you have free time, what do you usually find yourself doing?

8. What does living a "good life" mean to you?

9. How would you define success? (What would it take for you to feel that you were successful?)

10. How do you define happiness? (What would it take for you to feel happy?)

11. Do you have any heroes or anyone you admire, look up to, or feel has set an example worth following? (If yes, who and why?)

12. Would you rather be thought of as:

   a. Smart,

   b. Wealthy,

   c. Creative, or

   d. Caring?

(Rank from 1 to 4, with 1 being the highest)

From your responses to the above questions, identify a leadership role or position that's most compatible with your personal values. In the space below, note the role or position and the values that are compatible with it.

Exercise 1.3 *Awareness of Multiple Intelligences*

Review the types of intelligence in the box below and circle your strongest area.

Box 1.4

Multiple Forms of Intelligence

1. **Linguistic intelligence.** Ability to communicate through words or language. For example: verbal skills in the areas of speaking, writing, listening, or reading.
2. **Logical-mathematical intelligence.** Ability to reason logically and succeed in tasks that involve mathematical problem-solving. For example: skill for making logical arguments and following logical reasoning, or the ability to think effectively with numbers and make quantitative calculations.
3. **Spatial intelligence.** Ability to visualize relationships among objects arranged in different spatial positions and to perceive or create visual images. For example: forming mental images of three-dimensional objects; detecting detail in objects or drawings; artistic talent for drawing, painting, sculpting, and graphic design; or skills related to sense of direction and navigation.
4. **Musical intelligence.** Ability to appreciate or create rhythmical and melodic sounds. For example: playing, writing, or arranging music.
5. **Interpersonal (social) intelligence.** Ability to relate to others, to accurately identify others' needs, feelings, or emotional states of mind, and to effectively express one's emotions and feelings to others. For example: interpersonal communication skills, accurately "reading" the feelings of others, and meeting their emotional needs.
6. **Intrapersonal (self) intelligence.** Ability to self-reflect, become aware of, and understand one's own thoughts, feelings, and behavior. For example: capacity for personal reflection, emotional self-awareness, and self-insight into personal strengths and weaknesses.
7. **Bodily-kinesthetic (psychomotor) intelligence.** Ability to coordinate one's own body skillfully and to acquire knowledge through bodily sensations or movements. For example: skilled at tasks involving physical coordination, ability to work well with hands, mechanical skills, talent for building models and assembling things, or skills relating to technology.
8. **Naturalist intelligence.** Ability to carefully observe and appreciate features of the natural environment. For example: keen awareness of nature or natural surroundings; ability to understand causes or results of events occurring in the natural world.

Source: Howard Gardner (1993), *Frames of Mind: The Theory of Multiple Intelligences* (2nd ed.).

What leadership positions, roles, or tasks do you think best match your most well-developed form(s) of intelligence?

Exercise 1.4 *Leadership Information Interview*

Find someone to interview who holds a leadership position on or off campus, particularly someone who's considered to be an effective leader. Candidates for an interview include current peer leaders on campus or in the community, as well as friends or family members.

Ask some or all of the following questions during your interview. (Feel free to add or substitute questions of your own.)

1. What led you to choose or become involved with your current leadership role?

2. What advice would you give to others about how they could best prepare for assuming leadership responsibilities?

3. During a typical day or week, what are the types of leadership responsibilities or activities that consume most of your time?

4. What personal qualities or prior experiences have contributed most to your effectiveness as a leader?

5. What skills, perspectives, or attributes do you see as being critical for success in your particular leadership role, or for leadership in general?

6. What do you like most about your role as a leader?

7. What are the most difficult or frustrating aspects of your leadership role?

8. Are there any particular moral issues or ethical challenges that you tend to face in your leadership role?

9. Do your leadership responsibilities require you to interact effectively with members of diverse ethnic/racial groups and lifestyles?

10. What impact do your leadership responsibilities have on other aspects of your life (e.g., academic performance and personal life)?

11. What do you do to continue growing and developing as a leader?

12. Could you recommend someone you admire as a leader that I may speak with to obtain additional insight into the nature of effective leadership?

Personal Reflections on the Interview

1. What impressed you most about this leader?

2. What was the most useful thing you learned about leadership from conducting this interview?

3. Was there any information you received that surprised or concerned you about the process of leadership?

4. As a result of conducting this interview, did your interest in or motivation for leadership increase, decrease, or remain the same? Why?

Exercise 1.5 *Self-Assessment of Leadership Confidence*

1. How would you rate your leadership self-confidence right now? (Circle one)

    very confident   somewhat confident   somewhat unconfident   very unconfident

    a. Provide an explanation for your rating.

    b. Do you think that your leadership self-confidence rating is higher or lower than the self-ratings given by other peer leaders on campus? Why?

The Essence of Leadership
Foundational Principles, Practices, and Personal Attributes

Reflection 2.1

If you were to identify one characteristic or attribute that all effective leaders have in common, what would it be?

One you've completed this chapter, you should have a "big picture" overview (aerial view) of effective leadership and a broad-based understanding of the characteristics of effective leaders. You will see that being an effective peer leader involves a lot more than showing students "the ropes" or acquiring a laundry list of college-success "tips" to pass on to your students. Effective leadership is a larger enterprise that requires deep knowledge of research-based principles and skills that prepare you to meet the wide range of leadership challenges associated with different situations and contexts.

The Practice of Effective Leadership

Kouzes and Posner (2012) collected thousands of "at your personal best as a leader" stories from leaders about their most successful leadership experiences. Employing a research method known as *content analysis*, Kouzes and Posner read, reread, and picked apart the content of these stories. Their analysis revealed five universal themes or "exemplary practices" that characterized effective leaders in multiple contexts. Leaders who were able to make extraordinarily positive changes in the individuals and groups with whom they worked engaged in these five practices:

- Inspired a shared vision,
- Modeled the way,
- Enabled others to act,
- Challenged the process, and
- Encouraged the heart.

The five leadership practices are described below, along with specific actions associated with each of them.

1. **Inspire a shared vision.** Great leaders share "exciting and ennobling possibilities . . . and enlist others in a common vision appealing to shared aspirations" (Kouzes & Posner, 2002, pp. 14–16). They have a vision and they're on a mission; they're ambitious and optimistic about the possibilities for positive

> *Leadership is about a process that can be understood, grasped, and learned. Leadership, just like any other skill in life, can be strengthened through coaching and practice.*
>
> —Kouzes & Posner, *The Student Leadership Challenge*

> *If your actions inspire others to dream more, learn more, do more and become more, you are a leader.*
>
> —John Quincy Adams, sixth president of the United States

change for themselves and for the individuals, groups, and organizations of which they are a part. They encourage and inspire others to develop lofty aspirations and goals for themselves and their communities. They keep their vision and mission front and center, and they guide others to see and believe in their view of the future.

2. **Model the way.** According to Kouzes and Posner (2002), modeling the way means "demonstrating intense commitment to your beliefs with each and every action" (p. 63). Great leaders reflect on their values and consciously align their actions with their values. Great leaders do what they believe in: they "walk the talk" through their everyday behaviors. Their actions speak loudly!

> *I made sure to show people what to do rather than tell them what to do.*
>
> —Peer leader, cited in Kouzes & Posner (2008)

Reflection 2.2

In the leadership position you're holding or preparing for, what would you say are the most important actions or behaviors you need to display to serve as a positive role model for other students?

_____

> *To lead, one must follow.*
>
> —Lao Tzu, ancient Chinese philosopher and founder of Taoism, a philosophy that emphasizes thought before action

3. **Enable others to act.** Effective leaders "strengthen others by sharing power and discretion" (Kouzes & Posner, 2002, p. 301); they make others feel capable and powerful. Successful leaders help individuals and groups develop a plan by engaging them in the process, then gradually recede as others gain more ownership of the plan. An effective leader strengthens others and empowers others to become leaders.

4. **Challenge the process.** Effective leaders continually "search for opportunities to change, grow, and improve" (Kouzes & Posner, 2002, p. 194). Leaders do not assume that the world as it is represents the world as it could or should be. They seek to innovate and improve. They experiment and take risks. They learn and grow from their experiences—both setbacks and successes. Rather than settling for mediocrity, they expect the best from themselves and supportively challenge others to be the best they can be.

5. **Encourage the heart.** "We need heart because the struggle to the top is arduous. Our research tells us that if we're going to make it to the summit we need someone shouting in our ear, 'Come on, you can do it. I know you can do it!'" (Kouzes & Posner, 2003, p. xi). Effective leaders do not ignore the emotional dimension of leadership. Successful leaders also consistently recognize and acknowledge the achievements and accomplishments of others. When others experience setbacks, effective leaders help them remain optimistic and hopeful by noting small victories and encouraging resilience.

Remember that these five themes are not simply "ideas" or "concepts" about leadership: they are down-to-earth *practices* that effective leaders consciously use on a consistent basis. Throughout the book, suggestions will be made for applying these five exemplary practices in different leadership contexts, such as mentoring, group leadership, facilitating learning teams, and leading campus organizations.

Reflection 2.3

Look back at the five effective leadership practices identified by Kouzes and Posner. Which one of these practices best matches your previous ideas about effective leadership? Which practice did you least expect to find on the list? Why?

Myths and Realities of Effective Leadership

Contrary to the popular belief about "natural born" leaders, leadership is not an inherited personality trait or a genetic gift that just happens naturally (Bass, 1985). Leadership doesn't happen automatically and effortlessly; it's a learned skill that's developed over time through diligent practice and responsiveness to feedback (Arvey et al., 2003).

Moreover, leadership is not some inexplicable "magnetic" personality or "charisma" that a leader displays in all situations and circumstances. Instead, effective leaders adapt or model their approach to meet the specific demands of leading people in different contexts or situations—a quality that scholars refer to as *situational leadership* (Blanchard, 1992; Fiedler, 1993).

Core Characteristics and Attributes of Effective Leaders

A popular misconception about leadership is that effective leaders are extroverted, bold, forceful, or aggressive. While these traits may characterize some famous (or infamous) political and military leaders, effective leaders are not typically dominant, controlling, or power-driven: instead, they demonstrate their leadership skills in more subtle and socially sensitive ways (Daft & Lane, 2008).

Powerful leaders don't always roar; there are many "quiet leaders" who influence and empower others with a soft voice. Others become effective leaders without doing much talking at all; they lead by example, modeling positive behaviors and strategies that others imitate and emulate. To lead others successfully, you must first lead yourself. This puts you in the position to share what you've learned and to model successful behavior for others to emulate.

The bottom line: Leadership comes in a variety of forms and styles (Locke, 1991), and people can demonstrate different forms of leadership in different situations.

Personal Qualities and Attributes of Effective Leaders

Although leaders come in a variety of styles, certain personal qualities tend to characterize all effective leaders. Listed below are common characteristics of effective leaders that have been repeatedly identified by leadership researchers and scholars (Avolio & Luthans, 2006; Goleman, Boyatzis, & McKee, 2002; Kouzes & Posner, 2002; Northouse, 2009; Strang & Kuhnert, 2009; Wagner, 2007).

It's not the absence of leadership potential that inhibits the development of more leaders; it's the persistence of the myth that leadership can't be learned.

—Kouzes & Posner, *The Student Leadership Challenge*

The most dangerous leadership myth is that leaders are born—that people simply either have certain charismatic qualities or not. The opposite is true. Leaders are made rather than born.

—Warren G. Bennis, professor and founding chairman of the Leadership Institute at the University of Southern California

At times, we have confused 'leadership' with 'dominance.'

—David Boren, president of the University of Oklahoma and longest-serving chairman of the U.S. Senate Intelligence Committee

Leadership is based on inspiration, not domination.

—William Arthur Ward, American author and poet

Reflection 2.4

As you read the following common characteristics of effective leaders, place a plus sign next to the attributes that align with your previous beliefs or experiences about leadership and a negative sign next to those that do not.

> *If people don't believe in the messenger, they won't believe in the message.*
>
> —James Kouzes & Barry Posner, *Student Leadership Planner: An Action Guide to Achieving Your Personal Best*

> *If you help others with problems of time management but you are the one who is always late to meetings, or if you give [a] presentation on responsible drinking yet get picked up for a DUI, much [of] your credibility is quickly and decidedly undermined.*
>
> —Steven Ender & Fred Newton, *Students Helping Students*

> *Perhaps the most basic life trait that translates to leadership effectiveness is honest, authentic self-awareness that is open to growth, learning, and change.*
>
> —Komives, Lucas, & McMahon, *Exploring Leadership: For College Students Who Want to Make a Difference*

Credible and Authentic

Effective leaders are believable and inspire others to believe in them. They're also genuine—they "keep it real"—they don't pretend to be what they're not. Their actions and convictions coincide; what they profess in words, they express in deed. They are models of consistency, not hypocrisy. They don't just give "lip service" to their values and commitments by simply stating them; they truly embody them and live by them.

Accountable and Reliable

Good leaders hold themselves accountable to others; they can be counted on and relied upon to follow up and follow through on their commitments. They show up when and where they're expected to, and they do what they promise to do.

Knowledgeable and Resourceful

Effective leaders are knowledgeable about their positions, themselves, the people they lead, and the context in which their leadership takes place. Effective peer leaders know the expectations of their position, the needs and goals of their students, and their own values and habits (Sanft, Jensen, & McMurray, 2008).

Effective leaders are also willing to say, "I don't know, but I'll find out." They capitalize on their resources, are open to learn from others, and are willing to receive help from others so they can help others.

Dedicated and Committed

Effective leaders are driven and determined to be the best leaders they can be. They invest a high level of time, energy, and effort in their work. They are passionate about making a real difference in the individuals, groups, and organizations they lead.

Reflection 2.5

Think about something that you do with passion and intensity. What thoughts, attitudes, and behaviors do you display when you do it?

Do you see ways in which you could apply the same approach to your leadership role?

Respectful and Humble

Effective leaders are neither pompous nor pretentious; their egos aren't inflated by the power or prestige of the positions they hold. As a peer leader, you're in a position to exert tremendous influence. However, if you come across as an arrogant, overbearing know-it-all, you will lose your edge as a peer leader. Being knowledgeable also means knowing how much you don't know and still need to learn.

Remember: Leadership is not something automatically granted or bestowed on you by a formal title or powerful position: it's earned by what you do with and for others, and by what you accomplish in the position that you hold (Kouzes & Posner, 2008).

Enthusiastic and Optimistic

Effective leaders are positive and hopeful, and they maintain these qualities when their efforts seem to be going slowly, nowhere, or backwards. This is a normal and inevitable part of the leadership challenge. Even when leaders are fully committed, have a deep understanding of effective leadership principles, and use all the right strategies, positive change may not be the immediate result. We can't always influence the actions of others. Remember: Creating change in individuals, groups, or organizations is typically an evolutionary, not a revolutionary process. Effective leaders remain patient, positive, and supportive during the inevitable twists and turns that characterize the process of promoting positive change.

> *People don't respect know-it-alls. Hubris, excessive pride, is the killer disease in leadership. It's easy to be seduced by power and importance. Humility is the only way to resolve the conflicts and contradictions of leadership.*
> —James Kouzes & Barry Posner (2008), *Student Leadership Planner: An Action Guide to Achieving Your Personal Best*

> *Don't let the power go to your head.*
> —George Orwell, *Animal Farm*

Tale FROM THE Trenches

A lesson I am constantly learning: patience, patience, patience. And you know what? Just like with everything, finding patience is challenging. But I need more patience with myself. I need more of it with other people. I need more of it as I wait for results and outcomes—instant gratification isn't always an option, and it's not always what it's cracked up to be.

—PEER LEADER

Ethical

Great leaders are not just influential: they're ethical. According to *transformational leadership theory*, the hallmark of the most effective leaders is the ability to elevate others to higher levels of ethical conduct (Burns, 1978). Although great leaders are not moralistic—they don't impose narrow values or conventional moral standards on others—they do raise the bar by encouraging themselves and others to pursue higher ideals than personal gain and self-interest (Bass, 1990).

In short, effective leadership is grounded in and grows from personal *character.* According to the Josephson Institute of Ethics, a person of character is:

> *A leader takes people where they want to go. A great leader takes people where they don't necessarily want to go but ought to be.*
> —Rosalynn Carter, former United States first lady

- **Trustworthy**—honest, loyal, trustworthy, and demonstrates integrity;
- **Respectful**—courteous, accepting, non-prejudiced, and nonviolent;
- **Responsible**—accountable, pursues excellence, and shows self-restraint;
- **Fair**—just, equitable, reasonable, open, and unbiased;
- **Caring**—unselfish, kind, empathetic, and compassionate; and
- **A good citizen**—law-abiding, does his or her share for the community, and protects the environment (Jones & Lucas, 1994).

Reflection 2.6

What ethical or moral issues do you anticipate encountering in your leadership role? How well prepared do you think you are for dealing with these issues?

The Process of Effective Leadership: Common Themes

Although leadership involves occasional improvisation and modification to accommodate the nuances of specific people, situations, and organizations, there are recurrent themes about the process of effective leadership that are relevant to all leadership roles (Rost, 1991). Leadership is an art form, like playing jazz. Great musical artists learn the basic musical processes, such as learning scales and chords, which, in turn, enables them to creatively apply these basic processes in the moment. Similarly, leadership involves creative use of basic processes. In particular, four key processes characterize successful leadership. Effective leadership is (1) relational, (2) collaborative, (3) empowering, and (4) reflective. These four core characteristics of the leadership process are described below.

1. **Leadership is a *relational* process that involves development and deployment of effective social and emotional skills.** According to relational leadership theory, effective leadership is always relationship-based; it's grounded in the creation and cultivation of interpersonal relationships (Murrell, 1997; Uhl-Bien, 2006). (Detailed discussion of the social and emotional dimension of effective leadership is provided in Chapter 4.)

2. **Leadership is a *collaborative* process that is best shared or "dispersed" among other leaders and mentors (Schein, 2004).** The process of effective leadership involves creating and capitalizing on linkages with other leaders. No single leader can be all things to all people; it's inevitable that co-leaders are needed to bring special knowledge, a different perspective, or an alternative approach that will complement and augment the effectiveness of the "official" leader.

   Take stock of your social networks and interpersonal connections on campus. If a particular need emerges, but you are not sure who can help, ask other student leaders and campus professionals. Somebody always knows somebody. You never know who may be able to exert the most influence on whom, or what particular relationships will prove to be life-changing.

   Leadership becomes more powerful when it's not done independently by "the" leader, but interdependently by a team of leaders. As the old saying goes, "It takes a village."

3. **Leadership is a process of *empowering* others.** Great leaders enable those they lead to become leaders of themselves and others. According to servant-leadership theory, we are transformed into leaders when we focus primarily on helping others meet their needs and goals and reach their full potential (Greenleaf, 1977). The ultimate goal of servant leadership is to enable others to grow and develop into servant leaders themselves.

   "Thus, the process of becoming an effective leader involves a shift of the leader's identity from thinking 'I am *the* leader' or 'I am *not* the leader' to 'I am a leader' and 'I can engage in leadership with others'" (Komives, Lucas, & McMahon, 2007, p. 408). A leader doesn't view others as "followers," but as associates, partners, or teammates who are eventually liberated from dependence on the leader to become leaders themselves. The best mentors are those who empower others to become mentors themselves: they pass it on (Elmore, 2008; Gould & Lomax, 1993).

> No leaders truly accomplish anything worthwhile by themselves. We achieve more when we share credit and ownership with others.
>
> —David Boren, president of the University of Oklahoma and longest-serving chairman of the U.S. Senate Intelligence Committee

> The leadership paradox is that leaders turn their followers into leaders.
>
> —Kouzes & Posner, The Student Leadership Challenge

> The fundamental task of the mentor is a liberatory task. A mentor truly believes in the autonomy, freedom, and development of those he or she mentors.
>
> —Paulo Freire, influential Brazilian educator and activist, in Mentoring the Mentor

Author's Experience I was a ten-year-old boy growing up in New York when I saw the Iowa Hawkeyes win the Rose Bowl on national TV. I immediately became a fan of the team; I even attended the University of Iowa as a graduate student. I continued to root for that team throughout my life and began to notice that it seemed like a sizable number of today's college and professional football coaches once played football at the University of Iowa. I thought it must have been a coincidence until my brother-in-law sent me an article from the *Wall Street Journal* about Iowa's legendary football coach Hayden Fry. Apparently, the large number of successful football coaches who once played football for Iowa were players coached by Hayden Fry.

During his many years as a successful head coach at Iowa, Fry intentionally identified different players to serve as player-coaches for teammates who played the same position. His idea was to have the player-coaches develop leadership skills that would benefit the team's performance during games. As Coach Fry put it, "Those were the guys that the players would listen to, not an old coach like me" (Diamond, 2011, p. 5). The second phase of Coach Fry's leadership development process was to give his player-coaches positions on his staff as graduate assistants after they had graduated from the university. The result: more than a dozen of his former player-coaches went on to become successful professional coaches.

Coach Fry's approach to developing future leaders illustrates two important points made in this book: (1) the power of peer leadership, and (2) how effective leaders empower others to become leaders themselves.

— *Joe Cuseo*

4. **Leadership is a *reflective* process that involves ongoing review and revision.** Personal reflection and self-assessment are essential to the quest for success in any venture, including leadership. Continually assessing where we are in relation to where we want to go, and then devising strategies to get there, is essential to the process of becoming a successful leader (and a successful human being). Leadership starts with a vision followed by action, reflection, and revision. Effective leaders formulate thorough and thoughtful plans, but they also adjust and tweak those plans after putting them into action. Successful leaders continuously take stock of where they are, define what they need to know and do to get better, set goals for improving, take action to reach those goals, and monitor their progress along the way.

Like great coaches, great leaders review, revise, and utilize feedback to improve their own performance and the performance of those they lead. After a tough game—win or lose—a good coach replays the game film, reviews and analyzes what happened, deciphers what went well and what could be improved, and provides the team with feedback. Like great coaches, great leaders continuously seek ways to improve themselves and their teams. They don't fear feedback; they embrace it.

Effective leaders engage in ongoing reflection on the effectiveness of their leadership by regularly seeking out and using feedback from others. They use this feedback to accentuate their strengths and strengthen their weaknesses. In other words, successful leaders engage in a continuous process of self-assessment and self-improvement.

> *Without reflection, we go blindly on our way, creating more unintended consequences, and failing to achieve anything useful.*
>
> —Margaret Wheatley, *It's an Interconnected World*

> *Leaders aren't born, they are made. And they are made just like anything else, through hard work. And that's the price we'll have to pay to achieve that goal.*
>
> —Vince Lombardi, Hall of Fame football coach

Reflection 2.7

If you were to select one aspect or element of leadership on which you would like to receive ongoing feedback for continuous self-improvement, what would it be?

The Importance of Leadership Role Awareness

Effective leadership requires self-awareness and awareness of your particular leadership role, position, and situation (Goleman, Boyatzis, & McKee, 2002). Leadership research and theory suggest that effective leadership is situation-specific—i.e., it takes place in a specific leadership context (Hersey, Blanchard, & Johnson, 2007). Thus effective leaders must develop awareness of specific roles and the particular context or situation in which leadership takes place (Blanchard, 2001; Komives, Lucas, & McMahon, 2007).

Once you become self-aware of your particular leadership strengths and skills, as well as your limitations (McCauley, Noxley, & Velsor, 1998), you are positioned to identify those leadership roles or situations that best fit your leadership talents (Zaccaro, Foti, & Kenny, 1991) and you're ready to capitalize on your personal talents (Haas & Tamarkin, 1992). Research indicates that when people do what they are best at doing, they find more meaning and fulfillment in what they do and do it more successfully (Buckingham & Clifton, 2001; Kouzes & Posner, 2003).

Awareness of yourself and of your leadership roles also helps you to know when you may be spreading yourself too thin by taking on too many different leadership responsibilities.

Ambitious leaders can sometimes overextend themselves, and this can quickly lead to stress, burnout, and poor leadership results (Dugan & Komives, 2007). One national survey revealed that close to one-half of all peer leaders held more than one peer leadership position at the same time, and almost 10% held four or more positions (Keup, 2010). Effective leaders shoot for quality, not quantity, by focusing their efforts on leadership roles and situations that best match their leadership talents and values; they go for quality, not quantity.

> *I learned that everything I wanted to do, I can't do at one time . . . my plate's not big enough. That [being a peer mentor] taught me a lot about my limits . . . that I spread myself too thin, I won't do a good job at everything.*
>
> —Peer leader, quoted in Harmon (2006)

Summary and Conclusion

This chapter provides a "big picture" overview (aerial view) of effective leadership and a broad-based understanding of the characteristics of effective leaders. Its content demonstrates that effective peer leadership involves a lot more than showing students "the ropes" or acquiring a laundry list of college-success tips to pass on to your students. Instead, it's a larger enterprise that requires deep knowledge of research-based principles and skills that prepare you to meet the wide range of leadership challenges associated with different situations and contexts.

Kouzes and Posner (2012) collected thousands of "at your personal best as a leader" stories from leaders about their most successful leadership experiences and discovered five universal themes or "exemplary practices" that characterized effective leaders in multiple contexts:

1. **Inspire a shared vision.** They have a vision and they're on a mission; they encourage and inspire others to develop lofty aspirations and goals for themselves and their communities.
2. **Model the way.** They reflect on their values and consciously align their actions with their values; they "walk the talk" through their everyday behaviors.

3. **Enable others to act.** They make others feel capable and powerful by engaging them in the process, and then gradually recede as others gain more ownership of the plan; they empower those they lead to become leaders themselves.

4. **Challenge the process.** They don't assume that the world as it is represents the world as it could or should be; they seek to innovate and improve it.

5. **Encourage the heart.** They don't ignore the emotional dimension of leadership; when others experience setbacks, effective leaders help them remain optimistic and hopeful by noting small victories and encouraging resilience, and when others are successful, they recognize and acknowledge their success.

Although leadership comes in a variety of forms and styles, and people can demonstrate different forms of leadership in different situations, research suggests that the following personal qualities tend to characterize all effective leaders:

Credible and authentic. They're genuine; they "keep it real" and don't pretend to be what they're not.

Accountable and reliable. They're dependable and hold themselves accountable to others; they can be counted on to follow up and follow through on their commitments.

Knowledgeable and resourceful. They're knowledgeable about their positions, themselves, the people they lead, and the context in which their leadership takes place; however, they're also willing to say, "I don't know, but I'll find out," and are willing to use their resources and receive help from others so they can help others.

Dedicated and committed. They're driven and determined to be the best leaders they can be; they are passionate about making a real difference in the individuals, groups, and organizations they lead.

Respectful and humble. They're not pompous or pretentious; their egos aren't inflated by the power or prestige of the positions they hold.

Enthusiastic and optimistic. They're positive and hopeful, and they maintain these qualities when their efforts seem to be going slowly, nowhere, or backwards.

Ethical. They elevate others to higher levels of ethical conduct without being moralistic—they don't impose narrow values or conventional moral standards on others, but they do raise the bar by encouraging themselves and others to pursue higher ideals than personal gain and self-interest.

Research points to recurrent themes about the *process* of effective leadership. Four processes, in particular, characterize successful leadership:

1. **It's a *relational* process that involves development and deployment of effective social and emotional skills.** Effective leadership is grounded in the creation and cultivation of interpersonal relationships.

2. **It's a *collaborative* process that is best shared or "dispersed" among other leaders and mentors.** The process of effective leadership involves creating and capitalizing on linkages with other leaders; no single leader can be all things to all people. Leadership becomes more powerful when it's not done independently by "the" leader, but interdependently by a team of leaders.

3. **It's a process of *empowering* others.** Effective leadership enables those who are led to become leaders of themselves and others. It transforms "followers"

into associates, partners, or teammates who eventually become liberated from dependence on the leader to become leaders themselves.

4. **Leadership is a *reflective* process that involves ongoing review and revision.** Leadership starts with a vision followed by action, reflection, and revision. It begins with a thoughtful and well-formulated plan, but that plan is monitored and adjusted after it's put into action to maximize its impact.

Lastly, effective leadership requires self-awareness and awareness of one's particular leadership role, position, and situation. Research suggests that effective leadership is situation-specific—i.e., it takes place in a specific leadership context. Thus effective leaders must develop awareness of specific roles and the particular context or situation in which leadership takes place. When you become self-aware of your particular leadership strengths and skills, as well as your limitations, you are then positioned to identify those leadership roles or situations that best fit your leadership strengths and talents.

Internet Resources

For additional information related to the ideas discussed in this chapter, we recommend the following websites:

What Is Leadership? A New Leadership Mindset—Leadership for a New Era
www.leadershipforanewera.org/page/A+New+Leadership+Mindset

Principles of Transformative Leadership
www.aahea.org/bulletins/articles/transformative_leadership.htm

Characteristics of Effective Leaders
Holden Leadership Center, University of Oregon
www.leadership.uoregon.edu

Psych Web
www.psywww.com/sports/leader.htm

Exercise 2.1 *Journal Reflections*

1. Have you witnessed an example of leadership that was:
   a. exceptionally admirable?

   b. particularly despicable?

   What specific actions or behavior(s) did the leader display in each of these situations?

2. Reflecting back on your very first interactions as a new student with faculty, staff, and administrators on your campus:
   a. Do you recall anyone who impressed you as being a potential mentor?

   b. What did that person say or do that impressed you the most?

3. Think about other peer leaders in your program. Do you see any of them as being potential teammates to network with, share resources, and exchange feedback to improve each other's leadership development?

4. Think about your leadership experiences to date:
   a. What leadership strengths did you display?

   b. What positive effects have your leadership strengths had on your peers?

c. What could you do to further increase or maximize your strengths?

d. What would you say are leadership areas in which you need to improve?

e. What could you do to improve them?

5. Can you think of a situation in which you (1) had to take a stance on a value that was important to you, or (2) displayed ethical leadership behavior that could serve as a model for others to emulate?

Exercise 2.2 *Self-Assessment of Exemplary Leadership Practices*

Look back at the definitions and descriptions of the five "exemplary practices" of leaders identified by Kouzes and Posner (pp. 29–30).

1. Rate yourself on a scale from 1–5 (1 = lowest; 5 = highest) on the extent to which you engage in each of these practices.

2. Identify one of your highest-rated practices and provide a description or illustration of how you implement this practice well.

3. Identify one of your lowest-rated practices and provide a step you may take to begin developing your ability to implement this practice more effectively.

Exercise 2.3 *Self-Assessment of Leadership Qualities and Attributes*

The box below contains a set of key *personal qualities or attributes* that are likely to be relevant in a wide variety of leadership positions and situations. As you read these personal qualities, underline those you believe you already possess, and circle those that you believe you need to improve. (For a brief description of these five qualities, see pp. 32–33.)

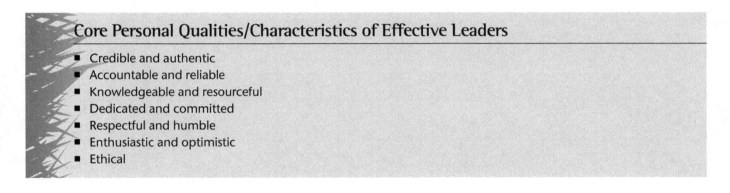

Core Personal Qualities/Characteristics of Effective Leaders

- Credible and authentic
- Accountable and reliable
- Knowledgeable and resourceful
- Dedicated and committed
- Respectful and humble
- Enthusiastic and optimistic
- Ethical

1. For each quality you underlined, provide a brief explanation or source of evidence that supports your belief that you already possess this quality.

2. For each quality you circled, provide a step you could take to begin developing this quality.

Exercise 2.4 *Gap Analysis of "Real" versus "Ideal" Leadership Qualities*

Identify one of the four processes of effective leadership described on pp. 34–35 for which there's the greatest gap between what you'd like to be doing (the ideal) and what you're actually doing (the reality). In the space below, identify short-range, mid-range, and long-range goals for reducing this gap.

To reduce this gap:

1. What *specific action*(s) can you take?

2. What *obstacles or roadblocks* would you have to overcome?

3. What *resources* could you draw upon for help and support?

E xercise 2.5 *Self-Assessment of Leadership Skills*

The following box contains sets of leadership skills that are likely to be relevant in a wide variety of leadership positions and situations. As you read these personal qualities, underline those you believe you already possess, and circle those that you believe you need to improve.

Personal Skills Relevant to Successful Leadership Performance

advising	evaluating	planning
coaching	explaining	problem solving
collaborating	initiating	producing
communicating	motivating	referring
coordinating	negotiating	resolving
creating	networking	summarizing
delegating	partnering	supervising
designing	persuading	synthesizing

Exercise 2.6 *Leadership Fit*

Using your *Student Handbook* or *College Catalog (Bulletin)*, list all the official peer leadership positions on your campus and their primary roles or responsibilities. After compiling the list, highlight the role(s) you think best match your interests, skills (talents), and values.

chapter 3

The College Experience
Applying Student Development Research and Theory to Promote Student Success

---

Reflection 3.1

What would you say are three major differences between high school and college?

During the 1960s, record numbers of baby-boom children attended college, and research on the college student experience began to explode. Studies continued over the next four decades, leaving us with more than 40 years of research on student development in college. The goal of this chapter is to synthesize the major findings of this research and help you apply it to your role as a peer leader.

The First-Year Experience: Transitioning from High School to Higher Education

The first year of college is a critical stage of the college experience. It's the time when students experience the greatest amount of learning and personal growth; it's also the time when they experience the most stress and the most academic difficulties and are most likely to withdraw from college (Cuseo, Fecas, & Thompson, 2010).

New students encounter different adjustments at different times during their first term in college; they are more likely to be receptive to information and advice that's delivered at times when they really need it. Simply stated, students are more willing and ready to acquire knowledge that's timely and immediately applicable to their current challenges and concerns. You can provide just-in-time support to students when they need it the most by thinking of students' first term on campus as unfolding in three major stages: Early, Middle, and Late.

The Early Stage (first six weeks of term)

Fitting in socially is very important to new students at the very start of their college experience. Research indicates that new students are most concerned about making interpersonal connections with their peers and other members of the college community (Brower, 1997; Simpson, Baker, & Mellinger, 1980; Tinto, 1988). These early social needs of new college students are consistent with psychologist Abraham Maslow's classic "need hierarchy" theory of human motivation, which stipulates that social acceptance and self-esteem are basic human needs that must be met before higher needs for personal growth and self-actualization can be realized (Maslow, 1954). (See **Figure 3.1**.)

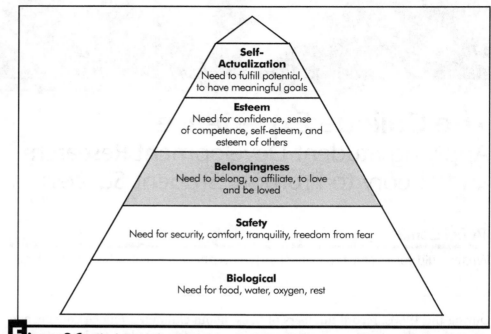

Figure 3.1   Abraham Maslow's Hierarchy of Needs resembles a pyramid. *Source:* Maslow (1954).

Thus, social needs (e.g., finding friends, overcoming shyness, and dealing with homesickness) are likely to be high-priority needs for students during the first few weeks of college. These needs may be met by creating early opportunities for new students to interact with peers, faculty, and student-support agents on campus (e.g., academic advisors and student development specialists).

Author's Experience It is ironic that I should be co-authoring this book. You see, I was a college dropout (or at least a stop-out) the first time around. I attended a rather large university that was about a five-hour drive from home. Unfortunately, campus housing availability was limited, so I wasn't able to live on campus. A few weeks before school started, I fell in love (or at least infatuation) with a girl back home. My heart and mind were not focused on school. By December, I was back at home.

I eventually returned and graduated, so my story had a happy ending. However, during my first turn at college I would have benefited immensely from a peer leader or mentor—someone whom I could have turned to, someone who could have helped me think through my decisions, or someone to connect me with a campus professional who, in turn, could have provided the support and direction I needed at that stage of my life.

— *Greg Metz*

> *As a peer leader I have seen students struggle with homesickness, pregnancy, forceful coaches, hostile roommates, death, and more. Freshmen have to deal with all of these issues while trying to adjust to an entirely new way of life. There are so many benefits from being a peer leader, but my favorite is providing hope for students that need a light at the end of the tunnel.*
>
> —Peer leader, quoted in Hamid & VanHook (2001)

The Middle Stage (the week before and after midterm exams)

The middle stage of the new-student experience may be defined as the time period just before and after midterm—the midpoint of the term when students are likely to encounter their first wave of college exams, assignment deadlines, and course grades. Research indicates that student satisfaction with college changes at different times during the term and an appreciable dip in student satisfaction tends to occur at midterm (Pennington, Zvonkovic, & Wilson, 1989).

This stage also marks the end of the "honeymoon period" for new students—when the novelty or rush of simply being in college (and attending lots of social gatherings and meeting lots of new people) is replaced by the pressure of meeting the academic demands and expectations of college. The terms *midterm slump* and *midterm crunch* have been coined to capture the stresses associated with this stage of the semester (Duffy & Jones, 1995).

As a peer leader, this is the time of the term to help students respond constructively to midterm grades and use their results as feedback for improving their future performance. Here are some questions you can use to get this process going:

- Were these the grades you expected to receive?
- Are you pleased or disappointed by them?
- Do you see any patterns in your performance that suggest what you're doing well or what you need to improve? (See Chapter 6, pp. 162–164 for more detailed strategies for helping students respond constructively to midterm grades.)

Midterm is also the time of the term when students are likely to be most receptive to your recommendations and referrals to academic support services on campus.

Reflection 3.2

Looking back at your first term in college:

1. During your first two weeks on campus, what were you most concerned about or worried about?

2. At midterm, were your concerns and worries the same, or had they changed to different issues?

The Late Stage (between midterm and final exam week)

Providing students with emotional support may be critical at this stage because anxiety and depression are more likely to surface toward the end of the term as students try to cope with the pressures of final projects, final exams, and returning home for the holidays (Thanksgiving and Christmas).

As a peer leader, the final weeks of the first term may be an especially critical time to be sensitive and responsive to the wellness needs of new students, because end-of-term projects, papers, and upcoming final exams are often accompanied by sleep loss (pulling all-nighters), disruption of normal eating and exercise routines, and stress related to academic performance anxiety or fear of failure. (See Chapter 7 for specific wellness strategies to share and model for your students.)

Research suggests that toward the end of the first term, most new students have settled in and are transitioning to concerns about the future (Brower, 1997). Thus, this may be the time of the term when they are most receptive to questions that ask them to reflect on their first term in college and identify what they did well and what they should do differently in the future. This may be a good time to ask them about setbacks or stumbling blocks they encountered during their first term in college, what they learned from those mistakes, and how they can avoid repeating them next term.

Being aware of the common issues that new students are likely to experience at different points in time (early, middle, and late stages) during their first term in college helps you anticipate their needs and respond to those needs in a timely fashion. However, it's important to remember that new students are likely to experience a variety of adjustment issues at the same time. For instance, while new students may be initially dealing with social questions about leaving home and fitting in, they are simultaneously confronted by the practical tasks of getting to class, taking notes in class, and doing the assigned readings. Even if students manage the initial task of overcoming homesickness and fitting in, they're likely to encounter new social challenges later in the term (e.g., sustaining early friendships, developing deeper relationships, and dealing with increasing social intimacy).

One strategy for being sensitive and responsive to the multiple adjustments of new students at any point in time during the first term is to remain mindful that college adjustments usually come in three major forms:

1. **Social adjustments** (Do I belong here?). Developing new relationships while maintaining or modifying relationships with their family and high school friends.
2. **Academic adjustments** (Will I make it?). Dealing with the heavier academic workload in college and the reality that their first grades in college are likely to be lower than those they earned in high school.
3. **Motivational adjustments** (Is it worth it?). Thinking about whether the benefits of college outweigh its costs (the time and money).

By asking them how things are going with respect to these three aspects of their college experience and supporting them in any areas where they may be in jeopardy, you should be able to remain aware of and responsive to the most important needs of new students throughout their first-year experience. You will find specific strategies for helping students with social adjustments in Chapter 4 and academic adjustments in Chapter 6. To help students who are struggling with the questions of whether college is really worth it, share with them the information contained in Box 3.1.

Box 3.1

Why College Is Worth It: The Economic and Personal Benefits of a College Education

Less than 30% of Americans have earned a four-year college degree. When college graduates are compared with others from similar social and economic backgrounds who did not continue their education beyond high school, research consistently shows that college is well worth the investment. College graduates experience numerous long-lasting benefits, such as those summarized in the following list:

1. **Career Benefits**
   - Career security and stability—lower rates of unemployment;
   - Career versatility and mobility—more flexibility to move out of a position and into other positions;
   - Career advancement—more opportunity to move up to higher professional positions;
   - Career interest—more likely to find their work stimulating and challenging;
   - Career autonomy—greater independence and opportunity to be their own boss;

- Career satisfaction—are more likely to enjoy their work and feel that it allows them to use their special talents; and
- Career prestige—hold higher-status positions (i.e., careers that more socially desirable and respected).

2. **Economic Advantages**
- Make better consumer choices and decisions;
- Make wiser long-term investments;
- Receive greater pension benefits; and
- Earn higher income: The gap between the earnings of high school and college graduates is *growing*. Individuals with a bachelor's degree now earn an average annual salary of about $50,000 per year—40% higher than high school graduates, whose average salary is less than $30,000 per year. When these differences are calculated over a lifetime, families headed by people with a bachelor's degree will take in about $1.6 million more than families headed by people with a high school diploma. That adds up to double the amount earned by those who complete only a high school diploma.

An investment in knowledge always pays the best interest.

—Ben Franklin, scientist, musician, inventor, political activist, and one of the founding fathers of the United States

3. **Advanced Intellectual Skills**
- Greater knowledge;
- More effective problem-solving skills;
- Better ability to deal with complex and ambiguous (uncertain) problems;
- Greater openness to new ideas;
- More advanced levels of moral reasoning;
- Clearer sense of self-identity—greater awareness and knowledge of personal talents, interests, values, and needs; and
- Greater likelihood they will continue learning throughout life.

4. **Better Physical Health**
- Better health insurance—more likely to be covered and receive more comprehensive coverage;
- Better dietary habits;
- Exercise more regularly;
- Lower rates of obesity; and
- Live longer and healthier lives.

5. **Social Benefits**
- Higher social self-confidence;
- Understand and communicate more effectively with others;
- Greater popularity;
- More effective leadership skills; and
- Greater marital satisfaction.

6. **Emotional Benefits**
- Lower levels of anxiety;
- Higher levels of self-esteem;
- Greater sense of self-efficacy—believe they have more influence and control over their life;
- Higher levels of psychological well-being; and
- Higher levels of personal happiness.

7. **Effective Citizenship**
- Greater interest in national issues—both social and political;
- Greater knowledge of current affairs;
- Higher voting participation rates; and
- Higher rates of participation in civic affairs and community service.

(continued)

> For the individual, having access to and successfully graduating from an institution of higher education has proved to be the path to a better job, to better health and to a better life.
>
> —College Board

8. **Higher Quality of Life for Their Children**
    - Less likely to smoke during pregnancy;
    - Provide better health care for their children;
    - Spend more time with their children;
    - More likely to involve their children in educational activities that stimulate their mental development;
    - More likely to save money for their children to go to college;
    - More likely that their children will graduate from college; and
    - More likely that their children will attain high-status and higher-paying careers.

Sources

Andres, L., & Wyn, J. (2010). *The making of a generation: The children of the 1970s in adulthood.* Toronto, Buffalo, and London: University of Toronto Press.

Astin, A. W. (1993). *What matters in college?* San Francisco, CA: Jossey-Bass.

Bowen, H. R. (1977, 1997). *Investment in learning: The individual & social value of American higher education.* Baltimore, MD: The Johns Hopkins University Press.

College Board. (2008). *Coming to our senses: Education and the American future.* Report of the Commission on Access, Admissions and Success in Higher Education. Retrieved August 5, 2009, from http://advocacy.collegeboard.org/college-admission-completion/access-admissions-success-education-and-american-future/publications/co

College Board. (2011). *Education pays 2010.* Washington, DC: Author.

Dee, T. (2004). Are there civic returns to education? *Journal of Public Economics, 88,* 1697–1720.

Feldman, K. A., & Newcomb, T. M. (1969, 1994). *The impact of college on students.* San Francisco, CA: Jossey-Bass.

Hamilton, W. (2011, December 29). College still worth it, study says. *Los Angeles Times*, p. B2.

Pascarella, E. T., & Terenzini, P. T. (2005). *How college affects students: A third decade of research* (Vol. 2). San Francisco, CA: Jossey-Bass.

Tomasho, R. (2009, April 22). Study tallies education gap's effect on GDP. *Wall Street Journal.*

U.S. Census Bureau. (2008). *Bureau of Labor Statistics.* Washington, DC: Author.

> A bachelor's degree continues to be a primary vehicle of which one gains an advantaged socio-economic position in American society."
>
> —Ernest Pascarella & Patrick Terenzini, *How College Affects Students*

Note well! Sacrifices made in the short run can bring long-run benefits that last a lifetime.

Reflection 3.3

Which of the eight benefits of college listed in Box 3.1 were you least aware of?

Which of the eight benefits do you think would be most important to the students you'll be working with in your leadership role?

Theories of College Student Development

What is a *theory*? A theory may be defined as a body of connected concepts and general principles that help us organize, understand, and apply knowledge in specific situations. How do theories come about? Over time, researchers begin to notice consistent patterns and sequences of human behavior that allow them to draw general conclusions. Thus, a theory is well supported by research evidence. Don't confuse a *theory*, which is supported by evidence, with a *hypothesis*, which is an informed guess about what *might* be true, but still needs to be tested to confirm whether it *is* true.

The Purpose and Value of Theories

Although theories are supported by evidence, no single theory can account for the whole truth or tell the whole story. This is why more than one theory exists in virtually every field of study. Different theories explain different portions of the total truth or knowledge that exists in any given field. If you find yourself thinking, "Why do we need all these theories anyway?" keep in mind that explaining and improving the human experience and the world around us isn't a simple process; it involves consideration of multiple factors and perspectives. To be able to comprehend and respond to these multiple factors and perspectives, more than one theory is needed.

Unfortunately, when people hear the word *theoretical*, they often think it's exactly the opposite of *practical*; they mistakenly conclude that a theory is something that is not useful in the "real world." However, the opposite is true. Theories have very practical benefits; they help us pull together separate, disconnected concepts and research findings and put them into an organized form that can be used to guide and improve the effectiveness of our practical efforts—including the efforts of peer leaders.

> *Nothing is more practical than a good theory.*
> —Kurt Lewin, social psychologist and first leading authority on group dynamics

Theories can help your understand, predict, and respond to what will take place in your leadership work with students. It's true that there is no substitute for experience, and you will learn much about leadership through hands-on trial-and-error experiences as a peer leader. However, you need to go into these experiences with some research-based clues that will enable you to put your day-to-day experiences into a broader context and make sense of them. To put it another way: you can't find your way through a dense forest without a map or a compass to guide you.

Familiarity with some essential theories about college student development provides a framework for helping you anticipate common patterns of student behavior and enables you to learn more from your leadership experiences. For example, college student development theories enable us to anticipate and appreciate the fact that students typically move through stages of personal and intellectual development during their college experience. Similarly, group development theory helps us understand that groups gradually move through different phases or stages (including some early conflict) before they perform effectively as a team. Leaders need to be aware of these theories, because without them, it's difficult (if not impossible) to prepare for and deal with these events effectively.

In this chapter, three major theories of college student development will be discussed that should provide you with a comprehensive overview of the key factors that affect and promote student success in college:

- Student Involvement Theory (Alexander Astin),
- Student Retention Theory (Vincent Tinto), and
- Student Identity Development Theory (Arthur Chickering).

Astin's Student Involvement Theory

To be successful, students need to become "actively involved" in their college experience. Alexander Astin, a prominent higher education research scholar, has developed an influential theory on how college success depends on students' depth of involvement in the college experience. Simply stated, involvement theory predicts that success in college is related to the amount of time and energy students invest in the learning process—both *inside* and *outside* the classroom (Astin, 1984, 1993). Thus, one of your goals as a peer leader should be to increase students' level of active involvement or engagement in the college experience. Here are some strategies for doing so.

Implications and Applications of Astin's Student Involvement Theory

Encourage students to *act* (engage in some action) on what they're learning. Students can be sure that they're actively involved in the learning experience if they engage in one or more of the following *actions* during the learning experience:

- **Writing**—when students write in response to what they're learning (e.g., taking notes on what they're reading, rather than passively underlining sentences).
- **Speaking**—when students say out loud what they're trying to learn (e.g., explaining a course concept to a study group partner, rather than just looking over it silently).
- **Organizing**—when students connect or integrate the ideas they're learning into an outline, diagram, or map.

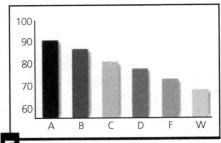

Figure 3.2 Relationship between Class Attendance Rate and Final Course Grades

Encourage students to get to class. Over the past 75 years, multiple studies have found a direct relationship between class attendance and course grades—as one goes up or down, so does the other (Anderson & Gates, 2002; Devadoss & Foltz, 1996; Grandpre, 2000; Launius, 1997; Moore, 2003, 2006; Moore et al., 2003; Shimoff & Catania, 2001; Wiley, 1992; Wyatt, 1992). **Figure 3.2** represents the results of a study conducted at the City Colleges of Chicago, which shows the relationship between students' class attendance during the first five weeks of the term and their final course grades.

Encourage students to become actively involved in class. During professors' lectures, the best way to apply the principle of active involvement is to engage in the action of taking notes. Writing down what the instructor is saying essentially forces students to pay closer attention to what's being said and reinforces their retention of what they've heard. Remind students that their role in the college classroom is not to be an absorbent sponge or passive spectator who simply sits back and soaks up information through osmosis. Instead, their role is more like that of an aggressive detective or investigative reporter who's on a search-and-record mission. They should actively search for knowledge, pick their instructor's brain, pick out their instructor's key points, and record their "pickings" in their notebook.

Encourage students to spend time twice as much time working on their courses outside of class as they spend in class. Studies clearly show that when college students spend more time on academic work outside of class, the result is better learning and higher grades (National Survey of Student Engagement, 2003). One study of over 25,000 college students found that the percentage of students receiving mostly "A" grades was almost three times higher for students who spent 40 or more hours per week on academic work than it was for students who spent 20 hours or less. Among students who spent 20 or fewer hours on academic work, the percentage receiving grades of "C" or below was almost twice as high as it was for students who spent 40 or more hours per week on academic work (Pace, 1990a, 1990b).

As a general rule, students should spend two hours out of class for every hour spent in class. For instance, if they're taking 15 credits, they're spending about 15 hours per week in class; thus, they should be spending almost 30 hours per week on their courses outside of class. Unfortunately, less than 40% of beginning college students report having studied for six or more hours per week during their final year in high school (Pryor et al., 2012), and only one-third expect to spend more than 20 hours per week preparing for class in college (National Survey of Student Engagement, 2009). This has to change if new college students are to earn good grades.

Reflection 3.4

Estimate how many hours per week you spent on schoolwork outside of class during your senior year of high school. How does this compare with the number of hours you spent on coursework during your first year of college?

If your students need further motivation to put in the time to earn good grades in college, remind them that there is a strong relationship between academic success in college grades and career success after college. Research on college graduates indicates that the higher their grades were in college, the higher (1) the status (prestige) of their first job, (2) their starting salary, and (3) their career mobility (ability to change jobs or move into different positions). This relationship between college grades and career advantages exists for students at all types of colleges and universities—regardless of the reputation or prestige of the institution that the students are attending (Pascarella & Terenzini, 1991, 2005). In other words, how well students do academically in college matters more to their career success than where they went to college.

Tinto's Theory of Student Retention

Over the past 40 years, the opportunity to attend college has expanded dramatically in the United States. The percentage of high school graduates that go on to enroll in college is increasing for all racial and income groups (NASH & Education Trust, 2009). Unfortunately, however, these gains in college *access* rates are not being matched by gains in college *success* rates (Hunt & Carruthers, 2004). The United States has one of the highest college-going rates in the world, yet its college completion rates (both two-year and four-year) rank near the bottom half of all industrialized nations (College Board, 2008a; National Governors Association, 2008). Only 35% of America's college students graduate with a bachelor's degree in four years and just over half (52%) graduate within six years (College Board, 2009). For students who attend college part time, the completion rate is even lower: less than 25% graduate within eight years (Complete College America, 2011). Viewing America's current college completion rates from an international perspective, the United States has dropped from number two in the world to number 12, and is in the process of dropping further (Complete College America, 2010). If this trend continues, the current generation of college-age Americans will be the first in U.S. history to be less educated than its parents (CCSSE, 2010).

One of the major reasons why campuses have developed peer leadership programs is to promote student retention—i.e., help students persist in college until they graduate. Vincent Tinto, an educational sociologist, has developed a widely adopted theory of student retention. His work has strongly influenced how campus leaders and student development professionals think about retention and take action to support it (Tinto, 1987, 1993). According to Tinto, understanding and promoting student retention requires consideration of student experiences that take place *before* and *at* (during) college.

Before–college factors. Students enter college with different sets of "pre-entry attributes," such as their family's prior educational experiences and their level of academic preparedness or readiness for college. For example, some students enter college with better developed reading and writing skills and have had greater exposure to family members who already graduated from college. These prior experiences can affect how much academic and personal support students need to succeed in college.

Students' initial intentions and level of commitment at college entry can also affect the likelihood that they will persist to graduation. Students who are less committed to college in general or to the specific college they are attending will need more guidance and assistance to hang in there and graduate.

At–college factors. Although before-college factors influence retention, Tinto asserts that students' experiences at college have the greatest effect on their persistence to graduation. Those experiences include interactions with faculty, student support professionals, and peer leaders.

Tinto's theory posits that a student's college experience take place in two general areas: academic and social. As their college experience unfolds, students become connected or "integrated" into the campus to various degrees. The greater their degree of academic and social integration, the more likely they will persist to graduation. Simply stated, when students become socially and academically integrated, they see themselves as integral members of a college family or community; as a result, they are more likely to remain in college and complete their degrees (Tinto, 1987, 1993; Braxton, Sullivan, & Johnson, 1997).

The powerful role that peer leaders can play in connecting new students to the campus community was highlighted in a national study of 41,000 first-year college students at 72 campuses. The study revealed that new students who were linked with peer leaders reported they were more connected with fellow students and faculty, were more involved in campus life outside the classroom, and felt a greater sense of "belonging" (Barefoot, 2003).

> *Call it a clan, call it a network, call it a tribe (or) call it a family. Whatever you call it, whoever you are, you need one.*
>
> —Elizabeth Jane Howard, award-winning British novelist

Implications and Applications of Tinto's Student Retention Theory

As a peer leader, you can intentionally promote students' academic and social integration by helping students make the following connections.

Connect Students with Faculty

Research repeatedly indicates that when students interact with faculty, they are more likely to remain in college and get more out of their college experience (Astin, 1993). Student-faculty contact outside of class is strongly associated with improved academic performance, increased critical thinking, greater college satisfaction, higher graduation rate, and stronger desire to continue education beyond college (Pascarella & Terenzini, 2005). As a peer leader, you can help students connect with faculty by:

- Encouraging them to use faculty office hours—for example, urge students to seek out their instructors for help with course concepts they find difficult, to clarify their understanding of course assignments, or to seek out opportunities for undergraduate research and internships. (New college students may need to be reminded that, unlike high school instructors, college instructors have office hours during which they make themselves available to students, and that students who go to their offices are not students who have fallen behind, are failing, or are being disciplined for misbehavior.)
- Sharing your personal experiences with faculty, including how you approached them and posed questions to them.
- Suggesting that students approach faculty members who share their educational and personal interests and faculty who you know are approachable and helpful.
- Encouraging students to attend events at which faculty will be present, such as scholarly presentations on campus.
- Advising students to participate in activities with faculty, such as field trips.
- Inviting faculty members as guests to meetings you hold with your students.

Students may have fears and preconceptions about college faculty—e.g., "they're not interested in spending time with inexperienced students" or "I would not know what to say to them." Students may need you to help them gain enough confidence to approach faculty, pose questions, and create relationships. Remind students that faculty are more likely to remember students who have approached them and show interest in their course material, and that faculty are more willing to write letters of recommendation for students who have interacted with them outside of class and whom they've come to know on a more personal basis.

Author's Experience When I teach first year courses, I instruct each of my students to visit during the office hours of each of their faculty at least three times during each semester. As a matter of fact, I make this a requirement for my particular class. At the end of the class I do an evaluation of my class based on student responses to a set of questions about content, instructon and suggestions of improvement. Each time, the number one positive statement students make is how helpful those office visits were. Indeed, they told me that it not only assisted them in understanding the material in each of their classes but it helped them to understand the value of college and how to navigate the sometimes turbulent waters that college students experience. Interacting with faculty in and out of the classroom is by far one of the strongest engagement strategies for learning lessons for success in college and success in life after college.

— *Aaron Thompson*

Connect Students with Academic Advisors

Regardless of your particular leadership role on campus, make a point of stressing to your students the importance of connecting with academic advisors. Too often, students view the role of academic advisors narrowly as folks you go to only for class scheduling or to check graduation requirements. Yes, they do those things, but advisors have so much more to offer. Advisors can:

- Help students choose or change majors.
- Alert students to opportunities relating to their major.
- Refer students to a broad array of campus resources.
- Direct and guide students to appropriate resources and opportunities at different stages of their college experience.
- Help students construct a plan to graduate and graduate on time.
- Assist students with choices, plans, and procedures related to opportunities after graduation.

In short, academic advisors can be much more than course schedulers: they can also serve as mentors, student support agents, and powerful partners for peer leaders to work with to help students succeed.

Connect Students to Campus Resources

Using campus resources is an important, research-backed principle of college success, and it is a natural extension of the principle of active involvement. Successful students are active learners not only inside the classroom, but outside of class as well. Active involvement outside of class includes making use of campus resources. Studies show that students who utilize campus resources report higher levels of satisfaction with their college experience and are more likely to continue college until they complete their degrees (Pascarella & Terenzini, 1991, 2005). Your campus is brimming with opportunities and possibilities for students. It's probably safe to say that after college, students will never again be a member of any other organization or community with as many resources and services that are intentionally designed to promote their learning, development, and success. If they capitalize on the campus resources available to them, and if they utilize effective college-going strategies (such as those suggested in this book), they can create a life-changing experience for themselves that will enrich the quality of their life for the remainder of their life.

As a peer leader, you can pay a key role in helping students connect with and capitalize on campus resources by:

- Making students aware of their purpose and the value of using them.
- Sharing positive experiences you have had with these resources or the positive experiences of other students who have used these resources.
- Actively referring students to these resources. (Specific strategies for making effective student referrals are discussed in Chapter 4.)

> *Do not be a PCP (Parking Lot—Classroom—Parking Lot) student. The time you spend on campus will be a sound investment in your academic and professional success.*
>
> —Drew Appleby, professor of psychology

Note well! Using campus resources is not only valuable, it's also "free" because the cost of these services has already been covered by college tuition. By investing time and energy in campus resources, students increase their prospects for success in college and maximize the return on their fiscal investment in college—they get a bigger bang for their buck.

Reflection 3.5

What are the most important connections—whether they be people or resources—that you have made thus far on campus?

_____

Have these connections benefited or changed you in any way? In your leadership role, will you have the opportunity to encourage students to make the same connections that benefited you?

An essential first step in making effective use of campus resources is to become aware of what they are and what they're designed to do. The following sections describe what key campus services are offered on most college campuses and provide reasons why students should utilize them.

Learning Center (a.k.a. Academic Support or Academic Success Center). This is the campus resource designed to strengthen students' academic performance. The individual and group tutoring provided here can help students master difficult course concepts and assignments, and the people working here are professionally trained to help you learn how to learn. While professors may have expert knowledge of the subject matter they teach, learning resource specialists are experts on the process of learning. These specialists can equip students with effective learning strategies and show them how they can adjust or modify their learning strategies to meet the unique demands of different courses and teaching styles they encounter in college.

> At colleges where I've taught, it's always been found that the grade point average of students who use the Learning Center is higher than the college average and honors students are more likely to use the center than other students.
>
> —Joe Cuseo, professor of psychology and co-author of this text

Studies show that college students who become actively involved with academic support services outside the classroom are more likely to attain higher grades and complete their college degrees, particularly if they begin their involvement with these support services during the first year of college (Cuseo, 2003). Also, students who seek and receive assistance from the Learning Center show significant improvement in academic self-efficacy—that is, they develop a stronger sense of personal control over their academic performance and higher expectations for academic success (Smith, Walter, & Hoey, 1992).

Despite the powerful advantages of using academic support services, these services are typically underused by college students, especially those students who need them the most (Cuseo, 2003; Knapp & Karabenick, 1988; Walter & Smith, 1990). Some students believe that seeking academic help is admitting they are not smart, self-sufficient, or unable to succeed on their own. Make sure students don't buy into this belief system. Using academic support services does not mean they're helpless or clueless; it indicates that they're motivated, resourceful, and striving for academic excellence.

Note well! The purpose of the Learning Center or Academic Support Center is not just to provide remedial repair work for academically underprepared learners or to supply academic life support for students on the verge of flunking out. It's a place where all learners benefit, including students who are well prepared and highly motivated.

Writing Center. Many college campuses offer specialized support for students who would like to improve their writing skills. Typically referred to as the Writing Center on most campuses, this is the place where you can receive assistance at any stage of the writing process, whether it be collecting and organizing ideas, composing a first draft, or proofreading a final draft. Since writing is an academic skill that students will use in many of their college courses, if they can strengthen their writing, they're likely to improve their overall academic performance. Thus, strongly encourage students to capitalize on this campus resource.

Disability Services (a.k.a. Office for Students with Special Needs). If students have a physical or learning disability that is interfering with their performance in college, Disability Services is the campus resource to consult for assistance and support. Programs and services typically provided by this office include:

- Assessment for learning disabilities;
- Verification of eligibility for disability support services;
- Authorization of academic accommodations for students with disabilities; and
- Specialized counseling, advising, and tutoring.

> *The next best thing to knowing something is knowing where to find it.*
>
> —Dr. Samuel Johnson, English literary figure and original author of the *Dictionary of the English Language* (1747)

College Library. The library is the campus resource for developing information literacy—the ability to locate, evaluate, and use accurate and scholarly information for completing research assignments (e.g., term papers and group projects). These are transferable skills that students can apply to any course and can use throughout their lives. Remind students that they can learn from library science professionals just as they can learn from any course instructor.

Academic Advisement Center. Whether or not students have an assigned academic advisor, the Academic Advisement Center is a campus resource for help with course selection, educational planning, and choosing or changing a major. Studies show that college students who have developed clear educational and career goals are more likely to persist in college until they complete their degrees (Willingham, 1985; Wyckoff, 1999). Research also indicates that beginning college students need help clarifying their educational goals, selecting an academic major, and exploring careers (Cuseo, 2005; Frost, 1991). For new college students, being undecided or uncertain about educational and career goals is nothing to be embarrassed about. However, they should start thinking about their educational future during their first year of college. Help first-year students connect early and often with an academic advisor to help them clarify their educational goals and find a field of study that's most compatible with their interests, talents, and values.

Office of Student Life (a.k.a. Office of Student Development). The Office of Student Life is the campus resource for student development opportunities outside the classroom, including student clubs and organizations, recreational programs, leadership activities, and volunteer experiences. Research consistently shows that experiential learning—which takes place outside the classroom—is as important to your personal development and future success as learning that takes place inside the classroom (Kuh, 1995; Kuh, Douglas, Lund, & Ramin-Gyurnek, 1994; Pascarella & Terenzini, 2005). This is why these out-of-class opportunities are now referred to as *co-curricular experiences* (co meaning "equal" or "equivalent"), rather than *extracurricular activities*. More specifically, studies show that students who become actively involved in co-curricular experiences outside of class are more likely to:

- Enjoy their college experience;
- Graduate from college; and
- Develop leadership skills that enhance their career performance beyond college (Astin, 1993).

When students devote a reasonable amount of their out-of-class time to co-curricular experiences, research shows that it doesn't interfere with students' academic performance. In fact, college students who become involved in co-curricular and volunteer experiences that total no more than 15 hours per week actually earn higher grades than students who do not get involved in any out-of-class activities (Pascarella, 2001; Pascarella & Terenzini, 2005).

Note well! *Co-curricular experiences are also resume-building experiences, and campus professionals with whom students interact while participating in co-curricular activities (e.g., the director of student activities or dean of students) are valuable resources for personal references and letters of recommendation to future schools or employers.*

Financial Aid Office. This campus resource is designed to help students finance their college education. If students have any questions about how to obtain assistance in paying for college, the staff of this office is there to guide them through the application process. The paperwork needed to apply for and secure financial aid can sometimes be confusing or overwhelming. Encourage students not to let this paperwork intimidate them from seeking financial aid; professionals in the Financial Aid Office can help them work through this process. Also, remind students that they can also seek help from this office to find:

- Part-time employment on campus through a work-study program;
- Low-interest student loans;
- Grants; and
- Scholarships.

Lastly, if students have any doubt about whether they're using the most effective plan for financing their college education, advise them to see a professional in the Financial Aid Office.

Counseling Center. Personal counseling can not only help students cope with the adjustments associated with the transition to college, but also help them gain greater self-awareness and enable them to reach their full potential.

Note well! *Personal counseling is not just for students who are experiencing emotional problems. It's for all students who want to enrich their overall quality of life.*

Health Center. Making the transition from high school to college often involves adjustments and decisions affecting students' health and wellness. Good health habits help students cope with stress and reach peak levels of performance. The Health Center is the campus resource for information on how students can maintain their physical health and personal wellness. It is also the place to go for help with illnesses, sexually transmitted infections or diseases, and eating or nutritional disorders.

Career Development Center (a.k.a. Career Center). Research on college students indicates that they're more likely to continue in school and graduate when they see a connection between their present academic experience and their future career goals (Levitz & Noel, 1989; Tinto, 1993; Wyckoff, 1999). Studies also show that most new students are uncertain about what careers they would like to pursue (Gordon & Steele, 2003). If the first-year students you're working with are uncertain about their future careers, remind them that they are members of a club that includes a very large number of other students. Their uncertainty is understandable and normal because they haven't had the opportunity for hands-on work experience in the real world of careers.

The Career Development Center is the place where students can go for help in finding meaningful answers to the important question of how to connect their current college experience with their future career goals. This campus resource typically provides such services as personal career counseling, workshops on career exploration and development, and career fairs where students are able to meet professionals working in different fields. Although it may seem like a career is light-years away because they're just beginning college, remind new students that the process of exploring, planning, and preparing for career success starts in their first year of college.

Reflection 3.6

Which of the campus resources described on pp. 62–66 do you think your students are (1) most likely to benefit from, and (2) least likely to take advantage of without your encouragement?

Connect Students with Each Other

As you know, students listen to other students, often more than they do to faculty, staff, and administrators. One of the most powerful things you can accomplish as a peer leader is facilitating long-lasting associations and friendships among students, which pave the way for social networks of mutual support. By doing so, you supply them with social capital—the sociological superglue that can bond them together until they graduate together.

The connections that students make with other students can have enormous impact on students' sense of campus community, their personal and social well-being, and the overall quality of their college experience. Strive to connect students with each other early and often, and in manners that are positive, productive, and supportive of their personal growth and development. You can be a catalyst for connecting students to students by:

- Bringing students together to share meals,
- Attending cultural or athletic events on campus together with your students,
- Playing sports or working out together, and
- Facilitating the formation of learning teams, which is described in more detail below.

Helping Students Form Learning Teams

Effective learners are *interactive* learners who interact and collaborate with others in the learning process to widen and deepen their knowledge. Research clearly demonstrates that college students learn as much from peers as they do from instructors and textbooks (Astin, 1993; Pascarella, 2005). When seniors at Harvard University were interviewed, nearly every one of them who had participated in learning teams considered the experience to be crucial to their academic progress and success (Light, 1990, 1992, 2001).

Remind students that learning teams are much more than study groups formed the night before an exam. Effective learning teams collaborate more regularly and work on a wide variety of academic tasks. Listed below are different types of learning teams that students can form to improve their performance on the key academic tasks in college. Encourage your students to join or form these types of teams.

Note-taking teams. Immediately after a class session ends, students can take a couple of minutes to team up with each other to compare and share notes. Since sustained listening and note-taking are demanding tasks, it's likely that an individual student will miss something that one of their teammates picked up and vice versa. Also, by teaming up immediately after class to review their notes together, the team has the opportunity to consult with the instructor about any missing or confusing information before the instructor leaves the room.

Author's Experience During my first term in college, I was having difficulty taking complete notes in my biology course because the instructor spoke rapidly and with an unfamiliar accent. I noticed another student (Alex) sitting in the front row who was trying to take notes as best he could, but he appeared to be experiencing the same difficulty. Following one particularly fast and complex lecture, we looked at each other, noticed that we were both shaking our heads in frustration, and began talking about it. We decided to team up immediately after every class and compare our notes to identify points we missed or found confusing. First, we helped each other by comparing and sharing our notes in case one of us picked up something that the other missed. If there were points that we both missed or couldn't figure out, we went to the front of class together to consult with the instructor before he left the classroom. At the end of the course, Alex and I finished with the highest grades in the course.

— *Joe Cuseo*

Reading teams. After completing their reading assignments, students can team up with each other to share their highlighting and margin notes. Students can compare notes on what they identified to be the most important points in the reading and what should be studied for upcoming exams.

Writing teams. Students can provide each other with feedback to revise and improve the quality of their writing. Studies show that when peers assess each other's writing, the quality of their writing and attitude toward writing improves (Topping, 1998). Students can form peer-writing teams to help at any or all of the following stages in the writing process:

1. **Topic selection and refinement**—to help each other come up with a list of possible topics and subtopics to write about;
2. **Pre-writing**—to clarify their purpose for writing and their reading audience;
3. **First draft**—to improve their general writing style and tone; and

4. **Final draft**—to proofread and correct mechanical errors before submitting their written work.

Library research teams. Many first-year students are unfamiliar with the process of conducting academic research at a college or university library. Some students may experience "library anxiety" and try to avoid even setting foot in the library, particularly if it's large and intimidating (Malvasi, Rudowsky, & Valencia, 2009). Forming library research teams is an effective way for students to develop social support groups that can make trips to the library less intimidating and transform library research from a solitary experience into a collaborative venture that's done as a team.

Note well! It's perfectly acceptable and ethical for students to team up with other students to search for and share resources. This isn't cheating or plagiarizing—as long as the final product is completed individually and what's turned in to the instructor represents the student's own work.

Test results–review and assignment–review teams. After receiving the results of course examinations and assignments, students can collaborate with peers to review their results as a team. By comparing answers, they're better able to identify the sources of their mistakes, and by seeing the answers of teammates who received maximum credit on particular questions, they get a clearer picture of where they went wrong and what they should do to get it right next time.

Encourage students to team up after tests and assignments *early* in the term because it will enable them to get a better idea of what the instructor expects from students throughout the remainder of the course. Students can use this information as early feedback to diagnose their early mistakes, improve their subsequent performances, and raise their course grades—while there's still plenty of time left in the term to do so.

Team-instructor conferences. Making team visits to instructors in their offices is an effective way to get additional assistance in preparing for exams and completing assignments. Seeing instructors in teams, rather than individually, has the following advantages:

- Students are more likely to feel comfortable venturing onto the instructor's "turf" in the company of peers than entering this unfamiliar territory on their own. As the old expression goes, "There's safety in numbers."
- When students make office visits as a team, the information shared by the instructor is heard by more than one person, so each student may pick up some useful information that someone else may have missed, misinterpreted, or forgotten to write down.
- Students save time for their instructors because it allows them to help multiple students at the same time, reducing the need for them to engage in "repeat performances" for individual students making separate visits at separate times.
- Students send a message to their instructor that they're serious about the course and are motivated because they've taken the time—ahead of time—to connect with their peers and prepare for the office visit.

Two heads are better than one, not because either is infallible, but because they are unlikely to go wrong in the same direction.
—C.S. Lewis, English novelist and essayist

Learning Communities

Your campus may offer students the opportunity to participate in a learning community program, whereby the same group of students registers for the same block of courses during the same term. If this opportunity is available on your campus, encourage students to take advantage of it because research suggests that students who participate in learning community programs are more likely to:

- Become actively involved in classroom learning,
- Form their own learning groups outside of class,
- Report greater intellectual gains, and
- Continue their college education (Tinto, 1997, 2000).

If learning community programs are not offered on your campus, suggest to new students that they create their own informal learning communities by finding other first-year students who are likely to be taking the same courses as they are (e.g., the same general education or pre-major courses). These students can get together before registration to see if they can enroll in the same two or three courses together. This will allow them to reap the benefits of a learning community, even though a formal learning community program may not be available to them on campus.

Connect Students with Key Members of the Campus Community

Summarized in **Box 3.2** are ten strategies to share with students to help them connect with different members of the college community who are likely to play key roles in promoting their college success.

In addition to connecting students with other members of the campus community, you can promote student success by keeping an eye and ear out for underlying causes of student dissatisfaction with your college or university. Peers are often more aware of students' intentions to leave the college—and their reasons for leaving—long before these intentions become apparent to faculty, staff, and administrators. As a peer leader, you can promote student retention on your campus by assuming any of the following roles:

- Helping gather information on students' campus experiences and sources of satisfaction or dissatisfaction (e.g., by conducting personal interviews or focus groups). Students are more likely to feel comfortable sharing their true feelings about the college with a trusted peer than with an older authority figure.
- Serving as a student representative on the college's retention committee.
- Serving as a retention ambassador who can articulate to other students: (1) the college's exceptional and distinctive features, (2) exciting campus opportunities and programs, and (3) the advantages of continuing their education at the college until they complete their degree.
- Identifying and interceding with students who show signs of intended withdrawal (e.g., students who have not pre-registered for next term's classes, or students who haven't reapplied for financial aid).
- Conducting "exit interviews" with students who are in the process of departing. (A peer is likely to receive more honest responses from departing students than a professional employee of the college.)
- Surveying students (by mail or online) who have withdrawn from the college to assess (1) their reasons for leaving, (2) whether there was anything the college could have done better to help them stay enrolled, and (3) if there is anything the college could do to help them return in the future.

Box 3.2

Making Connections with Key Members of the College Community

Studies consistently show that students who become socially integrated or connected with other members of the college community are more likely to remain in college and complete their degrees. Below is a list of ten tips you can share with students to help them make important interpersonal connections on campus. Help new students make these connections as soon as possible so that they can begin constructing a base of social support that will strengthen their performance during their critical first year in college.

Encourage your students to:

1. Connect with a student development professional that they may have met during orientation.
2. Connect with peers who commute to campus from the same geographical area. (If their schedules are similar, encourage them to carpool together.)
3. Join a college club, student organization, campus committee, intramural team, or volunteer service group whose members may share the same personal interests or career goals as they do.
4. Connect with more experienced students who are in their major or intended field of study (e.g., by joining a departmental club).
5. Connect with motivated classmates to work together in teams to take notes, complete reading assignments, and study for exams.
6. Connect with faculty in a field that they're considering as a major by visiting faculty during office hours, conversing briefly with them after class, or communicating with them via e-mail.
7. Connect with an academic support professional in the learning resource center to receive personalized academic assistance or tutoring in any course in which they'd like to improve their performance (even if it's to make a good grade better).
8. Connect with an academic advisor to discuss and further develop their future educational plans.
9. Connect with a college librarian to get early assistance and a head start on any research project that they've been assigned.
10. Connect with a personal counselor or campus minister to discuss any college adjustment or personal life issues that they may be experiencing (even if it's not yet a problem, but something they want to know more about and use as a source for personal growth).

Chickering's Theory of Student Identity Development

In addition to Astin's student involvement theory and Tinto's theory of student retention, Arthur Chickering has designed a highly regarded theory of student development in college that identifies seven key "vectors" of personal identity that take place during the college experience (Chickering, 1969; Chickering & Reiser, 1993). Listed below are short descriptions of Chickering's seven vectors with references to chapters in this text that address each of these vectors.

1. **Achieving competence:** Gaining a stronger sense of self-efficacy and self-confidence with respect to one's intellectual and interpersonal skills. (Chapters 5 and 6)
2. **Managing emotions:** Learning to recognize and control emotions, such as anxiety, anger, and frustration. (Chapters 4 and 7)
3. **Moving through autonomy toward interdependence:** Developing independence and less reliance on others to determine one's personal values, but at the same time growing to appreciate the value of working interdependently (collaboratively) with others. (Chapters 5 and 8)

4. **Developing mature interpersonal relationships:** Becoming open to developing new and closer interpersonal relationships, along with greater appreciation for intercultural differences and commonalities. (Chapters 4 and 9)
5. **Establishing identity:** Becoming comfortable with oneself (e.g., one's sexuality, ethnicity, or belief systems) and developing a personal identity that's self-created rather than determined by others. (Chapters 5 and 7)
6. **Developing purpose:** Finding one's calling or purpose in life and making intentional plans about the future. (Chapter 5)
7. **Developing integrity:** Developing a coherent system of personal values and ethical principles and acting in ways that are consistent with those values and principles. (Epilogue)

Reflection 3.7

Look back at Chickering's seven developmental challenges during the college years. Which ones do you think will pose the greatest challenge for the students with whom you'll be working?

Implications and Applications of Chickering's Theory of Student Identity Development

All of us will experience challenges and opportunities in Chickering's seven areas of development throughout our lives, but during the college years, these challenges come at a fast and furious pace. Chickering stresses that college students don't proceed through these vectors in a strictly sequential or linear fashion; instead, they typically "spiral" through them, going forward, then back, then forward, depending on their personal circumstances and college experience. Thus, it's best not to view these seven vectors as sequential stages of development. Instead, view them as general areas for targeting your peer leadership efforts, keeping in mind that student development in these areas will not always progress smoothly over time (and may actually regress from time to time). One of your key roles as a peer leader is to support students in their quest to meet each of these areas of challenge. In fact, another classic and very influential theory of college student development posits that students' growth is maximized when they experience a balance of challenge and support (Sanford, 1967).

As a peer leader, you, too, will continue to mature in these seven areas as you work to promote their development among the students you lead. This will advantage you as a peer leader because it will increase your ability to empathize and identify with your students (and they with you). To maximize this identification process, we encourage you to complete Exercise 3.3 at the end of this chapter.

Summary and Conclusion

New students encounter different adjustments at different times during their first term in college; they are more likely to be receptive to information and advice that's delivered at times when they really need it. Simply stated, students are more willing and ready to acquire knowledge that's timely and immediately applicable to their current challenges and concerns. You can provide just-in-time support to students when they need it the most by thinking of students' first term on campus as unfolding in three major stages: Early, Middle, and Late.

Early Stage (first six weeks of term). "Fitting in" socially is very important to new students at the very start of their college experience. Social needs (e.g., finding friends, overcoming shyness, and dealing with homesickness) are likely to be high-priority needs for students during the first few weeks of college. You can help students meet these needs by creating early opportunities for new students to interact with peers, faculty, and student support agents on campus (e.g., academic advisors and student development specialists).

Middle Stage (the week before and after midterm exams). This stage may be defined as the time period just before and after midterm—the midpoint of the term when students are likely to encounter their first wave of college exams, assignment deadlines, and course grades. The terms *midterm slump* and *midterm crunch* have been coined to capture the stresses associated with this stage of the semester. As a peer leader, this is the time of the term to help students respond constructively to midterm grades and use their results as feedback for improving their future performance. Midterm is also the time of the term when students are likely to be most receptive to your recommendations and referrals to academic support services on campus.

Late Stage (between midterm and final exam week). Providing students with emotional support may be critical at this stage because anxiety and depression are more likely to surface toward the end of the term as students try to cope with the pressures of final projects, final exams, and returning home for the holidays (Thanksgiving and Christmas). As a peer leader, the final weeks of the first term may be an especially critical time to be sensitive and responsive to the wellness needs of new students, because end-of-term projects, papers, and upcoming final exams are often accompanied by sleep loss (pulling all-nighters), disruption of normal eating and exercise routines, and stress related to academic performance anxiety or fear of failure.

It's also important to remember that new students experience a variety of adjustment issues at the same time. One strategy for being sensitive and responsive to the multiple adjustments of new students at any point in time during the first term is to remain mindful that college adjustment usually come in three major forms.

1. **Social adjustments** (Do I belong here?). Developing new relationships while maintaining or modifying relationships with their family and high school friends.
2. **Academic adjustments** (Will I make it?). Dealing with the heavier academic workload in college and the reality that their first grades in college are likely to be lower than those they earned in high school.
3. **Motivational adjustments** (Is it worth it?). Thinking about whether the benefits of college outweigh its costs (the time and money).

By asking students how things are going with respect to these three aspects of their college experience and supporting them in areas where they may be in jeopardy, you should be able to remain aware of and responsive to the most important needs of new students throughout their first-year experience.

Theories can help you understand, predict, and respond to what will take place in your leadership work with students. Familiarity with some essential theories about college student development provides a framework for helping you anticipate common patterns of student behavior and enables you to learn more from your leadership experiences. In this chapter, three major theories of college student development were discussed to provide you with a comprehensive overview of the key factors that affect and promote student success in college.

Student Involvement Theory (Alexander Astin). Simply stated, student involvement theory predicts that success in college is related to the amount of time and energy students invest in the learning process, both *inside* and *outside* the classroom. Thus, one of your goals as a peer leader should be to increase students' level of active involvement or engagement in the college experience.

Student Retention Theory (Vincent Tinto). According to Tinto, student retention and graduation are influenced by student experiences that take place *before* and *at* (during) college. Before-college factors include students' level of academic preparedness or readiness for college and their family's level of educational attainment. These prior experiences can affect how much academic and personal support students need to succeed in college. Although before-college factors influence retention, Tinto asserts that students' experiences at college have the greatest effect on their persistence to graduation. His theory posits that a student's college experience take place in two general areas: academic and social. The greater the degree of students' academic and social integration (connection), the more likely they are to persist to graduation. Simply stated, when students become socially and academically integrated, they see themselves as integral members of a college family or community; as a result, they are more likely to remain in college and complete their degrees. As a peer leader, you can promote students' academic and social integration by connecting students with faculty, advisors, campus resources, and supportive peers.

Student Identity Development Theory (Arthur Chickering). Chickering's theory of student development in college identifies seven key "vectors" of personal identity that take place during the college experience:

1. **Achieving competence:** Gaining a stronger sense of self-efficacy and self-confidence with respect to one's intellectual and interpersonal skills.
2. **Managing emotions:** Learning to recognize and control emotions, such as anxiety, anger, and frustration.
3. **Moving through autonomy toward interdependence:** Developing independence and less reliance on others to determine one's personal values, but at the same time growing to appreciate the value of working interdependently (collaboratively) with others.
4. **Developing mature interpersonal relationships:** Becoming open to developing new and closer interpersonal relationships, along with greater appreciation for intercultural differences and commonalities.
5. **Establishing identity:** Becoming comfortable with oneself (e.g., one's sexuality, ethnicity, or belief systems) and developing a personal identity that's self-created rather than determined by others.
6. **Developing purpose:** Finding one's calling or purpose in life and making intentional plans about the future.
7. **Developing integrity:** Developing a coherent system of personal values and ethical principles and acting in ways that are consistent with those values and principles.

These seven vectors can serve as general areas for targeting your peer leadership efforts, keeping in mind that student development in these areas will not always progress smoothly over time (and may actually regress from time to time). You, too, will continue to mature in these seven areas as you work to promote their development among the students you lead.

Internet Resources

For additional information related to the ideas discussed in this chapter, we recommend the following websites:

Differences between High School and College
smu.edu/alec/transition.asp

Different Stages of Student Challenges/Adjustments during the First Year of College
www.altoona.psu.edu/fts/docs/WCurve.pdf

Benefits of the College Experience and College Degree
trends.collegeboard.org/education_pays

Theories of College Student Development
www.hpcnet.org/dos/theory_psychosocial

Exercise 3.1 *Journal Reflections*

1. If you were to make a presentation to high school seniors about the major *differences* between high school and college, what would be the top three differences on your list?

2. If you were asked to share your top three tips for college success with new students during orientation, what would be your top three suggestions?

3. Based on your experiences as a first-year student on your campus, what do you think will be the most difficult or challenging situations your students will face?

4. a. What practices or policies on your campus do you think are working to *increase* student satisfaction and retention? Why?

   b. What practices or policies on your campus do you think are working to *decrease* student satisfaction and retention? How could these practices or policies be improved? As a peer leader, do you see any way you could help make these improvements happen?

Exercise 3.2 *Identifying College Stressors*

Read the list of college stressors below and rate them on a scale from 1 to 5 (1 = lowest level of stress; 5 = highest level) in terms of how stressful each one is likely to be for the students you are leading or mentoring.

Potential Stressor	*Stress Rating (1= lowest; 5 = highest)*
Tests and exams	1 2 3 4 5
Writing assignments	1 2 3 4 5
Class workload	1 2 3 4 5
Pace of courses	1 2 3 4 5
Performing up to expectations	1 2 3 4 5
Speaking up in class or in front of groups	1 2 3 4 5
Handling personal freedom	1 2 3 4 5
Time pressure (e.g., meeting deadlines)	1 2 3 4 5
Financial pressure (e.g., not enough money)	1 2 3 4 5
Organizational pressure (e.g., losing things)	1 2 3 4 5
Living independently	1 2 3 4 5
The future	1 2 3 4 5
Decisions about a major or career	1 2 3 4 5
Moral and ethical decisions	1 2 3 4 5
Finding meaning in life	1 2 3 4 5
Emotional issues	1 2 3 4 5
Physical health	1 2 3 4 5
Intimate relationships	1 2 3 4 5
Sexuality	1 2 3 4 5
Family responsibilities	1 2 3 4 5
Family conflicts	1 2 3 4 5
Peer pressure	1 2 3 4 5
Family pressure	1 2 3 4 5
Loneliness or isolation	1 2 3 4 5
Roommate conflicts	1 2 3 4 5
Conflict with professors	1 2 3 4 5
Campus policies or procedures	1 2 3 4 5
Transportation	1 2 3 4 5
Technology	1 2 3 4 5
Safety	1 2 3 4 5
Other stressors you would add to this list:	
_____	1 2 3 4 5
_____	1 2 3 4 5
_____	1 2 3 4 5

Review your highest ratings and identify:

1. The time or stage during the first year when students are most likely to experience this source of stress

2. A coping strategy you would suggest to your students for dealing with each source of stress

3. A campus resource to which you could refer students to help them deal with that source of stress

Exercise 3.3 *Facilitating Students' Social Integration*

Construct a short "sales pitch" or "elevator speech" you could share with students to persuade them to make a personal connection with:

1. A faculty member

2. An academic advisor

Deliver your pitch to a fellow student leader or friend and ask for feedback on its persuasiveness.

Exercise 3.4 *Applying Chickering's "Seven Vectors" of Development*

Think of a situation or scenario that students are likely to experience in each of Chickering's seven vectors of development (described on pp. 70–71).

Write a description of this scenario that includes information relating to each of the following questions:

1. How does the scenario relate to the challenges of that particular vector of Chickering's theory?

2. What could you do to help students manage the scenario and advance to a higher level of maturity with respect to that particular vector?

chapter 4

Social and Emotional Intelligence
The Foundation of Effective Leadership

Reflection 4.1

When you think about someone who's "intelligent," what personal characteristics come to mind?

Human intelligence was once considered to be one general trait that could be detected and measured by a single intelligence test score. The singular word *intelligence* has now been replaced by the plural word *intelligences* to reflect the fact that humans can display intelligence (mental ability) in many forms other than performance on an intelligence quotient (IQ) test. One of these alternative forms of human intelligence is *social intelligence*, also known as interpersonal intelligence, which refers to the ability to communicate and relate effectively to others (Gardner, 1993, 1999). Research indicates that this type of human intelligence is a better predictor of personal and professional success than intellectual ability (Goleman, 2006), and leadership scholars have long noted the importance of interpersonal relationship skills for successful leadership (Bass & Avolio, 1994; Feidler & Chemers, 1984).

Another form of human intelligence is *emotional intelligence*, which refers to the ability to recognize our own emotions, the emotions of others, and how our behavior affects the emotions of others (Salovey & Mayer, 1990). Research on this form of intelligence reveals that it's a better predictor of personal and occupational success than performance on intellectual intelligence tests (Goleman, 1995). Research also shows that emotional self-awareness—a key element of emotional intelligence—is essential for effective leadership (Avolio & Luthans, 2006; Goleman, Boyatzis, & McKee, 2002; Higher Education Research Institute, 1996).

> *Relationships are the key to leadership effectiveness. . . . Leadership is inherently relational.*
> —Komives, Lucas, & McMahon, *Exploring Leadership: For College Students Who Want to Make a Difference*

> *Knowing and managing your emotional response while helping another is crucial to your own well-being and to your ability to help.*
> —Steve Ender & Fred Newton, *Students Helping Students*

Key Elements of Social and Emotional Intelligence

Successful leadership rests on a solid foundation of interpersonal communication and human relations skills (Hogan et al., 1994; Johnson & Bechler, 1998). Leaders in all contexts and roles need to be skilled at initiating and developing relationships with those whom they lead. As a peer leader, if you develop these skills, your students will be more likely to trust you and be receptive to your mentoring and leadership.

Relationship development doesn't happen by chance, but through an intentional process of (1) initiating interpersonal interaction, (2) getting to know others as unique individuals, and (3) showing genuine interest in others by asking questions about them.

Initiating and Developing Interpersonal Relationships

Creating and sustaining open and deep relationships with students is a key component of effective peer leadership and mentoring. Here are some specific strategies for starting this important relationship-building process.

- If you're working as a peer leader in the classroom, arrive early to strike up conversations with students and stick around afterward to interact with them.
- Periodically invite your students for informal get-togethers at places that are comfortable and conducive to conversation. For your first get-together, suggest a short meeting (e.g., not longer than an hour) so that it doesn't seem as if you're asking for a major commitment. You can always go overtime if the conversation is going well.
- On the day before the get-together, remind your students about the time, place, and purpose of your meeting. Reminders work wonders for both stimulating students' memory and confirming their commitment to attend.
- At your first meeting, learn about your students' backgrounds, interests, experiences, and goals.
- Keep track of what you learned in this initial meeting and build on it to guide your conversations in future meetings. (See Chapter 5 for a wide range of questions you could ask students to learn about them as individuals.)

Effective and Professional Communication Strategies

In any leadership role, the ability to communicate effectively with others is vital. Communication skills enhance your credibility with your students, keep your partners in the loop, and demonstrate your commitment and competence to other members of the campus community. Listed below are some key suggestions for communicating effectively with your students and leadership partners.

- When you first meet your students, ask them for their contact information and their preferred modes of communication (e.g., e-mail, Facebook, cell phone). Don't rely exclusively on a single mode of communication; be willing to utilize multiple mediums to maximize the probability that your message is received and read by all individuals for whom it's intended.
- Establish mutual agreements (norms) about what your students can expect from you with respect to your communication and what they will commit to in terms of reading and responding to your communications.
- Communicate regularly (e.g., at least once a week) with your students to:
  1. Keep them informed about upcoming events, activities, and meetings. (Consider developing a website for your program that includes planned activities, key resources, and helpful links.)

> *In all helping situations, the interaction between two people—the quality of the relationships—is probably the most important factor in the success and helpfulness that occurs.*
>
> —Steve Ender & Fred Newton, *Students Helping Students*

Tale FROM THE Trenches

For each student, I met for a minimum of a half-hour, usually to grab lunch, and discussed what they have going on outside of classes, how they feel about the upcoming year, and if they've thought about what they'll do with their education/degree. Initially I was just a little bit nervous to meet individually with some of my students, but it went well and I did just fine facilitating conversation.

—PEER LEADER

> *Leadership is interpersonal influence, exercised in a situation, and directed, through the communication process.*
>
> —Tannenbaum, Weschler, & Massarik, *Leadership and Organization: A Behavioral Science Approach*

2. Help them stay on track with respect to their tasks and goals.
3. Seek feedback about their needs or areas of concern.
4. Acknowledge their achievements, accomplishments, birthdays, and milestones—e.g., completing their first term or year in college.

- Personalize your communications; make them sound less like a formal business memo and more like a personal letter that's coming from one human being to another (e.g., type the name of the person(s) at the start of the message and your name at the end of the message).

- Unless your communication is confidential, keep partners and supervisors in the loop by copying messages to them about what your program or organization is doing. This serves to heighten others' interest and sense of involvement with your program, and it gives them the opportunity to provide you with advice and resources. Students may prefer to communicate via informal texting or Facebook, but communication with professional partners and supervisors may require use of standard campus media (e.g., campus e-mail or Blackboard).

- When communicating with others online, use the same human relations skills that you would use when communicating in person. The terms *e-mail etiquette* and *netiquette* have made their way into our current vocabulary because some people forget to apply principles of social etiquette and interpersonal sensitivity when they communicate electronically. In fact, it's probably even more important to use effective verbal communication skills when communicating online because we don't have nonverbal communication channels available to us to support and clarify our written words. Thus, when communicating electronically, we need to be especially careful about choosing our words thoughtfully and delivering our messages sensitively.

- At all times and in all communication media, keep it professional. Use appropriate language and be sure not to make negative remarks about any student or member of the campus community. Others will judge you on the quality and professionalism of your communications. Don't forget that your e-mails and Facebook posts can be instantaneously transmitted anywhere and to anybody. Using insensitive slang, slurs, or profanity is not only counter to the higher expectations that the community has for peer leaders as student role models, but may also violate campus codes of conduct and place the peer leader at risk of facing judicial consequences.

Reflection 4.2

Would you say you're good at initiating relationships? Why?

Which strategies for initiating relationships cited on pp. 89–91 would you feel most comfortable using in your particular peer leadership role?

The Power of Listening

Although being a dynamic and eloquent speaker can be helpful in certain leadership roles, spectacular oratory skills are less important than effective listening and human relations skills. Others will not hear you if they don't believe that you're committed to hearing them. Students may be interested in your wisdom

> *We have been given two ears and but a single mouth in order that we may hear more and talk less.*
>
> —Zeno of Citium, ancient Greek philosopher and founder of Stoic philosophy

and advice, but they're likely to be even more interested in being heard; they're far more likely to listen to you (and to each other) if they feel listened to.

Human relations experts often recommend that we spend less time talking and more time listening and listening well (Nichols, 1995; Nichols & Stevens, 1957). When people are asked to cite the attributes of their best friends, being a good listener always ranks among the top attributes cited (Berndt, 1992). It's also one of the top skills employers look for when hiring and promoting employees (Maes, Weldy, & Icenogle, 1997; Winsor, Curtis, & Stephens, 1997).

Active Listening Strategies

Because most people can listen at a rate that's at least four times faster than the average rate at which people speak, if we're not actively doing something while listening, it's easy to drift off or lapse into *passive listening*—hearing the words with our ears, but not thinking about those words because our minds are partially somewhere else. While listening, we need to remain aware of the natural tendency of the mind to drift off to other places and consciously combat this tendency by working hard at focusing our thoughts on the speaker's message. This process is referred to as *active listening*, and it's crucial in all leadership and mentoring roles. More specifically, active listening involves (1) listening with attention focused on the speaker's message (rather than focusing on what you want to say next), (2) listening with attention to both the verbal and nonverbal messages being sent by the speaker, and (3) listening with empathy (personal interest and concern).

Active listening doesn't just happen naturally. It's a skill that must be prepared for and practiced until it becomes a regular habit. To develop the habit of active listening, engage in the following practices:

- Prior to your conversations with students, consciously remind yourself to listen intently.
- During your conversations, monitor whether you're actually thinking about what the speaker is saying. Good listeners take personal responsibility for listening with understanding and interest; in contrast, poor listeners put all the responsibility on the speaker to make the message clear and interesting.
- To check if you're following the speaker's message, occasionally summarize or paraphrase what you hear the speaker saying in your own words (e.g., "What I hear you saying is . . ."). This ensures the speaker that you're understanding the message and taking it seriously.
- Actively engage with the speaker by occasionally asking questions (e.g., "Can you tell me a little more about that?"). This demonstrates your interest and encourages the speaker to continue communicating and elaborate on their ideas.
- Pause after you ask questions to allow the speaker time to formulate a thoughtful response. (Be patient with occasional periods of silence.)
- If you pose a question that doesn't trigger an initial response, rephrase it in a different way.
- Avoid the urge to interrupt the speaker when you think you have something important to say. Wait until the speaker pauses or has completed his/her train of thought.
- If the speaker stops and you start to say something at the same time the speaker begins to speak again, don't overpower the speaker by speaking louder; let the speaker continue before you express your ideas.

- Check to be sure you're understanding what the person is feeling in addition to what they're saying (e.g., "I'm sensing that you're feeling . . .").
- Be sensitive to nonverbal messages, such as tone of voice and body language, because they can often provide clues to the feelings behind the speaker's words. (For instance, speaking at a high rate and with high volume may indicate frustration or anger, and speaking at a low rate and with low volume may indicate dejection or depression.)
- Be sure that your own nonverbal messages convey to the speaker that you're interested and non-judgmental. (See **Box 4.1** for ways to send positive nonverbal communication signals while listening.)

Box 4.1

Nonverbal Behaviors Associated with Active Listening

Effective listening not only involves receiving messages from the speaker, but also involves sending messages to the speaker. Good listeners listen with their whole body and use their body language to signal their attention and interest. The acronym "SOFTEN" can be used as a mnemonic device (memory improvement strategy) for remembering the different body language signals we should send while listening.

S = Smile. Smiling sends a signal of acceptance and interest; however, you should smile periodically, not continually. (A sustained smile can come across as a synthetic or artificial pose.)

Sit Still. Fidgeting and squirming send the message to the speaker that you're feeling anxious or bored.

O = Open Posture. Avoid closed-posture positions, such as crossing your arms or folding your hands; they can send a message that you're not open to what the speaker is saying or passing judgment on what is being said.

F = Forward Lean. Leaning back can send a signal that you're not "into" what the person is saying or evaluating (psychoanalyzing) the person saying it. In contrast, leaning forward sends the message that you're looking forward to what the speaker is going to say next.

Face the Speaker Directly. Line up your shoulders with the speaker's shoulders, rather than turning one shoulder away, which can send the message that you want to get away or give the speaker the "cold shoulder."

T = Touch. An occasional light touch on the arm or hand can be a good way to communicate warmth—but avoid repeated touching, stroking, or rubbing, which could be interpreted as inappropriate intimacy (or sexual harassment).

E = Eye Contact. Lack of eye contact sends the message that you're looking around for something more interesting or stimulating than the speaker. However, eye contact shouldn't be continuous or relentless because that becomes close to staring or glaring. Instead, strike a happy medium by making periodic eye contact.

N = Nod Your Head. Slowly and periodically nodding your head while listening sends the signal that you're following what is being said and affirming the person who is saying it. However, avoid rapid and repeated head nodding, because this may send the message that you want the speaker to hurry up and finish up so you can start talking!

Sources

Barker, L., & Watson, K. W. (2000). *Listen up: How to improve relationships, reduce stress, and be more productive by using the power of listening.* New York, NY: St. Martin's Press.

Nichols, M. P. (1995). *The lost art of listening.* New York, NY: Guilford Press.

Purdy, M., & Borisoff, D. (Eds.). (1996). *Listening in everyday life: A personal and professional approach.* Lanham, MD: University Press of America.

Reflection 4.3

Are there any effective nonverbal listening messages cited in Box 4.1 that you weren't already aware of, or that you need to work on?

Oral Communication Skills

In addition to listening skills, relationship building requires effective *speaking* skills—the ability to verbally communicate our ideas to others. Described below are our top recommendations for strengthening verbal communication skills. Some of these strategies may appear to be very basic or fundamental, but they're also very powerful. In fact, it's probably because they're so basic that people overlook them or forget to use them consistently. Don't be fooled by the seeming simplicity of the following suggestions, and don't underestimate the power of their impact on your social interactions and relationships.

Communicate your ideas precisely and concisely. When you speak, your goal should be to get to your point, make your point, get "off stage," and shift the focus of conversation back to your students. Great leaders occasionally have great things to say, but they shouldn't use their leadership positions to become "stage hogs" who dominate the conversation and gobble up more than their fair share of conversation time.

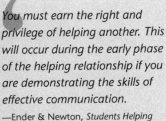

Note well!   Leadership isn't about you, it's about them.

Our verbal messages become less time-consuming and concise when we avoid tangents, unnecessary details, and empty fillers such as *like, kinda like, I mean, I'm all,* and *you know.* Fillers such as these just "fill up" and waste conversation time while adding nothing substantial or meaningful to the speaker's message. Excessive use of fillers may also result in the listener losing patience, interest, and respect for the speaker (Daniels & Horowitz, 1997).

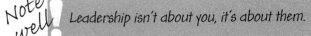

Box 4.2   Avoiding the Three "Egos": The Type of Leader (and Person) You Don't Want to Be

Egocentric—an egocentric person views the world as if he or she is always at the center of it (including every conversation), showing little interest in or empathy for others. The words *me* and *I* appear with relentless frequency when an egocentric person speaks, and you get the feeling that this person is not talking *with* you but *at* you.

Egotist—an egotistical person is basically *conceited*, a braggart who boasts, shows off, and spends lots of conversation time talking about his or her outstanding features or personal accomplishments.

Egoist—an egoistic person is basically *selfish*, i.e., unwilling to share time or resources with others or do things for others.

Take time to think about what you're going to say before you say it. Silent spells during a conversation can often make us feel uncomfortable. To relieve the discomfort of silence, it's tempting to rush in and say anything that will get the conversation going again. Although this may be well intended, it can result in speaking before (and without) thinking. More often than not, it's better to hold back your words and think them through before blurting them out.

Silent spots in the conversation shouldn't always be viewed as a "communication breakdown." Instead, they may indicate that the people involved in the conversation are pausing to think deeply about what they are saying and are comfortable enough with each other to allow these reflective pauses to take place.

Reflection 4.4

Would you say that you're a good conversationalist?

If yes, what makes you so?

If no, why not?

Human Relations Skills (a.k.a. People Skills)

How do you build relationships that allow students to see you as trustworthy and credible? The first step in the process is to get to know students and demonstrate interest in their lives, their well-being, and their development. Students may be interested in what you know, but they're more likely to be interested in knowing whether you're interested in them.

Work hard at remembering the names of your students and leadership partners. When you remember someone's name, you acknowledge that person's uniqueness and individuality. It makes others feel less like anonymous faces in a crowd and more like special individuals with distinctive identities.

You've likely heard people claim they don't have a good memory for names; however, there's no evidence that ability to remember names is some kind of natural gift, talent, or inherited trait. Instead, it is a learned skill that's developed through personal effort and consistent use of effective memory-improvement strategies. The following strategies can be used to help you remember the names of your students and leadership partners:

- Consciously pay attention to the name of each person you meet. When you first meet someone, listen intently for the person's name rather than focusing on the impression you're making on that person, the impression that person is making on you, or what you're going to say next. Often, when people say, "I forgot that person's name," what they really mean is they never *got* that person's name in the first place because they weren't paying attention to it when they first heard it.

- Reinforce your memory of the person's name by saying it or rehearsing it within a minute or two after you first hear it. For instance, if your friend Gertrude has just introduced you to Geraldine, you might say, "Geraldine, how long have you known Gertrude?" By using a person's name soon after you've heard it, you intercept memory loss at the time when it's most likely to occur—immediately after information is first received and processed.

- Strengthen your memory of an individual's name by associating it with other information you've learned or know about the person. For instance, you can associate the person's name with (1) your first impression of the individual's personality, (2) a physical characteristic of the person, (3) your topic of conversation, (4) the place where you met, or (5) a familiar word that rhymes with the person's name. By making a mental connection between the person's name and some other piece of information, we make the name more meaningful and more memorable.

> People don't care how much you know until they know how much you care.
>
> —John C. Maxwell, speaker, pastor, and author of more than 60 books, primarily focusing on leadership

> We should be aware of the magic contained in a name. The name sets that individual apart; it makes him or her unique among all others. Remember that a person's name is to that person the sweetest and most important sound in any language.
>
> —Dale Carnegie, author of the bestselling book *How to Win Friends and Influence People* and founder of the Dale Carnegie Course, a worldwide leadership training program for business professionals

- We write down things we want to be sure to remember. We can do the same for remembering names by keeping a name journal that includes the names of new people we meet plus some information about them (e.g., what they do and what their interests are). Whenever you meet someone new, make note of that person's name by recording it in a name journal, along with the situation or circumstances in which you met.

> **Note well!** Developing the habit of remembering names is not only a social skill that can bring you friends and improve your social life, it's also a powerful professional tool that can promote your career success in whatever field you may pursue.

Refer to people by name when you greet and interact with them. When you greet a person, be sure to use the person's name in your greeting. Saying, "Hi, Waldo," will mean a lot more to Waldo than simply saying "Hi" or "Hi, there," which sounds like you just saw some object or unknown person "out there" (like sending a letter "to whom it may concern"). By continuing to use people's names after you've learned them, you continue to send them the message that you haven't forgotten who they are and you continue to strengthen your memory for their names.

Reflection 4.5

Do you know the names of all the students and campus partners you work with in your leadership role?

If not, what could you do right now to learn and remember their names?

Show interest in others by remembering information about them. Ask people questions about their personal interests, plans, and experiences. Listen closely to their answers, especially to what seems most important to them, what they care about, or what interests them, and use this information as topics of conversation with them. For one person that topic may be politics, for another it may be sports, and for another it may be relationships.

When you see that person again, ask about something that was brought up in your last conversation. Try to get beyond the standard, generic questions that people routinely ask after they say "Hello" (e.g., "What's going on?"). Instead, ask about something specific you discussed with them last time you spoke (e.g., "How did you make out on that math test you were worried about last week?"). You can use informal encounters to continue to build rapport with others by showing that you remember them and care about them. Our memories often reflect our priorities—we're more likely to remember what's important to us. When you remember people's names and something about them, it lets them know that they're important to you.

Furthermore, when you show interest in others, you're likely to find that others start showing more interest in you; you're also likely to start hearing others say that you're a good listener and a great conversationalist.

Studies show that college students' success is enhanced when students experience *personal validation*—when they feel significant, recognized, and affirmed as individuals and believe that they matter to the college or that the college cares about them (Rendón, 1994; Schlossberg, Lynch, & Chickering, 1989; Terenzini et al., 1996). One of the most effective ways to provide students with personal validation is to know them (by name) and show interest in them.

> *Note well!* Good human relations skills also include leaders saying little things like "please" and "thank you" to others, such as administrative assistants, who may not rank high in the "organizational pecking order," but who routinely perform critical jobs and services for those in leadership positions.

The Art of Questioning

Demonstrating interest in other students by asking questions about them is an effective way to build rapport and gradually deepen relationships. There is no fool-proof set of "best questions" or sequence of questions to ask students. However, if you plan ahead for the types of questions you will ask others, you can increase the likelihood that the conversation will flow smoothly and that you'll receive the types of information you need to most effectively support your students.

1. **"Check-in" questions.** A check-in is a type of question that can get conversation going in one-on-one and group situations. A check-in question involves sharing responses to a prompt, such as:

   - What's your favorite bumper sticker and why?
   - What's your favorite movie?
   - What's the most hilarious thing you've experienced in college thus far?
   - What would you do tomorrow if you won the lottery?
   - What weather forecast would describe how you are feeling today?

   Check-ins can get the conversation going because they're non-threatening. If you do a Google search with the phrase *conversation starters*, you'll find hundreds of check-in prompts; the possibilities are endless.

> *Note well!* Conversations can only become meaningful and reach a deeper level after the conversationalists have become comfortable with each other on a surface level.

2. **"How's it going" questions.** A simple way to show interest in others and promote dialogue with them is by posing "how's it going" questions with respect to:

   - Social life (e.g., roommates, friends, and family)
   - Academic life (e.g., classes, tests, and assignments)
   - Emotional life (e.g., their stress level)
   - Physical well-being (e.g., their health)
   - College life (e.g., "Was it what you expected it to be?" "Are you happy you came here?" "What's been your biggest adjustment or challenge thus far?")

3. **"Open-ended" questions.** After your students have become comfortable talking to you, you may start conversations or meetings by asking a question like "What would you really like to talk about today?" This is called an *open-ended question* because it gives the respondent the freedom to answer it in different ways and plenty of room to elaborate. In contrast, *closed-ended*

questions are those that can be answered in a single word. Compare the following two types of questions:

a. "What grade did you get on your last chemistry test?" (closed-ended question)

b. "Could you have done anything differently to improve your performance on your last chemistry test?" (open-ended question)

The first question calls for a one-word response and the second question invites elaboration and full statements. The second question also allows the peer leader to learn more about the student's study or test-taking strategies and help improve the student's future performance.

Reflection 4.6

Design three open-ended questions that you could use in your specific leadership role on campus.

_____

4. **"Probing" questions.** Probing is a conversational process that invites and encourages others to share more details about their experiences, needs, concerns, attitudes, or feelings. Coming to understand others' experiences in more detail and depth will position you to better assist them. Probes are often used spontaneously during the course of a conversation and cannot always be scripted. However, you can plan ahead to use effective probes like the following:

a. "That's interesting. Can you tell me more about _____."

b. "It seems like there's a lot going on with _____. Can you give me some details?"

The process of probing may feel awkward initially and it may seem like you're violating the person's privacy. Certainly, you don't want to force others to elaborate; however, by using probes occasionally and sensitively, you can encourage students to open up to you. Conversations often develop like a spider's web; you can weave them into more intricate and elaborate patterns through artful probing.

Tale FROM THE **T**renches

So far, the biggest thing I have noticed is how the conversation has evolved beyond just the questions I had prepared and how willing the students are to talk. All of them feel open talking to me about whatever problems they are facing. It has been cool to see them open up. I can now ask them more focused questions and interact with them on a deeper level.

—PEER LEADER

Asking Deeper, More Meaningful Questions

Initially, you just want to make your students feel comfortable talking about anything, but after you've built rapport and solidified your relationship with them, you are positioned to pose more meaningful or significant questions. As a peer leader, here are some deeper questions that you can pose to students:

- How do you feel you have done with adjusting to life as a college student so far and all that it entails? What have you done well? What could you do differently?

- Who are you connected to on campus so far? Do you think that you're developing relationships that will contribute to your success? What can you do to expand your connections to other people or resources on campus?

- How are things going academically? What learning strategies are working well for you and what are areas in which you need to improve?

- What would you say are the major sources of stress in your life right now? Have you been able to keep these sources of stress at a manageable level?
- Do you feel you are changing (or have changed) as a person since coming to college? Why?

Keep track of the types of questions that tend to generate elaborate and passionate responses from your students. Very detailed and strongly expressed responses can serve as clues to what's most important or meaningful to the students you're working with and areas in which they would be most receptive to your support, guidance, or leadership.

Reflection 4.7

Design some "deep" questions of your own that would be pertinent to your leadership role on campus.

Briefly explain why you think these questions would stimulate deeper dialogue.

Emotional Intelligence

In addition to social skills such as listening, speaking, and questioning, effective leadership requires an ability to relate to people with emotional sensitivity and emotional intelligence. Listed below are suggestions for relating to others in ways that are sensitive to their feelings, enabling them to feel emotionally "close" to you, and strengthening their sense of trust in you.

Be caring and compassionate. Show authentic concern for your students' feelings. For example, instead of asking the routine question "How are you?" or "How's it going?", ask, "How are you feeling?". Really listen to what they say in response to your question. Showing genuine concern for others not only helps them feel more comfortable about sharing information with you, it also helps to create more opportunities for you to learn from and about the people you meet. Studies show that when people share their feelings with others, it helps them feel understood and feel better about themselves (Reis & Shaver, 1988).

Be willing to share information about yourself. How often have you witnessed this rapid, ritualistic interchange between two individuals?

Person A: "Hi, how's it going?"
Person B: "Fine, how you doing?"

No real personal information is shared by either person, and chances are that neither person expects or wants to hear about how the other person is truly feeling (Goffman, 1967). Such social rituals are understandable and acceptable when two people first interact with each other. However, if they continue interacting and want to move their relationship forward, they need to move beyond these ritualistic routines toward mutual sharing of personal experiences.

As you have more contact and conversations with your students, engage in some self-disclosure—share or disclose a little more of yourself. If someone asks you, "How's it going?" or "How are you?", take these questions seriously and respond by sharing something meaningful about yourself. By so doing, you model

> *The leaders who have the most influence on people are those who are the closest to them.*
>
> —Kouzes & Posner, *The Student Leadership Challenge*

> *I've learned that people will forget what you said, people will forget what you did, but people will never forget how you made them feel.*
>
> —Maya Angelou, African American poet, educator, and best-selling author

what you'd like your students to do for you. By sharing information about yourself, you pave the way for others to do the same. Sharing your aspirations, fears, success stories, and stumbling blocks can encourage mutual sharing. Naturally, you want to do this gradually and in small doses, rather than blowing others away with sudden "hot blasts" of intimacy and private details about your personal life.

Selectively and gradually sharing more about yourself shows others you trust them well enough to share a part of yourself. Building up close and meaningful relationships through this give-and-take process of progressively sharing personal information is referred to by human relations specialists as the *intimacy spiral* (Cusinato & L'Abate, 1994). You can start the sharing process by noticing the little things that students share and respond by sharing something similar about yourself that's a little more personal or intimate. Relating a similar experience of your own demonstrates *empathy*—your ability to understand the feelings of others. It also lets others know that you have something in common, which, in turn, encourages them to share more of themselves with you (Adler & Towne, 2001).

Be complimentary. Look for the positive in others and praise it when you see it. Giving students sincere compliments provides them with personal validation, elevates their self-esteem, and increases the probability that they'll continue doing what you complimented them for doing. Simply stated, people like to be around others who make them feel good about themselves.

Remember that you can compliment others for many things besides their physical appearance. Complimenting others about their actions or inner character is more meaningful than complimenting them on their outer appearance because you're recognizing them for something less superficial and more substantive.

As you notice students improving and succeeding, acknowledge them with kind words, a quick e-mail or Facebook message, or a modest celebration. Even the smallest victories can be noted, such as students consistently getting to class, completing a major assignment, or visiting a professor during office hours. These simple gestures reinforce success-promoting behavior and strengthen your relationship with the students. Little, unexpected compliments can often have a big, unexpected impact on your students and their impression of you.

Stay positive and enthusiastic. Simply stated, people prefer to be around others who are upbeat and enthusiastic. Studies show that others are more likely to respond positively to us if we're in a good mood (Byrne, 1997). As the old adage goes, "Enthusiasm is contagious"—others can "catch" our good mood and, when they do, their own mood improves. In contrast, when we're pessimistic, angry, or "down," we bring others down with us, and we drive down our chances of connecting with them and influencing them in a positive way. In a major study of effective student leaders, it was discovered that one of their most distinguishing characteristics was their enthusiasm—and their ability to spread that enthusiasm to the students with whom they worked (Kouzes & Posner, 2008).

> *People are more willing to follow someone they like and trust. To be trustworthy, you must trust and be open both with and to others. That means . . . telling people the same things you'd like to know about them.*
> —Kouzes & Posner, *The Student Leadership Challenge*

> *Be kind, warm and willing to offer unconditional positive regard. People thrive when they feel safe, valued and well supported.*
> —Carl Rogers, an influential American psychologist and among the founders of the humanistic approach to psychology

> *Kind words can be short and easy to speak, but their echoes are truly endless.*
> —Mother Teresa of Calcutta, Albanian Catholic nun and winner of the Nobel Peace Prize

Reflection 4.8

In your particular leadership role, what could you say or do to maintain optimism and enthusiasm among your students?

Helping Students with Personal Issues and Problems

Good leaders and mentors are willing and able to help others in need. Given your leadership position on campus, it's very likely that students will come to you for advice or assistance about personal issues, particularly if you've taken the time to establish a relationship with them. Listed below are strategies for helping you help others who may seek your support:

- First and foremost: Be a good listener and lend an empathetic ear. If you act as a sounding board and let others "bounce" their thoughts and feelings off you, a solution may bounce right back to them. Simply giving others a chance to get their personal feelings out in the open and allowing them the opportunity to think out loud can lead them to discover effective solutions on their own. Their problem may be solved with your doing little more than listening in a concerned and compassionate way.

- Before beginning to suggest strategies for solving the problem, help the students (and help yourself) clarify the problem. To do so, use phrases such as "It seems like . . ." "Could it be that . . . ?" "I get the impression that . . .". An effective helper assists others in understanding and discovering solutions to their own problems. Often, the best help we can provide others is to ask the right question, rather than giving the right answer. Good questions help others help themselves by leading them to see their problem more clearly, which, in turn, can lead them to an effective solution.

- If you've experienced a similar problem, or have had other students come to you with a similar problem, share that experience. It's always nice for people to know that they're not the only ones who are facing challenges, have worries, or stumble once in a while. Don't be afraid to let your students know that others have encountered similar obstacles and difficulties.

   Sharing a similar experience of your own can help others feel that their problem isn't unusual and give them more confidence about solving it. However, avoid using the common expression "I know how you feel." Although this statement may be well intended, it's presumptuous to say that you *know* how someone else feels because it's impossible to get into that person's head and actually experience what that person is currently feeling.

- Be sure not to dismiss or minimize the person's feelings. Avoid saying things like "Oh, don't worry about it, everything will be all right." or "You'll get over it." Comments like these make it sound like the person's feelings are unjustified or exaggerated (e.g., "you're making a mountain out of a molehill"), or being discounted.

- Try to avoid directly instructing or dictating to others what they should do. An effective helper is someone who helps students see their options clearly but allows them to make their own decisions. When students make their own choices, they "own" their decisions, and when they take action on those deci-

> *A friend is a person with whom I may be sincere. Before him, I may think aloud.*
>
> —Ralph Waldo Emerson, American author, philosopher, and orator

> *A problem well-defined is half solved.*
>
> —John Dewey, influential philosopher, psychologist, and educational reformer

> *When I ask you to listen to me and you begin to tell me why I shouldn't feel that way, you are trampling my feelings.*
>
> —Author unknown

> *The point of being a mentor is not to create dependency but to promote self-responsibility, not to decide for someone, but to encourage self-direction.*
>
> —Ender & Newton, *Students Helping Students*

sions, their sense of self-control and self-esteem is strengthened. Rather than becoming dependent on you to solve problems for them, they're more likely to become independent thinkers and self-helpers who gain self-confidence in their ability to solve their own problems.

 You're not an "expert" and your job is not to save or rescue students: you're a facilitator whose job is to respect and empower students.

- If supportive listening and questioning are not enough to help solve the person's problem, then "Plan B" would be to help the student identify possible solutions. Brainstorming can serve as an effective method for generating possible solutions to personal problems. (See **Box 4.3** for a quick overview of the key steps in the brainstorming process.)

Box 4.3

The Process of Brainstorming

Key Steps

1. List as many ideas as you can, generating them rapidly without stopping to evaluate their validity or practicality. Studies show that worrying about whether an idea will work often blocks creativity (Basadur, Runco, & Vega, 2000). So, at this stage of the process, just encourage students to let their imaginations run wild and don't worry about whether the ideas generated are impractical, unrealistic, or impossible.
2. Help students use the list of ideas or strategies they generate as a springboard to trigger additional ideas, or combine two or more ideas into one strategy.
3. After students run out of ideas, help them critically evaluate the list of ideas they've generated and eliminate those that they think would be least effective or realistic.
4. From the remaining list of ideas, ask them to choose the best idea or best combination of ideas.

The point of brainstorming is to create as many good options as possible and allow the students to choose those one that they're most comfortable with, believe in, and find most consistent with their values (you don't impose your values). Helping students identify options and make their own choices serves to respect their individuality and promotes their sense of control or ownership of the choices they make. Students can use the process of brainstorming to solve any other problem they may encounter. Thus, by exposing students to the process, you not only help students solve their current problem, you empower them with a strategy they can use to solve future problems on their own.

- After you help students lay out all their options, if they still cannot make a decision and ask for your advice about what choice to make, start by sharing strategies that have worked for you or other students in the past. Be sure to offer your advice as a concerned friend, not as an expert authority. For instance, before giving your advice, introduce it by saying, "This is just a suggestion . . ." or "I wonder if this might . . .". Offer your recommendations as reasonable possibilities rather than surefire solutions. The last thing you want to do is give the impression that you're a professional psychotherapist by saying things like "What your problem is . . ." or "What you need to do is . . .". Statements such as these can make the person feel like a patient who is receiving your expert "diagnosis and treatment."

- Before ending your discussion, sum up what next steps will be taken to solve the problem or resolve the issue (e.g., what actions will be taken and when those actions will be taken).

- If the problem is too serious or beyond your capability to deal with, encourage the student to seek professional help (e.g., from an advisor or counselor on campus). Know your limitations; don't be afraid to say, "I don't know, but I can refer you to someone who does know." An intermediate step would be to consult with a campus professional who has more knowledge than you about the type of problem the student has come to you with, and come back to the student with different options suggested by the professional. (As a courtesy, you should inform the student that this is what you'd like to do.)

- Last and most importantly, if someone comes to you for help or assistance with a personal problem, any information that person shares with you must remain confidential. This isn't only the legally correct thing to do; it's also the ethically responsible thing to do because it respects the person's privacy and reinforces the person's trust and respect in you. The only exception to this rule is when a student shares information with you that indicates the student is in danger or is putting others in danger.

Note well! The *Family Education Rights and Privacy Act* (often referred to as *FERPA* or the "Buckley Amendment") legally prohibits communicating student information to others. If you have any doubt about whether you can share information about a student, before sharing it, check with your program supervisor.

Reflection 4.9

Do you often find people coming to you for advice?

If yes, what issues do they come to you for help with, and what do you think this says about where your leadership strengths or talents may lie?

Serving as an Effective Referral Agent

In some cases, you will be able to help students solve problems, but often you'll need to connect them with other resources and professionals on campus. You can strengthen your ability to be a connection catalyst by (1) asking students about their needs, concerns, and interests, (2) continually acquiring knowledge about the people, support resources, and student opportunities on your campus, and (3) referring students to campus partners who are most qualified to address their needs or concerns.

Learn about the support services available to your students. Familiarize yourself with the campus catalog (whether in print or online), especially the portions that relate directly to the students with whom you work. Also, review the key contacts and resources listed in any program handbook that may be available for the particular program you're representing as a student leader. In addition, peruse websites (and Facebook pages) for campus- and community-based resources that may be relevant to your students' needs. If you know where to refer students,

I have helped students close the gap between their potential and performance by listening to their concerns and giving them information about things that can help them, whether it is the counseling center on campus, the tutoring services, or the student groups they can get involved in.

—Peer Leader

The next best thing to knowing something is knowing where to find it.

—Samuel Johnson, author of *A Dictionary of the English Language* (1755), considered to be one of the greatest single achievements of scholarship.

they're less likely to get the "runaround" and more likely to get around and use the resources available to them.

Note well! *For your students, you're likely to be the resource for all resources on campus. You provide the first line of defense for your students, and by providing accurate and timely referrals, you can intercept their problems and issues before they turn into full-blown crises.*

Get to know the student support professionals on your campus. A leader need not be a superhero or a superstar. You cannot do everything for everybody. You have partners who can help you in your efforts to help others. Introduce your students to other people, opportunities, and resources, and encourage them to build networks of support. These relationships include other students, peer leaders, graduate students, faculty, teaching assistants, advisors, career professionals, and professionals in the local community.

Visit the people associated with the resources your students are most likely to use. Successful people have lots of mentors. Your goal is to strengthen your students' social network and stock of "social capital." You shouldn't assume total responsibility for supporting your students. It takes a community, and your college community consists of multiple members who have the experience, wisdom, resources, and knowledge to serve as "campus partners" to help you help students. Know who the professionals are—the supervisors of your leadership or mentoring program, course instructors, academic advisors, personal counselors, etc. Have their contact information handy, cultivate relationships with them, and connect students to them. Some of your key campus partners include:

- Faculty
- Academic Advisors
- Career Counselors and Specialists
- Student Life Professionals
- Residence Advisors and Assistants
- Personal Counselors
- Campus Ministers
- Financial Aid Counselors
- Community Service Specialists
- Graduate Teaching and Research Assistants
- Working Professionals in the Local Community

Get copies of their brochures and program descriptions, and ask them about what they do, the challenges they face, their most essential advice for students, and how you can most effectively partner with them.

If you're not sure whom to connect your student to, take the time to ask somebody who does know. When in doubt, find out! Somebody on campus almost always has an answer or can refer you to someone who does. Students will appreciate the time and effort you take to find the right answer or steer them in the right direction.

Make referrals strategically. To be an effective resource-and-referral agent, not only do you need to know what the resources are, you need to motivate students to use them. There's an art and science to the process of making effective referrals that goes well beyond simply relaying information about resources. An effective referral agent inspires students to capitalize on their resources by providing students with a compelling rationale for the resources, instilling a sense of confidence in the referred person or resource, and equipping them with a set of strategies for taking action on the referral.

Note well! *Your ability to make referrals effectively can empower students to develop the skill of resourcefulness—a life skill that can be used to solve problems and promote success beyond college.*

Box 4.4 contains a summary of key strategies for making effective referrals.

Box 4.4

Top Strategies for Making Effective Referrals

1. **First, take time to *listen* closely to the student's problem before making the referral.** Don't refer so quickly that it appears as if you're giving the student the "brush-off"—sending a message that you're disinterested or unconcerned.

2. **Respect and maintain student confidentiality.** Make it explicitly clear up front that you intend to keep your conversation private and confidential.

3. **Explain *why* you're referring the student rather than trying to help the student yourself.** For example, make it clear that you cannot provide that advice because the issue or problem is beyond your area of expertise or qualifications, so you're making a referral to ensure that the student receives the best advice and support.

4. **Provide a description of the resource and its purpose.** Establishing a sense of purpose is an essential leadership principle. You can apply this principle to the referral process by explaining why the resource exists, how it relates to the student's current issue or concern, and what good things are likely to take place if the student uses it. Students can have reservations, doubts, and sometimes skepticism about utilizing resources and approaching people ("faculty are not interested in talking to freshmen," "tutoring is just for dummies," etc.). When you provide a clear rationale for using the service and paint a positive picture of what the resource can do for students, you increase the likelihood that they'll actually follow through on your referral.

5. **Personalize the referral: Refer students to *a person,* rather than a position or office.** Here's where knowing people really helps. Referring students to Donnie or Doug or Barbara is far more powerful than referring them to an "advisor" or "counselor." Referring students to a real person, rather than an anonymous entity, serves to humanize the referral process and increases the student's sense of personal connection with the recommended resource.

6. **Reassure students that the person you're referring them to is caring, concerned, and qualified.** Vouch for the credibility and character of the person. A calculus tutor knows calculus and knows how to explain it to students. Academic advisors understand academic requirements and options, and they know how to help students make informed educational decisions about their course work. Personal counselors understand how to help students cope with and heal from a crisis. Better yet, share your experiences or the experiences of other students who have benefited from seeing the support-service professional. For instance, say, "I went to Doug and he laid out exactly what I needed to do to apply for law school. He's a real good guy, really cares and knows his stuff."

   Use your best judgment about what particular support professional on campus would best fit the student's personality and needs. If you're unsure who that person might be, seek input from fellow peer leaders or other campus partners.

7. **Help students take the steps needed to make an appointment.** When students come to you for support, this may be the very time that they'll be most willing to act on your referral and get the support they need. So, "strike while the iron is hot" and help students make the appointment while you're with them. If they're unwilling to make the appointment immediately, let them know you're ready and willing to help set up the appointment whenever they're ready.

8. **Help students prepare for the first visit.** Assist them with identifying what information to share, what questions to ask, and how to approach the resource person. This should serve to increase students' confidence and increase their likelihood of following through with the appointment.

(continued)

9. **If possible, walk the student to the referred person's office.** This will ensure that the student knows where to go and how to get there; it may also provide the student with the social support needed to actually get there.

10. **Compliment students for making the effort to seek support and strive for self-improvement.** Delivering such reinforcing comments serves to raise student awareness that help-seeking is not a sign of weakness, but a sign of personal strength and resourcefulness.

11. **Follow up with the referred student.** Encourage students to get back to you about how the referral went (in general). If you don't hear from a student, consider contacting that student to ask if they saw the referred person and if there's anything else you can do to help. Even if students don't act on your initial recommendation or don't get back to you, following up with them serves to remind them to follow through on your referral and that you're still thinking about them.

 Note well! Always respect the boundaries of your position. You're not a professional counselor or therapist; you're more like a trusted friend and resource agent who helps students connect with key campus services and student support professionals.

Reflection 4.10

What student issues would you say are beyond the professional boundaries of your position and should be referred to a professional on campus?

Where do you draw the line?

Making Crisis Referrals

> *When written in Chinese, the word 'crisis' is composed of two characters. One represents danger and the other represents opportunity.*
>
> —John F. Kennedy, 35th president of the United States

As students come to know and trust you, it's possible that highly serious and sensitive matters may be brought to your attention, such as issues involving relationships and sexuality, alcohol and drug abuse, anxiety, depression, or suicidal thoughts. Although it's unlikely you'll be dealing with crises on a regular basis, you need to be prepared for the possibility. Specific guidelines and procedures for dealing with crises are likely to be provided in a peer leadership handbook or handouts you received during leadership training. In addition to information you may have received from these resources, we offer the following guidelines for making crisis referrals.

- Let the student know that you are concerned and are there to listen to her or his concerns. In difficult situations, you can help most by simply being available, asking questions, listening (and listening some more), and reaffirming your encouragement and support.
- Encourage the student to make an appointment immediately with a personal counselor or advisor. If possible, escort the student to the appropriate office, or remain with the student until an appropriate professional becomes available.
- If the student elects not to act on your urgent recommendation to seek help and you fear that he/she is putting him/herself or others in danger, immediately and discreetly inform your program supervisor. If that person cannot be reached, inform the campus police. If the student is in a crisis situation, that

student's right to privacy or confidentiality is outweighed by the need to ensure the student's safety and the safety of others.

- Keep a record of the steps you took during the crisis and the parties you contacted.

Summary and Conclusion

Human intelligence was once considered to be one general trait that could be detected and measured by a single intelligence test score. However, humans display intelligence (mental ability) in many forms other than performance on an IQ test. One of these alternative forms of human intelligence is *social intelligence* (a.k.a. interpersonal intelligence)—the ability to communicate and relate effectively to others. Another form of human intelligence is *emotional intelligence*—the ability to recognize our own emotions, the emotions of others, and how our behavior affects the emotions of others. Research indicates that these forms of human intelligence are better predictors of personal and professional success than intellectual ability as measured by performance on traditional intelligence tests.

Successful leadership rests on a solid foundation of interpersonal communication and human relations skills. Leaders in all contexts and roles need to be skilled at initiating and developing relationships with those whom they lead. However, relationship development doesn't happen by chance, but through an intentional process of (1) initiating interpersonal interaction, (2) getting to know others as unique individuals, and (3) showing genuine interest in others by asking questions about them.

Relationship building requires effective *speaking* skills—the ability to verbally communicate our ideas to others. In any leadership role, the ability to communicate effectively with others is vital. Communication skills enhance your credibility with your students, keep your partners in the loop, and demonstrate your commitment and competence to other members of the campus community. Although being a dynamic and eloquent speaker can be helpful in certain leadership roles, spectacular oratory skills are less important than effective listening and human relations skills. Others will not hear you if they don't believe that you're committed to hearing them.

Relationship building involves getting to know students and demonstrating interest in their lives, their well-being, and their development. Students may be interested in what you know, but they're more likely to be interested in knowing whether you're interested in them. Work hard at learning the names of your students, show interest in them by asking questions, and share information about yourself, which serves to model and encourage your students to do the same.

Good leaders and mentors are willing and able to help others in need. Given your leadership position on campus, it's very likely that students will come to you for advice or assistance about personal issues, particularly if you've taken the time to establish a relationship with them. In some cases, you will be able to help students solve problems, but often you'll need to connect them with other resources and professionals on campus. You can strengthen your ability to be a connection catalyst by (1) asking students about their needs, concerns, and interests, (2) continually acquiring knowledge about the people, support resources, and student opportunities on your campus, and (3) referring students to campus partners who are most qualified to address their needs or concerns.

To be an effective resource-and-referral agent, not only do you need to know what the resources are, you need to motivate students to use them. There's an art and science to the process of making effective referrals that goes well beyond simply relaying information about resources. An effective referral agent inspires students to capitalize on their resources by giving them a compelling rationale for the resources, a sense of confidence in the referred person or resource, and a set of strategies for taking action on the referral.

The interpersonal communication skills discussed in this chapter provide the essential underpinnings for all leadership roles in any campus context. Moreover, these skills will be vital to you beyond college as a friend, family member, and citizen.

Internet Resources

For additional information related to the ideas discussed in this chapter, we recommend the following websites:

Social Intelligence and Interpersonal Relationships
www.articles911.com/Communication/Interpersonal_Communication/
hodu.com/ECS-Menu1.shtml

Active Listening and Leadership
www.uky.edu/GetInvolved/Leadership/pdf/Active%20Listening.pdf

Verbal and Nonverbal Communication Skills
www.skillsyouneed.co.uk/IPS/What_is_Communication.html

Crisis Referral Strategies
www.blinn.edu/counseling/Faculty_Referral_Resources.pdf

Exercise 4.1 *Journal Reflections*

Should peer leaders be friends with their students on Facebook?

Should student leaders limit access to certain parts of their social networking profiles? (If yes, what privacy settings should be used?)

Should peer leaders filter their comments, group members' comments, and photograph albums? If yes, in what way(s)?

What uses of social networking sites would be inappropriate or unethical for peer leaders?

Should peer leaders give out their cell phone numbers?

What would be a reasonable time frame for peer leaders to respond to student phone calls or text messages?

Source: Johnson, M. (2012). Integrating technology into peer leader responsibilities. In J. R. Keup (Ed.), *Peer leadership in higher education* (pp. 59–71). San Francisco, CA: Jossey-Bass.

Exercise 4.2 *Constructing a Master List of Student Support Resources*

1. Construct a master list of all student support resources available on your campus. Your final product should be a list that includes the following information:

Campus Resource	Types of Support Provided	Campus Location	Contact Person
_____	_____	_____	_____

2   After you complete this master list, save it for future use in making referrals.

3. List what you think are the most common problems or issues experienced by students on your campus, and next to each of them, list the campus resource or support professional that's best qualified to deal with that problem or issue.

Exercise 4.3 *Probing Simulation*

Get together with a fellow student—preferably one who is also involved in some form of leadership on campus—and practice the process of questioning, listening actively, and probing (described on pp. 91–92). Switch roles and give each other feedback on strengths and strategies for improvement.

Exercise 4.4 *Relationship Self-Assessment*

On a scale of 1–5 (1 = low; 5 = high), rate yourself on each of the following characteristics:

_____ I effectively initiate relationships.

_____ I am accessible.

_____ I am approachable.

_____ I am a good listener.

Provide a reason or explanation for each of your ratings that indicates (1) what you're doing well, (2) what you'd like to improve, and (3) how you could improve or from whom you might seek assistance.

Exercise 4.5 *Crisis Referral Role-Play*

Partner with a fellow student leader or just a friend. Think of an incident or scenario that would call for crisis referral. Either you or your partner makes the referral using the steps outlined on pp. 100–101. The other provides feedback on how effectively the partner implemented the process of an effective crisis referral.

Exercise 4.6 *Verbal Communication Self-Assessment*

Rate your level of self-confidence about communicating orally in the following situations:

1. Large Groups (e.g., asking a question in a class of 30 or more students):

    highly anxious   somewhat nervous   fairly relaxed   very relaxed

2. Small Groups (e.g., speaking in a discussion group of three to five students):

    highly anxious   somewhat nervous   fairly relaxed   very relaxed

3. Pairs (e.g., talking over an assignment with an individual student):

    highly anxious   somewhat nervous   fairly relaxed   very relaxed

Do your responses to the above questions suggest that you are ready to assume the verbal communication responsibilities of your leadership position, or do they suggest that you need to strengthen your communication skills in certain social situations?

If there are social situations in which you think you need to strengthen your communication skills, what are the first steps you could take to do so?

chapter 5

Setting Goals, Managing Time, and Maintaining Motivation

Reflection 5.1

What does being "successful" mean to you?

Deep within them, most students have the passion to succeed, but they often may need a leader or mentor to help them discover their passion and transform it into action. As a peer leader and mentor, you can inspire students to reach high and keep climbing. Challenge them to set ambitious, yet realistic goals. Dare them to dream, but also encourage them to convert their dreams into specific goals, to create plans for achieving their goals, and to take action on the plans they create.

> Student leaders breathe life into the hopes and dreams of others and enable them to see the exciting possibilities that the future holds.
>
> —Kouzes & Posner, *The Student Leadership Challenge*

Goal Setting and Success

The word *success* derives from the Latin root *successus*, meaning "to follow or come after," as in the word *succession.* Thus, by definition, success involves an order or sequence of actions that lead to a desired outcome; the process starts with identifying an end (goal) and then finding a means (sequence of steps) to reach that goal. Studies consistently show that setting personal goals is a more effective self-motivational strategy than simply telling ourselves to "try hard" or "do our best" (Boekaerts, Pintrich, & Zeidner, 2000). Achieving success begins with setting goals; successful people set goals on a regular basis (Locke & Latham, 1990).

Effective goal setting involves two key processes: (1) self-awareness—insight into who we are, and (2) self-projection—a vision of whom we want to become. When students engage in both of these processes, they begin to see a clearer connection between where they are now and where they want to go in the future.

> The tragedy of life doesn't lie in not reaching your goal. The tragedy of life lies in having no goal to reach.
>
> —Benjamin Mays, minister, scholar, activist, president of Morehouse College

Remind students that setting goals and developing plans to reach them doesn't mean that those plans can never be adjusted or modified. Goals can change as students change and develop, acquire new knowledge and skills, and discover new interests and talents. Setting goals doesn't mean they are locking themselves into premature plans that limit their flexibility or options. Instead, goal setting simply supplies students with a map that (1) enables them to "see" the future they'd like to have for themselves, (2) provides a sense of direction about how to get there, and (3) starts them moving in the right direction. More specifically, effective goal setting involves a sequence of five key steps:

1. **Awareness of self**—insight into personal interests, abilities and talents, and values.
2. **Awareness of goal options**—knowledge of different goal options available to you.

3. **Awareness of the options that best fit you**—the particular goals that are most compatible with your personal abilities, interests, values, and needs.
4. **Awareness of the process**—the major steps that must be taken in order to reach your chosen goal.
5. **Awareness of a time frame**—a timeline for completing each of the major steps toward the goal.

What follows are specific strategies for helping students take each of these five steps in the goal-setting process.

Step 1. Self-Awareness

> *Know thyself.*
> —Plato, ancient Greek philosopher

Helping students succeed involves far more than sharing tips. Strategies are meaningless unless students know and believe in the "why"—i.e., when they develop a clear understanding of who they are, where they want to go, and why they want to get there.

The goals students choose to pursue say a lot about who they are and what they want from life. Thus, self-awareness is the critical first step in the process of goal setting. Students must know themselves before they can know what goals they want to pursue. While this may seem obvious, self-awareness and self-discovery are often overlooked aspects of the goal-setting process. By helping students deepen their self-awareness, you'll put them in a better position to choose goals and to pursue a personal path that's true to who they are and what they want to be.

> *To thine own self be true.*
> —William Shakespeare in *Hamlet*

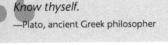 **Self-awareness is the first and most important step in the goal-setting process. Personally meaningful goals and good personal choices are built on a deep understanding of oneself.**

> *The unexamined life is not worth living.*
> —Socrates, ancient Greek philosopher and a founding father of Western philosophy

As a peer leader, you can increase your students' self-awareness by asking them self-examining questions that cause them to introspect and reflect on their inner qualities and personal priorities. Self-searching questioning can launch students on an inward search or quest for self-insight, self-discovery, and discovery of goals that are personally meaningful and significant. For instance, finding a gainful career is likely to be an important long-range goal for your students. You can help them launch their quest toward this goal by asking them self-examining questions related to their personal:

> *In order to succeed, you must know what you are doing, like what you are doing, and believe in what you are doing.*
> —Will Rogers, Native American humorist and actor

- **Interests**—what they *like* doing;
- **Abilities and talents**—what they're *good* at doing; and
- **Values**—what they believe is *worth* doing.

For a personal goal to be attainable, the person has to possess the interest, ability, and passion to attain it. You can use the questions listed in Exercise 2.1 (p. 39) to get students thinking about their personal interests, talents, and values. After students answer these questions, have them reflect on their answers by posing this follow-up question: "Based on your responses to the preceding questions, what is one long-range goal you could pursue that would be *compatible (consistent)* with your *interests, talents,* and *values*?"

Step 2. Awareness of Goal Options

The second critical step in the goal-setting process is for students to become aware of their options for long-range goals. For example, if a long-term goal for your students is a fulfilling future career, they need to be aware of what career options are available to them and have a realistic understanding of the types of work performance required by these careers. (To gain this knowledge, they'll need to capitalize on available resources, such as those provided by the career development office on campus.)

Step 3. Awareness of Options That Provide the Best Personal "Match" or "Fit"

For instance, college students have multiple courses and majors from which to choose. To deepen their awareness of what majors or academic fields are a good fit for them, they could take a course in each field to test out how well it matches their interests, values, talents, and learning style. Ideally, they should select a field that closely taps into, or builds on, their strongest skills and talents because choosing a field that's compatible with their strongest abilities will enable them to master the skills required by that field more efficiently and successfully. Their success should, in turn, strengthen their self-esteem, self-confidence, and personal drive to continue their pursuit of that goal. You've probably heard of the proverb "if there's a will, there's a way"—i.e., when we're motivated to achieve something, we're more likely to achieve it. It's also true that "if there's a way, there's a will"—when we can do something well, we're motivated to continue doing it.

> *Set yourself earnestly to discover what you are made to do, and then give yourself passionately to the doing of it.*
>
> —Martin Luther King, Jr., American clergyman, prominent leader in the African American civil rights movement, and winner of the Nobel Peace Prize

Reflection 5.2

Would you say that the leadership goals you're attempting to accomplish "fit" or "match" your talents and values?

If yes, why? If no, why not?

Step 4. Awareness of the Characteristics of a Well-Designed Goal

Before students jump into the process of setting goals, they need to know what a well-designed goal looks like. The acronym SMART is a popular mnemonic device (memory strategy) for recalling all the key components of a well-designed goal (Doran, 1981; Meyer, 2003). Box 5.1 describes each component of a SMART goal.

Box 5.1

The SMART Method of Goal Setting

A **SMART** goal is one that is:

Specific—it states precisely what the goal is and what the person will do to achieve it.

Example: I'll achieve at least a "B" average this term by spending 25 hours per week on my course work outside of class and by using the effective learning strategies recommended to me by my peer mentor. (This is a much more specific goal than saying, "I'm really going to work hard this term.")

Meaningful (and **M**easurable)—the goal really matters to the person, and progress toward reaching the goal can be steadily measured or tracked.

Example: I'll achieve at least a "B" average this term because it will enable me to get into the major I want, and I'll measure my progress toward this goal by keeping track of the grades I'm earning in all my courses from beginning to end of the term.

Actionable (i.e., **A**ction-Oriented) —it identifies the concrete actions or behaviors the person will engage in to reach the goal.

Example: I will achieve at least a "B" average this term by (1) attending all classes, (2) taking detailed notes in all my classes, (3) completing all reading assignments before their due dates, and (4) studying in advance for all my major exams (rather than cramming).

Realistic—the goal is attainable and the person is aware of the amount of time, effort, and skill it will take to attain it, as well as obstacles likely to be encountered along the way.

Example: Achieving a "B" average this term will be a realistic goal for me because my course load is manageable and I will be working at my part-time job for no more than 15 hours per week.

Time-Framed—the goal has a deadline and a timeline or timetable that includes a sequence of short-range, mid-range, and long-range steps.

Example: To achieve at least a "B" average this term, first I'll acquire the information I need to learn by taking complete notes in my classes and on my assigned readings (short-range step). Second, I'll study the information I've acquired from my notes and readings in short study sessions held in advance of major exams (mid-range step). Third, on the day before my exams, I'll hold a final review session for all information previously studied, and after my exams are returned, I'll review the results carefully to determine where I lost the most points; I'll use this information as feedback to improve my future performance and ensure that I maintain at least a "B" average (long-range step).

Note: The SMART process can be used to set goals for any aspect or dimension of one's life, including health-related goals such as losing weight, social goals such as meeting new people, fiscal goals such as saving money, or any element of self-development described in Chapter 7 (p. 176).

Author's Experience I intentionally and systematically lost 35 pounds in seven months. I wanted to get from 210 to about 175. My goal was:

Specific—I had a clear target to shoot for (175 pounds)

Meaningful—I wanted to improve my health (lower my cholesterol) and be a quicker basketball. player, and **M**easurable—I could measure my progress in terms of pounds lost

Actionable—I exercised more and consumed fewer calories.

Realistic—175 pounds is a reasonable weight for someone of my height and body type, and

Timed—I set out to lose 1–2 pounds per week.

It worked!

— *Greg Metz*

Step 5. Awareness of All Major Steps Needed to Reach the Goal

Long-range goals are achieved in a sequence of steps, not a single leap. For example, the long-range goal of achieving a college degree requires completion of a series of courses in general education and a particular major. Students need to be aware of what these courses are. Similarly, if students have a long-range career goal, they need to know what majors lead to that career and be aware that some careers require a specific major, but other careers may be entered through a variety of different majors.

> *Whoever wants to reach a distant goal must take many small steps.*
>
> —Helmut Schmidt, former chancellor of West Germany

Note well! Effective goal setting is a strategic process that could and should be applied to any goal we set for ourselves at any stage of our lives.

Goal Setting and Time Management

Setting goals is one thing, but doing what needs to be done to reach those goals is quite another matter. Time is a critical personal resource; when we gain greater control of it, we gain greater control of our lives and our ability to reach our goals. If we are to have any realistic chance of achieving our goals, we need an intentional and strategic plan for spending our time in a way that aligns with and enables us to make steady progress toward our goals. Thus, setting goals, reaching goals, and managing time are interrelated skills.

Reaching goals requires managing time because it takes time to successfully complete the series of steps and tasks that leads to goal achievement. This time-and-task management process requires answers to the following questions: What is my long-range goal? How can that goal be broken into smaller, more manageable steps? What tasks do I need to do over time to reach each step? How much time is each step likely to take?

This process requires a timeline that identifies *when* each of the key steps toward your goal is to be completed. An effective goal-setting timeline should break down the process into the following components or stages:

- Long-range goals (e.g., tasks to be completed within the next five years);
- Mid-range goals (e.g., tasks to be completed by the end of the current academic term);
- Short-range goals (e.g., tasks to be performed during the next few weeks);
- Weekly goals (e.g., tasks to be completed by the end of the week); and
- Daily goals (e.g., to-do lists for tasks to be completed by the end of the day).

> *Ultimately, a student (and all of us) should craft a 'dream' but the dream must be broken down into bite-size pieces.*
>
> —Brad Johnson & Charles Ridley, *The Elements of Mentoring*

Long-term goals are important, but they're achieved through incremental efforts and accomplishments on a day-to-day and week-to-week basis. Each day, whether we are aware of it or not, we make decisions about *what* we will do that day. To reach our goals, we must be mindful about whether our daily actions move us in the direction of our personal goals. This practice of ongoing (daily) assessment of personal progress is a simple, yet powerful form of personal reflection that is associated with successful goal completion. Research on successful people reveals that they reflect regularly on their daily progress to ensure that they're on track and making steady progress toward their goals (Covey, 1990).

As a peer leader and mentor, one of your key roles is to help students design day-to-day strategies for achieving their long-range goals. Most college students will struggle to at least some extent with time management, particularly first-year students who are transitioning from the lockstep schedules of high school to the more unstructured "free time" associated with college course schedules. Personal time-management skills grow in importance when one's time is less structured or controlled by others and more responsibility is placed on the individual to decide how personal time is spent.

Even for older first-year students who have lived on their own for some time, managing time remains a crucial skill because they're likely to be juggling work and family responsibilities in addition to school. Thus, it's not surprising that research points to time management as a skill that plays a crucial role in the success of all college students (Erickson, Peters, & Strommer, 2006; Light, 2001).

Reflection 5.3

What do you think will be the biggest time-management challenge you'll face in your peer leadership role or position?

Strategies for Managing Tasks and Time

Effective task and time management involves three key processes:

1. **Itemizing**—listing all key tasks that need to be accomplished along the path toward that goal.
2. **Prioritizing**—attacking tasks in their order of their importance.
3. **Scheduling**—deciding when tasks are to be started and completed.

To help students complete these three key steps, share the following strategies with them. These strategies should help students open up more time in their schedules and discover ways to use their time more productively.

To become more aware of how your time is being spent, break it down into smaller units. How often have you heard someone say, "Where did all the time go?" or "I just can't seem to find the time."? One way to find out where our time goes and find the time to do what needs to be done is by taking a personal time inventory—analyzing how we spend our time by tracking what we do and when we do it. By mapping out how we spend time, we become more aware of how much total time we have and where it goes, including patches of wasted time during which we get little or nothing accomplished. Time analysis only has to be done for a week or two to give us a good idea of where our time is going and find better ways to use our time productively.

Identify *what* tasks you need to accomplish and *when* you need to accomplish them. When we want to be sure not to forget items we need at the grocery store or people we want to invite to a party, we make a list. This same list-making strategy can be used for goal-related tasks so we don't forget to do them, or forget to do them on time. Studies of successful people show that they are list makers; they write out lists not only for grocery items and wedding invitations, but also for things they want to accomplish each day (Covey, 2004).

Encourage your students to identify and itemize the tasks on their lists by using any of the following time-management tools:

- **Small, portable planner.** Students can use this device to list all their major assignments and exams for the term, along with their due dates. By pulling together all work tasks required in all courses and getting them in one place, it's easier to keep track of what they have to do and when they have to do it.

- **Large, stable calendar.** This should be posted in a place that's seen every day (e.g., bedroom or refrigerator). In the calendar's date boxes, students should record their major assignments for the academic term. If students consistently look at the things they have to do, they're less likely to overlook them, forget about them, or subconsciously push them out of their minds because they'd really prefer not to do them.

- **PDA or cell phone.** Students can use either of these devices to do more than just check social networking sites and send or receive text messages. They can use the calendar tools to record due dates and set up alert functions to remind them of deadlines.

  Many PDAs and smartphones will also allow the user to set up task or "to-do" lists and to set priorities for each item entered.

A variety of other technological tools are now available that can be used to plan tasks and track time spent on tasks. Encourage your student to use them, but at the same time, keep in mind that planners do not plan time; people do. Effective planning of tasks and time must flow from a clear vision of whom the planner wants to become. Successful people manage their time and tasks in a way that's intentionally connected to their life goals.

Reflection 5.4

Do you have a calendar that you carry with you, or do you use the calendar tool on your PDA or cell phone?

If no, why not?

Rank tasks in order of their importance. Once work has been itemized by listing all tasks that need to be done, the next step is to *prioritize* these tasks—i.e., determine the order or sequence in which they'll be done. Prioritizing basically involves ranking tasks in terms of their importance, with the highest-priority tasks placed at the top of the list to ensure they're tackled first.

How do we determine which tasks are most important and should be ranked highest? Two criteria (standards of judgment) can be used to help determine which tasks should be our highest priorities:

- **Urgency.** Tasks that are closest to their deadline or due date should receive high priority. For example, finishing an assignment that's due tomorrow should receive higher priority than starting an assignment that's due next month.

- **Gravity.** Tasks that carry the heaviest weight (count the most) should receive highest priority. For example, if an assignment worth 100 points and another worth 10 points are due at the same time, the 100-point task should receive higher priority. We want to be sure to invest our work time in tasks that matter most. Just like investing money, we should invest our time in tasks that yield the greatest payoff.

One strategy you can suggest to students for prioritizing their tasks is to divide them into "A," "B," and "C" lists (Lakein, 1973; Morgenstern, 2004). The "A" list is reserved for *essential* tasks—what *must* be done now. The "B" list is for *important* tasks—what *should* be done soon. Finally, the "C" list is for *optional* tasks—what *could* or *might* be done if there's time remaining after we've completed the more important tasks on the A and B lists. Organizing tasks and time in this fashion can help students decide how to divide their labor in a way that ensures they "put first things first." They shouldn't waste time doing unimportant things to deceive themselves into thinking that they're "getting something done," when, in reality, they're just "keeping busy" and distracting themselves (and subtracting time) from doing the things they should be doing.

Note well! Developing awareness about how our time is spent is more than a brainless, clerical activity. When it's done well, it becomes an exercise in reflective thinking and values clarification—how we spend our time is a true test of what we really value.

Developing a Time-Management Plan

Humans are creatures of habit. Routines help us organize our time and gain control of our lives. When we decide to spend our time by design, rather than leaving it to chance or accident, we take an important first step toward taking charge of our time (and our lives).

Make sure your students don't fall for the myth that taking time to plan how they'll spend their time is wasting time because they could spend that planning time actually working on things they need to get done. Time-management experts estimate that the amount of time we spend planning our work reduces our total work time by a factor of three, i.e., for every one unit of time we spend planning, we save three units of work time (Goldsmith, 2010; Lakein, 1973). For example, five minutes of planning time will typically save us 15 minutes of total work time, and 10 minutes of planning time will save us 30 minutes of work time. As the proverb goes, "A stitch in time saves nine." Planning how to spend time represents the "stitch" (unit of time) that saves us nine additional stitches (units of time). Like successful chess players, successful time managers plan ahead and anticipate their upcoming moves.

By taking time to plan our tasks and time, we end up saving time in the long run because we're left with a clearer picture of what needs to be done and the order of steps needed to get it done. This clearer sense of direction and progression reduces the likelihood that we'll make "false starts"—starting off in the wrong (not most productive) direction. If we have no plan of attack, we run the risk of starting off on the wrong track and being forced to backtrack (and lose time).

Elements of a Comprehensive Time-Management Plan

Once your students have accepted the idea that taking time to plan their time will save them time in the long run, you're ready to help them design an effective time-management plan. Listed below are specific strategies you can share with students for creating a comprehensive, well-designed plan for managing their time.

An effective time-management plan should include short-, mid-, and long-range goals. For instance, a good time-management plan for the academic term should include:

1. A *long-range* goal (e.g., deadline dates for final exams, reports and papers to be completed by the end of the term);
2. A *mid-range* goal (e.g., tasks to be completed by midterm); and
3. A *short-range* goal (e.g., tasks to be completed by the next class session).

A good time-management plan should balance work time with recreation (play) time. Students shouldn't only plan to work; they should plan time to relax, refuel, and recharge. A time-management plan shouldn't turn us into robotic, obsessive-compulsive workaholics. Instead, it should represent a balanced blend of work and play, which includes planned activities that promote our mental and physical wellness, such as relaxation, recreation, and reflection. A good time-management plan works as a self-motivational plan when play time is scheduled to follow work time, thus allowing play activities to serve as a reward for completing our work activities.

An effective time-management plan also functions as an effective stress-management plan. It should help students stress less, learn more, and earn higher grades while reserving time for other things that are important to them, enabling them to attain and maintain balance in their lives.

> *From my perspective it's this: time management. It's about efficiently accomplishing the necessary things in the time you've got so that the free time you've allotted is stress free.*
> —Peer leader

Note well! *If our time-management plan includes the things we like to do, we're more likely to complete the things we have to do.*

A good time-management plan is one that gets transformed into an action plan. Once we've planned the work, the next step is to work the plan. A time-management plan turns into an ongoing action plan by (1) previewing what we intend to do, (2) reviewing whether we actually did what we intended to do, and (3) closing the gap between our intentions and actions. We can begin to implement an action plan by constructing a daily to-do list, bringing that list with us as the day begins, and checking off items on the list as we get them done throughout the day. At the end of the day, the list should be reviewed to determine what got done and what still needs to be done. The uncompleted tasks then become high priorities for the following day's to-do list.

If, at the end of the day, students find many unchecked items still remaining on their daily to-do lists, this could mean that they're spreading themselves too thin by trying to do too many things in a day. They may need to be more realistic about the number of items they can accomplish per day by shortening their daily to-do lists. Not being able to complete many of their intended daily tasks may also mean that they need to modify their time-management plans by adding more work time or subtracting activities that are drawing time and attention away from their work (e.g., responding to phone calls and text messages during their planned work times).

Encourage students to reflect on their daily to-do lists, and engage them in conversations about what they may have to sacrifice in order to achieve their daily goals (e.g., TV, video games, Facebook).

Reflection 5.5

At the end of a typical day, how often do you find that you accomplished most of the important tasks you hoped to accomplish? (Circle one.)

never   seldom   often   almost always

If you circled "often" or "almost always," what personal strategies could you share with other students to help them do the same?

> *Some people regard discipline as a chore. For me, it is a kind of order that sets me free to fly.*
>
> —Julie Andrews, Academy Award–winning English actress who starred in the Broadway musicals *Mary Poppins* and *The Sound of Music*

A good time-management plan should have some flexibility. Students often get immediately turned off by the idea of developing a schedule and planning their time because they feel it over-structures their lives and limits their freedom. It's only natural for us to prize our personal freedom and resist anything that appears to restrict it in any way. However, a good time-management plan shouldn't limit freedom; it should preserve it by helping us get done what we must do to ensure that we have "free time" for us to do what we want and like to do.

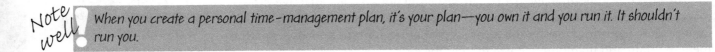

Note well! When you create a personal time-management plan, it's your plan—you own it and you run it. It shouldn't run you.

An effective time-management plan shouldn't be rigid; it should be malleable enough to allow us to occasionally bend it (without breaking it). Just as work commitments and family responsibilities can crop up unexpectedly, so, too, can opportunities for fun and enjoyable activities. Our time-management plan should allow us the freedom to occasionally modify our schedule so that we can take advantage of these spontaneous opportunities and experiences. However, we should plan to make up the work time that we traded for play time. In other words, we can "trade" work time for play time, but we shouldn't "steal" it. If we cancel work we planned to do, we should re-plan to do it at another time.

Box 5.2

Summary of Top Time-Management Tips to Share with Students

- Carry a portable device that can accurately and instantly tell you the time and date (e.g., watch, cell phone, or PDA). You can't even begin to manage time if you don't know what time it is, and you can't plan ahead if you don't know what date it is. (Try setting the time on your watch or cell phone slightly ahead of the actual time to help ensure that you arrive to class, work, or meetings on time.)

- Use an *organizational system* that helps you pull together, track, and follow through on your commitments (e.g., calendar, planner, and daily to-do lists).

- Carry a *small calendar, planner, or appointment book* at all times. This will enable you to record commitments and appointments made on the run during the day, as well as sudden recollections of things you need to do and creative ideas for doing them that may "pop" into your mind at unexpected times.

- Carry *portable work* with you that can be completed in any place at any time (e.g., carry material with you that you can read while sitting and waiting for appointments or transportation). This will enable you to take advantage of "dead time" during the day, "resurrect" this dead time, and transform it into "live" (productive) work time. Carrying portable work is not only a good time-management strategy, it's also a good stress-management strategy because it allows you to gain control of wait time rather than letting it control you and feeling frustrated, anxious, or bored while sitting and waiting.

- Find a partner—a time-management buddy—with whom you can discuss your daily progress and maintain commitment to your plan.

Note: In addition to passing on these tips to students, share and model time-management strategies that have worked well for you, and encourage your students to do the same.

Note well! *Time management is rooted in goal commitment. When these roots are strong, effective strategies can be learned and grow into lifelong habits.*

Helping Students Deal with Procrastination

A major enemy of effective time management is procrastination. Procrastinators don't abide by the proverb, "Why put off until tomorrow what can be done today?". In fact, their philosophy is just the opposite: "Why do today what can be put off until tomorrow?". Adopting this philosophy promotes a perpetual pattern of postponing what needs to be done until the last possible moment, forcing them to rush frantically to finish their work on time and turn in a product that's a far cry from their best work (or not turn in a finished product at all).

Research shows that 80% to 95% of college students procrastinate (Steel, 2007) and almost 50% report that they procrastinate consistently (Onwuegbuzie, 2000). Procrastination is such a serious issue for college students that some campuses have opened "procrastination centers" to provide help exclusively for students experiencing problems with procrastination (Burka & Yuen, 2008). To help combat procrastination, here are five key strategies you could share with your students.

126   Chapter 5   Setting Goals, Managing Time, and Maintaining Motivation

Strategies for Preventing and Overcoming Procrastination

1. **Continue practicing effective time-management strategies.** When effective time-management practices (such as those cited in this chapter) are implemented consistently, they turn into regular habits. Research indicates that when procrastinators repeatedly practice effective time-management strategies with respect to tasks that they procrastinate on, their procrastination tendencies gradually fade and are replaced by good time-management habits (Ainslie, 1992; Baumeister, Heatherton, & Tice, 1994).

2. **Make the start of work as inviting or appealing as possible.** Getting started, or getting off the starting blocks, is often the major stumbling block for procrastinators. It's common for procrastinators to experience "start-up stress"—when they're about to start a task, they start to experience negative feelings about the task being unpleasant, difficult, or boring (Burka & Yuen, 2008). If your students have trouble starting their work, suggest that they may give themselves a "jump start" by ordering their work tasks in a way that allows them to start their work on tasks that they find more interesting or are more likely to succeed in. By getting started on these easier and more appealing tasks, they overcome inertia and initiate some momentum. They can then ride this initial momentum to attack other tasks they find less appealing and more daunting.

   Also, when they make some progress toward getting work done, their anxiety begins to subside, and when they encounter the work they dreaded, it often turns out not to be as difficult, boring, or time-consuming as they thought it would be. As with many experiences in life that are feared and avoided, the anticipation of the event turns out to be worse than the event itself. One study of college students who didn't start a project until just before it was due revealed that they experienced anxiety and guilt while they were procrastinating, but once they began working, these negative emotions subsided and were replaced by more positive feelings of progress and accomplishment (McCance & Pychyl, 2003).

3. **Divide the work into manageable pieces.** Work becomes less overwhelming and stressful when it's handled in small chunks or segments. Students can conquer procrastination for large tasks by using a "divide and conquer" strategy: divide the large task into smaller, more manageable subtasks, and then attack and complete these subtasks one at a time.

   Remind your students not to underestimate the power of short work sessions; they can be more effective than longer sessions because it's easier to maintain concentration and momentum for shorter periods of time. Dividing their work into short sessions will enable them to take quick jabs and poke small holes in it, reducing its overall size with each successive punch. By continuing to jab at a tall task in short strokes, students will experience the sense of satisfaction that comes from knowing that they're making progress and moving in the right direction, which reduces the pressure and anxiety associated with having to go for a big knockout punch right before the final bell (deadline).

4. If students have difficulty maintaining or sustaining commitment to their work until it's finished, suggest that they schedule easier and more interesting work tasks *in the middle or toward the end* of their planned work

> *The secret to getting ahead is getting started.*
>
> —Mark Twain (Samuel Clemens), American humorist and author of *The Adventures of Huckleberry Finn* (1885), a.k.a. "the *Great American Novel.*"

> *Did you ever dread doing something, then it turned out to take only about 20 minutes to do?*
>
> —Conversation between two college students overheard in a coffee shop

> *To eat an elephant, first cut it into small pieces.*
>
> —Author unknown

time. While procrastinators often have difficulty starting work, they may also have difficulty continuing and completing the work they've started (Lay & Silverman, 1996). As previously mentioned, if students have trouble starting work, it might be best for them to first do tasks that they find most interesting or easiest. In contrast, if students tend to experience procrastination later in the work process, it might be better for them to take on tasks of greater interest and ease at a time later at their work session, which may serve to restore or revive their interest and energy. Also, doing the most enjoyable and easiest tasks last can provide an incentive or reward for students to complete their less enjoyable tasks first.

5. **If students are close to completing a task, encourage them to "go for the kill"—urge them to finish it then and there, rather than stopping and attempting to finish it later.** It's often harder to restart a task than it is to finish a task that we've already started because we've overcome the initial inertia needed to get started and we can ride the momentum we've created to finish what we started. Furthermore, finishing a task can give us a sense of *closure*— the feeling of personal accomplishment and self-satisfaction that comes from knowing that we "closed the deal." Placing checkmarks next to completed tasks also serves as a visible form of positive reinforcement that can increase our motivation to keep going and complete the remaining tasks on our to-do list.

> *I'm very good at starting things but often have trouble keeping a sustained effort.*
> —First-year college student

Reflection 5.6

How often do you procrastinate? (Circle one.)

rarely   occasionally   frequently   consistently

If you procrastinate, what's the usual cause?

Have you developed any anti-procrastination strategies that have worked well for you that you could share with your students?

Helping Students Build Motivation and Maintain Progress toward Their Goals

Setting goals and managing time create the potential for success, but it takes motivation to turn this potential into reality by converting intention into action. The word *motivation* derives from the Latin *movere*, meaning "to move." Thus, motivation involves overcoming inertia, initiating movement toward a goal, and maintaining that movement until a goal is reached.

Reaching a long-range or distant goal requires particularly strong motivation, perseverance, and resiliency. Listed below are strategies you can share with students to help them build a strong motivational foundation that will support and sustain their commitment to achieving their future goals.

Encourage students to visualize reaching long-range goals. Inspire students to visualize the goals that really matter to them and the future they want for themselves by creating mental images of future success. For example, if their goal is to achieve a college degree, they could visualize a crowd of cheering family, friends, and faculty at their graduation and how they'll cherish this proud memory for the rest of their life. (They could add musical inspiration by playing a motivational song in their head to keep them going—e.g., "We Are the Champions" by Queen.) Ask them to imagine themselves in careers that their college degrees enabled them to enter and visualize a typical workday going something like this: they wake up in the morning and are excited about their upcoming day at work. When they're at work, time flies by, and before they know it, the day's over. When they go home that night and reflect on their day, they feel good about what they did and how well they did it.

Advise students to put their goals in writing. When we put our goals in writing, we're more likely to remain aware of them and remember to pursue them. Written goals can serve almost like a written contract that holds us accountable for following through on our commitments.

Encourage students to place their written goals where they can't help but see them on a daily basis (e.g., their laptop, refrigerator, or bathroom mirror). If they're constantly in sight, they'll be kept constantly in mind.

Note well! *The next best thing to accomplishing something that can't be accomplished right away is to write down our intention to do it.*

Encourage students to keep a record of their progress. Research indicates that the mere act of monitoring and recording progress toward our goals can increase motivation to continue pursuing them (Locke & Latham, 2005; Matsui, Okada, & Inoshita, 1983). Keeping a regular record of personal progress increases motivation because it provides us with frequent feedback about whether we're on track and positive reinforcement for staying on track and moving toward our target (long-range goal) (Bandura & Cervone, 1983; Schunk, 1995).

Encourage students to mark down their accomplishments in red on a calendar, or keep a journal of the short- and mid-range goals they've reached. These markings can serve as benchmarks, supplying them with concrete evidence of their progress. Students could also mark their progress on a chart or graph, which would provide them with a very visible display of their upward trends and patterns of progress. Suggest that they keep the chart or graph where they can see it on a daily basis and use it as an ongoing source of inspiration and motivation.

Remind students to reward themselves for reaching milestones on the path toward their long-range goal. Reward is already built into reaching a long-range goal because it represents the end of the trip; it lands us at our desired destination. However, short- and mid-range goals are often not self-rewarding ends in themselves because they're merely the means or steps needed to be taken to reach our long-range goal. Consequently, we need to intentionally reward ourselves for climbing the smaller stepping stones along the path to the mountain peak (ultimate goal). When your students achieve short- and mid-range goals, encourage them to check them off and reward themselves for their accomplishments (e.g., celebrate successful completion of midterms or finals by treating themselves to something they really enjoy).

Like any other behavior, persistence and perseverance through all the intermediate steps needed to reach a long-range goal is more likely to occur if it's followed by reward (positive reinforcement). The process of setting small goals, recognizing that each stepping stone is a milestone along the path to our ultimate goal, and rewarding ourselves for successfully climbing each of these steps is a simple, but powerful self-motivational strategy. It helps us maintain momentum over an extended period of time, which is exactly what's required to reach our long-range goals.

Urge students to capitalize on resources that can help them stay on track and moving toward their goal. Research indicates that student success in college involves a combination of what students do for themselves (personal responsibility) and how well they capitalize on resources available to them (Pascarella & Terenzini, 1991, 2005). Successful people are *resourceful*: they seek out and take advantage of resources to help them reach their goals. Remind and encourage students to use campus (and community) resources that can help them achieve their long-range goals (e.g., academic advising and career counseling).

Encourage students to use their peers as a social resource for achieving their goals. The power of social support groups for helping people achieve personal goals is well documented by research in different fields (Brissette, Cohen, & Seeman, 2000; Ewell, 1997). Encourage students to ask, "Who can help me stick to my plan and complete the steps needed to reach my goal?". Students can harness the power of social support by surrounding themselves with peers who are committed to successfully achieving their educational goals and by avoiding "toxic" people who are likely to poison their plans or dampen their dreams.

Advise them to find motivated peers with whom they can make mutually supportive "pacts" to help one another reach their goals. These mutual-support pacts may be viewed as "social contracts" signed by "co-witnesses" whose job is to help each other stay on track and moving toward their long-range goals. Studies show that making a public commitment to a goal increases our commitment to it, probably because it becomes a matter of personal pride that's seen not only through our own eyes but also through the eyes of someone else (Hollenbeck, Williams, & Klein, 1989; Locke, 2000).

Inspire students to convert setbacks into comebacks. After we experience a setback, our reaction to it will affect what action we subsequently take in response to it. For instance, students can react to a poor test grade by knocking themselves down with a self-putdown ("I'm a loser.") or by building themselves back up with positive self-talk ("I'm going to learn from my mistakes on this test and rebound with a stronger performance on the next one.").

The root of the word *failure* is *fallere*, meaning "to trip or fall," and the root of the word *success* is *successus*, meaning "to follow or come after." Thus, failing at something doesn't mean we've been defeated; it just means we've stumbled and taken a spill. Success can still be achieved after the fall if we get up, don't give up, and continue to take the succession of steps needed to successfully reach the goal. If students view poor academic performance and other setbacks (particularly those occurring early in their college experience) not as failures but as learning opportunities, they put themselves in a position to bounce back and transform their setbacks into comebacks.

It's noteworthy that the word *problem* derives from the Greek root *proballein*, meaning "to throw forward," which suggests that a problem is an opportunity to move ahead. You can help students take this approach to problems by having

Develop an inner circle of close associations in which the mutual attraction is not sharing problems or needs. The mutual attraction should be values and goals.

—Denis Waitley, former mental trainer for U.S. Olympic athletes and author of *Seeds of Greatness*

Tale FROM THE Trenches

I gave the students a worksheet to write down their individual goals. They created academic, professional, and social goals, and they could have been short term or long term. I had them put their goals into an envelope and hand them to me. I chose this process because I would be able to have their goals with me and be able to keep up with them during meetings. We are going to have an evaluation of their goals during the middle of the term and near the end. I will be sending out emails to them to see how they are doing and always check in on them to see if they are working toward their goals.

—PEER MENTOR

What happens is not as important as how you react to what happens.

—Thaddeus Golas, *Lazy Man's Guide to Enlightenment*

them reword or rephrase each problem in terms of a positive goal statement. (For example, "I'm flunking math" can be reframed as "My goal is to get a grade of C or better on the next exam to pull my overall course grade into passing territory.")

Reflection 5.7

What would you say is the biggest personal setback or obstacle you've overcome in your life?

How did you overcome it? (What action did you take to get past it or prevent it from holding you back?)

Do you think you learned something from this experience that you could share with your students to help them deal with their setbacks?

> You've got to think about 'big things' while you're doing small things, so that all the small things go in the right direction.
>
> —Alvin Toffler, American futurologist and author who predicted the future effects of technology on our society

Remind students to keep their eyes on the prize. To be successful in the long run, we need to stay focused on the big picture—our dreams. At the same time, we need to focus on the little details—the due dates, to-do lists, and day-to-day duties that require perspiration but keep us on track and moving toward our goals. Setting meaningful life goals and steadily progressing toward them require two focus points. One involves a narrow-focus lens that allows us to focus in on the details immediately in front of us. The other is a wide-angle lens that gives us a big-picture view of what's further ahead of us (our long-range goals). Achieving success requires alternating between these two perspectives so that we continually view our small, short-term chores and challenges (e.g., completing an assignment that's due next week) in light of the larger, long-range picture (e.g., college graduation and a successful future).

> Self-discipline is the ability to make yourself do the thing you have to do, when it ought be done, whether you like it or not.
>
> —Thomas Henry Huxley, 19th-century English biologist

Successful people think big but start small; they take all the small steps and diligently do all the little things that need to be done, which, in the long run, add up to a big accomplishment—achieving their long-range goal. They're willing to tolerate short-term strain or pain for long-term gain. They maintain the self-control and self-restraint that's needed to resist the impulse for instant gratification or the temptation to do what they feel like doing instead of what they need to do. They're willing to sacrifice their immediate or short-sighted needs and desires to do what's necessary to get them where they want to be in the long run.

Note well! *Sometimes we've got to do what we have to do in order to get to do what we want to do.*

Reflection 5.8

Think about something you do with great commitment, effort, and intensity.

Do you see ways in which you could apply the same approach to achieving your goals in college and as a peer leader?

Provide students with motivating feedback. Success in any endeavor requires continual assessment of the gap between our current level of performance and the performance level we need to achieve in order to reach our goals. Feedback is essential to this process because it provides students with the information they need to assess whether they're on track and moving in the direction of their ultimate goal. As a peer leader and mentor, you can help students by providing them with feedback related to the goals they've set for themselves. These goals are reference points or touchstones for the self-improvement process.

When you provide feedback to your students about their goals, keep the following six attributes of motivating feedback in mind.

Box 5.3

Six Attributes of Motivating Feedback

1. **Proactive**—it's delivered in the *early stages* of the goal-setting process while there's still time for students to make corrections and improvements before they veer too far off track or fall too far behind.
2. **Prompt**—it's delivered *soon after* key steps toward the goal are taken.
3. **Precise**—it focuses *exactly* on what needs to be *corrected or improved to stay on track* and overcome setbacks.
4. **Practical**—it provides suggestions for improvement that are *manageable*, targeting behaviors that can be *realistically* changed (without having to change the student's entire character).
5. **Persuasive**—it provides good reasons *why* improvement should be made, which serves to *motivate* students to take action on the feedback provided.
6. **Positive**—it begins and ends in a *warm, non-threatening* manner; it preserves students' self-esteem, recognizes their personal *accomplishments*, and reinforces their *progress*.

How can you deliver feedback that's positive yet challenging? How can you remain positive and optimistic, while at the same time being honest and realistic about things that your students need to change? One strategy for doing so is using the following "warm-cool-warm" sequence:

1. Warm (compliments)
2. Cool (challenges)
3. Warm (compliments)

Start with a positive comment (e.g., about the student's effort and progress), follow it with a challenging yet supportive suggestion (e.g., about what the student could do better), and end on a positive or optimistic note (e.g., remind the student about what he/she's doing well and express confidence that by considering your suggestions, he/she can do even better). By starting with positive feedback, a positive "first impression" is created that can defuse defensiveness and increase student receptivity to the constructive criticism that follows. Concluding the interchange on an optimistic note creates a positive "last impression" that can inspire the student to act on the feedback you've provided.

When is it hardest to stay upbeat, enthusiastic, and deliver positive feedback? When students are really "messing up"! Don't give up on students when they stumble, and don't give up as a leader when things do not go according to your hopes and plans. Keep in mind that each student's pace of development will be affected by his or her unique circumstances and degree of readiness for the college experience—academically, socially, and emotionally. Continue to challenge your students to commit to their goals and to behave in ways that are consistent with their aspirations, but continue to do so by providing them with positive, empathetic, and effective feedback. Your leadership experiences will test your confidence and resilience; it's all about how you deal with it. Continue to believe in your students' potential to improve and continue to believe in your ability to make a difference.

Reflection 5.9

What leadership challenges do you think will provide the strongest test of your confidence and resiliency as a peer leader?

Lastly, keep in mind that just as your students can improve their performance by receiving feedback from you, you can improve your own leadership performance by receiving feedback from them. Make it clear that you're receptive to their feedback and make the effort to seek it out. You can obtain feedback from your students through various methods, including personal conversations, short surveys, e-mails, and social networking. Use whatever methods supply you with the most honest, open, and useful feedback. Here are some open-ended questions you could use to solicit feedback from your students:

- How is this going for you?
- Is this helping you make progress on your goals?
- Is there anything I could be doing that I'm not doing?
- Do you have any needs or interests that I have not yet addressed?
- Do you have any questions of me?
- Do you have any suggestions for me?

You can share the feedback you receive with fellow student mentors and leaders, and ask them to do the same. You can begin by meeting regularly with a fellow student leader or small group of leaders you respect and trust. In these meetings, discuss your most difficult challenges and most successful practices, and ask for feedback on your own leadership self-assessment.

Note well! Don't forget that a vital source of feedback for self-improvement is YOU! Take time to pause, reflect, assess, and use your self-assessment to continually improve your performance as a peer leader.

Summary and Conclusion

As a peer leader and mentor, one of your roles is to inspire and challenge students to set ambitious, yet realistic goals. Studies consistently show that setting personal goals is a more effective self-motivational strategy than simply telling ourselves to "try hard" or "do our best." Achieving success begins with setting goals, and successful people set goals on a regular basis.

Remind students that setting goals and developing plans to reach them doesn't mean that those plans can never be adjusted or modified. Goals can change as students change and develop, acquire new knowledge and skills, and discover new interests and talents. Setting goals doesn't mean they are locking themselves into premature plans that limit their flexibility or options. Instead, goal setting simply supplies students with a map that (1) enables them to "see" the future they'd like to have for themselves, (2) provides a sense of direction about how to get there, and (3) starts them moving in the right direction. More specifically, effective goal setting involves a sequence of five key steps:

1. **Awareness of self**–insight into personal interests, abilities and talents, and values.
2. **Awareness of goal options**–knowledge of different goal options available to you.
3. **Awareness of the options that best fit you**–the particular goals that are most compatible with your personal abilities, interests, values, and needs.
4. **Awareness of the process**–the major steps that must be taken in order to reach your chosen goal.
5. **Awareness of a time frame**–a timeline for completing each of the major steps toward the goal.

The acronym SMART is a popular mnemonic device (memory strategy) for recalling all the key components of a well-designed goal. A SMART goal is one that is:

Specific–it states precisely what the goal is and what the person will do to achieve it.

Meaningful (and Measurable)–the goal really matters to the person, and progress toward reaching the goal can be steadily measured or tracked.

Actionable (or Action-Oriented)–it identifies the concrete actions or behaviors the person will engage in to reach the goal.

Realistic–the goal is attainable and the person is aware of the amount of time, effort, and skill it will take to attain it, as well as obstacles likely to be encountered along the way.

Time-Framed–the goal has a deadline and a timeline or timetable that includes a sequence of short-range, mid-range, and long-range steps.

Goal setting gets students going, but time management is needed to get things done. Time is one of our most powerful personal resources; the better we manage it, the more likely we are to achieve our goals and gain control of our lives. Remind students that managing time effectively involves three key mental processes:

1. **Analysis**–breaking down time and becoming aware of how it's being spent;
2. **Itemization**–identifying the specific tasks that need to be accomplished and their due dates; and
3. **Prioritization**–tackling tasks in their order of importance.

Setting goals and managing time are the keys to igniting motivation, but maintaining motivation after it's been ignited requires use of effective self-motivational strategies. You can help your students maintain their motivation through such strategies as:

- Visualizing reaching their long-range goals;
- Putting their goals in writing;
- Creating a visual map of their goals;
- Keeping a record of their progress;
- Rewarding themselves for making progress toward their long-range goals;
- Converting their setbacks into comebacks by using positive self-talk and maintaining positive expectations;

- Keeping an eye on the long-term consequences of their short-term choices and decisions; and
- Providing students with motivating feedback.

Keep in mind that just as your students can improve their performance by receiving feedback from you, you can improve your own leadership performance by receiving feedback from them. Make it clear that you're receptive to their feedback and make the effort to seek it out.

Lastly, don't forget that a vital source of feedback for self-improvement is YOU! Take time to pause, reflect, assess, and use your self-assessment to continually improve your performance as a peer leader.

Internet Resources

For additional information related to the ideas discussed in this chapter, we recommend the following websites:

Goal Setting
www.siue.edu/SPIN/activity.html

Self-Motivational Strategies
www.selfmotivationstrategies.com

Time-Management Strategies
www.pennstatelearning.psu.edu/resources/study-tips/time-mgt

Beating Procrastination
www.mindtools.com

Exercise 5.1 *Helping Students Clarify Their Goals*

Take a moment to answer the following questions honestly. Ask your students to do the same.

1. What are my highest priorities?

2. What competing needs and priorities do I need to keep in check?

3. How will I maintain balance across different aspects of my life?

4. What am I willing or able to give up in order to achieve educational and personal success?

5. How can I maintain motivation on a day-to-day basis?

6. Whom can I collaborate with to reach my goals (and what will that collaboration involve)?

Exercise 5.2 *Prioritizing Important Life Goals*

Rank the following life goals in order of their priority for you (1 = highest; 5 = lowest):

_____ Emotional well-being

_____ Spiritual growth

_____ Physical health

_____ Social relationships

_____ Rewarding career

What were the primary reasons behind your first- and last-ranked choices?

Have you established any short- or mid-range goals for reaching your highest-ranked choice? If yes, what are they? If not, what could they be?

Ask your students to complete this exercise as well.

E xercise 5.3 *Setting Goals for Reducing the Gap between Your Ideal Future and Your Current Reality*

Think of an aspect of your life where there's a significant gap between what you'd like it to be (the ideal) and what it is (the reality). On the lines that follow, identify goals you could pursue to reduce this gap:

Long-range goal: _____

Mid-range goal: _____

Short-range goal: _____

Use the list below to identify strategies for reaching each of these three goals:

Long-range goal: _____

- Actions to be taken:

- Available resources:

- Possible roadblocks:

- Potential strategies for overcoming roadblocks:

Mid-range goal: _____

- Actions to be taken:

- Available resources:

- Possible roadblocks:

- Potential strategies for overcoming roadblocks:

Short-range goal: _____

- Actions to be taken:

- Available resources:

- Possible roadblocks:

- Potential strategies for overcoming roadblocks:

Exercise 5.4 *Designing a SMART Leadership Goal*

Think about a leadership goal that you'd like to reach this year, and apply the SMART method of goal setting (described on pp. 117–118) to create a plan for achieving it.

chapter 6

Becoming a Learning Coach
Helping Students Learn Deeply and Think Critically

Reflection 6.1

When you hear the term *deep learning*, what comes to mind?

Learning is the fundamental mission of all colleges and universities. Students must be able to meet higher expectations for higher levels of learning and thinking set by college faculty, as well as adjust to the challenge of becoming more independent, self-directed learners. However, learning isn't a hat that students take off after they graduate. It's a lifelong process that has become essential for success in the 21st century. The ongoing information-technology revolution and increasing global interdependence are creating a greater need for humans to develop effective learning skills that they'll use throughout life and apply those skills in diverse cultural and occupational contexts. Companies and organizations now seek employees who have "learned how to learn" and are willing to continue being "lifelong learners" (SECFHE, 2006). Indeed, the learning skills and strategies discussed in this chapter aren't merely "study skills" or "college success strategies," they're lifelong learning skills and life success strategies.

What Is Deep Learning?

Deep learning is not about surface-level memorization or pouring information into the brain as if it were an empty jar; it's about connecting new ideas to ideas that are already stored in our brains. In fact, when we learn deeply, our brains make actual biological connections between different nerve cells (Alnon, 1992). (See **Figure 6.1**.) What do deep learners do? They build mental bridges between what they're trying to learn and what they already know (Piaget, 1978; Vygotsky, 1978). They dive below the surface of shallow memorization to reflect, evaluate, and apply what they've learned.

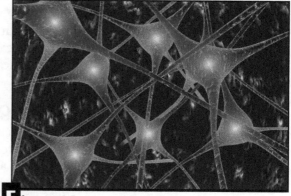

© Jurgen-Ziewe, 2013. Used under license from Shutterstock, Inc.

Figure 6.1 Network of Brain Cells

Numerous studies suggest that most college students don't engage in deep learning (Becker, 1968; Kuh, 2005; Moffatt, 1989; Nathan, 2005). They may show up for class most of the time, cram for their exams, procrastinate on their assignments, and get them done right before they're due. These learning strategies may enable them to survive in college, but not thrive in college and achieve academic excellence.

Do you really want to learn or do you just want to get by?

—Question posed by a student to another student in a coffee shop

Change is needed in the culture of learning on college campuses. Peer leaders can be key catalysts in this change process. They can assume the role of a *learning coach* by inspiring, modeling, and enabling students to develop the attributes of deep, lifelong learners. All student leaders—regardless of their specific leadership role on campus—should embrace the role of learning coach by (1) sharing their knowledge of effective leaning practices with others, (2) modeling effective learning practices for others to emulate, (3) providing effective feedback to other learners, and (4) encouraging others to value learning and to continue learning throughout life.

Note well! The word *educate* derives from the root *educere*, meaning "to bring out or lead forth." Thus, being a leader and being an educator are closely related concepts; both involve promoting positive change in others.

Reflection 6.2

Do you think most students on your campus engage in deep learning?

What kinds of changes in student behavior, teacher behavior, and/or college policies do you think would strengthen students' commitment to deep learning on your campus?

Sharing and Modeling Effective Learning Strategies

Academically successful students invest a significant amount of time, effort, and energy at each of the following key stages in the learning process: (1) acquiring information (by active listening in class and active reading outside of class), (2) learning that information deeply (through effective study strategies), and (3) thinking about what they've learned at a higher level (e.g., evaluating and applying it). You can serve as a learning coach by sharing and modeling effective learning strategies at each of these three stages in the learning process.

Coaching for Note-Taking

One academic task that students will be expected to perform at the start of their first term in college is taking quality notes in class. Studies show that professors' lecture notes are the number one source of test questions (and test answers) on college exams (Cuseo, Fecas, & Thompson, 2010). As a learning coach, promote student self-awareness about the importance of notes, advocate and demonstrate ways students can do it, and inspire them to take note-taking seriously. You can offer to review a student's notes and provide feedback, or attend class with students, take notes, and compare notes. (Ask the professor for permission first.) In addition, you can supply students with specific strategies to boost the quality of their note-taking, such as those cited in **Box 6.1.**

Box 6.1

Strategies for Effective Listening and Note-Taking in the College Classroom

1. **Get to class!** Whether or not your college instructors take roll, students are responsible for all material covered in class. Remember that a full load of college courses (15 units) only requires that you be in class about 13 hours per week. If you consider college to be a full-time job, any job that requires you to show up someplace for only 13 hours a week is a pretty sweet deal. It's a deal that supplies you with much more educational freedom than you had in high school. It's an abuse of this educational freedom to miss class sessions in college when you're required to spend so little time in class.

2. **Get to every class on time.** During the first few minutes of a class session, instructors often share valuable information, such as reminders, reviews, and previews.

3. **Get organized.** Bring the right equipment to class. Get a separate notebook for each class, write your name on it, date each class session, and store all class handouts in it.

4. **Get in the right position.**
   - The ideal *place* to sit is in the front and center of the room, where you're in the best position to hear and see what's going on.
   - The ideal *posture* is upright and leaning forward, because your body influences your mind. If your body is in an alert and ready position, your mind is likely to follow suit and assume an alert and ready frame of mind.
   - The ideal *social position* is to sit near people who will not distract you or detract from the quality of your note-taking.

5. **Get in the right frame of mind.** Get psyched up! Come to class with attitude—an attitude that you're going to pick your instructor's brain, pick up answers to test questions, and build up your course grade.

6. **Get it down (in writing).** Actively look, listen, and record important points at all times in class. Pay special attention to whatever information instructors put in writing, whether it's on the board, on a slide, or in a handout.

7. **Don't let go of your pen or keyboard.** When in doubt, write it out or type it out; it's better to have it and not need it than to need it and not have it.

Note well! Most college professors don't put every piece of important information on the board or on PowerPoint for you; instead, they expect you to listen carefully to what they're saying and write it down for yourself.

8. **Finish strong.** During the last few minutes of class, instructors often share valuable information, such as reminders, reviews, and previews.

9. **Stick around.** As soon as class ends, don't just bolt out: instead, hang out for a few moments and quickly review your notes, by yourself or with a classmate. This quick end-of-class review will help your brain "lock in" the information it just received. If you find any gaps, check them out with your instructor before the instructor leaves the classroom.

Finish class with a rush of attention, not a rush out the door!

Reflection 6.3

What would you say to students who believe that writing notes in class actually interferes with their ability to pay attention to what their instructor is saying?

The Cornell Note-Taking System

This method of note-taking was developed at Cornell University in 1949 by education professor Walter Pauk. Frustrated by his students' poor test scores, he designed a system for taking notes that his students could later use as effective study guides. His system has since become the best-known note-taking system in higher education. Following are the key steps:

1. On a single 8½" x 11" page of notepaper, have students draw a vertical line about 2½ inches from the left edge of the page and a horizontal line about 2 inches from the bottom edge of the page (as depicted in the scaled-down illustration below), resulting in three areas—labeled below as areas A, B, and C.

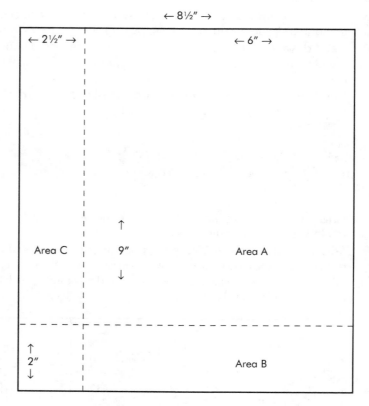

2. Area A (right side of the vertical line) is used to record notes during a lecture, presentation, or discussion.
3. Area B (bottom of page) is used to summarize the main points. This should be done as soon after class as possible.
4. Area C (left side of the page) is used to formulate questions about the material after the class. The material in areas A and B is used to answer these questions.

Using the questions they've created, students can then quiz themselves, quiz each other, or go to professors to ask if the questions they posed are relevant and represent higher-level thinking (See pp. 158–160 for a list of potential higher-level thinking questions that students could ask about their class notes.)

The Cornell System of note-taking promotes deep learning by getting students to become active and reflective leaders, and by challenging them to restate the material in their own words, as opposed to mimicking and memorizing the instructor's words.

While the Cornell method is an effective note-taking strategy, it's not the only one. Some students may prefer a more visual method that diagrams connections among key points, which are often referred to as "concept maps" or "mind maps." (For example, see **Figure 6.2**.)

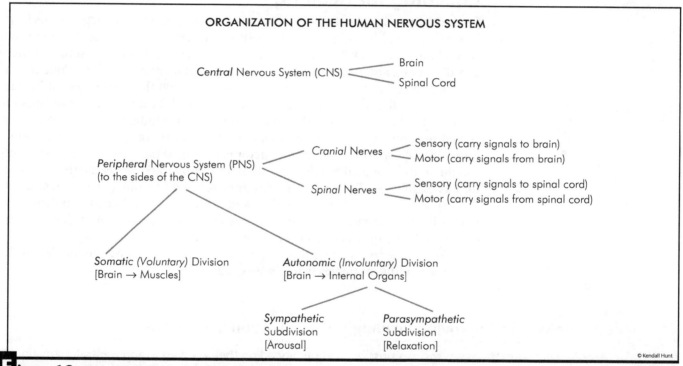

Figure 6.2   Concept Map for the Human Nervous System

Whatever particular method students choose to use, what's most important is for them to fully commit to a note-taking system that promotes active and deep learning. One of your key roles as a learning coach is to help students develop this commitment.

Author's Experience Frankly, I did not consciously think about study skills such as reading and note-taking when I was in college. However, I always attended classes and took thorough notes. Not only did taking notes help me review later; it kept me attentive in classes. Later, when I became a graduate student, I began to teach first-year seminar classes and became more conscious of the learning process and specific methods of reading and note-taking (such as Cornell notes). I began to employ these methods as a learner in my graduate classes while teaching them to my students. Wow—I realized this stuff really works!

Greg Metz

You can also promote effective note-taking by facilitating note-taking teams among students. After classes, encourage your students to form "cooperative note-taking pairs"—one member of the pair summarizes notes for the other, who, in turn, adds missing information obtained from the partner; then the partners reverse roles, allowing the other member to add missing information (Johnson, Johnson, & Smith, 1991). Thus, both members obtain something from their partner's notes and include it in their own.

Suggest that the partners ask each other questions such as "What main ideas did you take away? What did you feel was most important? What did you find challenging or confusing? What would you consider to be an essay question (or problem) that could come out of these notes?" (Johnson, Johnson, & Smith, 1995).

Coaching for Reading

Second only to lecture notes as a source of test questions on college exams is information found in assigned readings (Brown, 1988; Cuseo, Fecas, & Thompson, 2010). Students are likely to find exam questions in their reading that their professors didn't talk about specifically in class (or even mention in class). College professors often expect students to relate or connect what they lecture about in class with material that they've assigned students to read. Furthermore, professors often deliver class lectures with the assumption that students have done the assigned reading, so if they haven't done it, students are more likely to have more difficulty following what your instructor is talking about in class. Thus, students should do the assigned reading and do it according to the schedule their instructor has established. By completing assigned reading in a timely manner, students will (1) be better positioned to understand class lectures, (2) acquire information that is likely to appear on exams but not covered in class, and (3) improve the quality of their contributions to class discussions.

You can serve as a learning coach for reading by sharing and modeling the effective reading strategies listed in **Box 6.2**.

Box 6.2

Top Strategies for Improving Reading Comprehension and Retention

1. **Acquire course textbooks as soon as possible and get ahead on their reading assignments.** Information from reading assignments ranks right behind lecture notes as a source of test questions on college exams. If you've done the assigned reading, you can build on that knowledge to help you understand class lectures and take better class notes.

2. **Read with the right equipment.**
   - Bring tools to record and store key information obtained from your assigned reading. Always bring a writing tool (pen, pencil, or keyboard) to record important information and a storage space (notebook or computer) in which you can save and retrieve information acquired from your reading for later use on tests and assignments.
   - Have a dictionary nearby to quickly find the meaning of unfamiliar words that may interfere with your ability to comprehend what you're reading. Looking up definitions of unfamiliar words not only helps you understand what you're reading, it's also an effective way to strengthen your vocabulary. A strong vocabulary will improve your reading comprehension in all college courses, as well as your performance on standardized tests, such as those required for admission to graduate and professional schools.
   - Make use of the textbook's glossary. The glossary of terms contained at the back of a textbook is more than an ancillary or frill. It's a key resource for helping you comprehend technical concepts. Each academic subject or discipline has its own terminology; knowing the precise definitions of these terms is often the key to understanding the concepts covered in the text. Consider making a photocopy of the

glossary of terms at the back of your textbook so that you can have a copy of it in front of you while you're reading, rather than having to repeatedly stop, hold your place, and go to the back of the text to find the glossary.

3. **Get in the right reading position.** Sit upright and have light coming from behind you, over the side of your body opposite your writing hand. This will reduce the distracting and fatiguing effects of glare and shadows.

4. **Get a sneak preview.** Start each chapter by first reading its boldface headings and any chapter outline, summary, or end-of-chapter questions that may be provided. This will supply you with a mental map of the chapter's important ideas (the "whole forest") so you don't get lost in the trees.

5. **Use boldface headings and subheadings.** Headings provide a "heads up" for important information. Don't ignore them; use them as cues or clues to key ideas by turning them into questions and then reading to find their answers. This will launch you on an answer-finding mission that will keep you mentally active while reading and enable you to read with a purpose. Turning headings into questions is also a good way to prepare for tests because you're practicing exactly what you'll be expected to do on tests—answer questions.

6. **Pay special attention to the first and last sentences of each paragraph.** These sentences often contain an important introduction and conclusion to the material covered in that section of the text.

7. **Finish each of your reading sessions with a short review.** Rather than trying to cover a few more pages at the end of your reading session, use the last few minutes of reading time to "lock in" the most important information you've read (e.g., highlighted sentences and margin notes).

Note well! *Your goal when reading should be to discover the most important information, and the final step in the reading process should be to review (and lock in) the most important information you've discovered.*

Reflection 6.4

When you do academic reading, do you usually have the following tools on hand? (First answer these questions for yourself and then answer them in terms of how you think other students would respond.)

Highlighter:	yes	no
Pen or pencil:	yes	no
Notebook:	yes	no
Class notes:	yes	no
Dictionary:	yes	no
Glossary:	yes	no

Study Strategies for Learning Deeply and Remembering Longer

Key steps in the learning-and-memory process are to (1) acquire knowledge, (2) retain that knowledge, and (3) retrieve that knowledge (bring it back to mind) when you need it—e.g., test time. Learning isn't just a short sprint that takes place just before test time. Instead, it's the final lap of a long-distance run. Studying for a test represents the last step in a sequence of test-preparation steps that includes successful completion of a series of important academic tasks that take place well before test time, such as (1) taking accurate and complete notes in class, (2) doing the assigned reading, and (3) seeking help from professors or peers along the way for any concepts that are unclear or confusing. After these steps have been taken, students are then well-positioned to study the material and learn it deeply.

Described below is a series of study strategies that you can share with students to promote deep and durable (long-lasting) learning.

Give learning your undivided attention. The human attention span has limited capacity; we have only so much of it available to us at any point in time, and we can give all or part of it to whatever task(s) we're working on. If study time is spent engaging in other activities at the same time (e.g., listening to music, watching TV, or text-messaging friends), the total amount of attention devoted to studying is subtracted and divided among the other activities. In other words, studying doesn't receive your undivided attention.

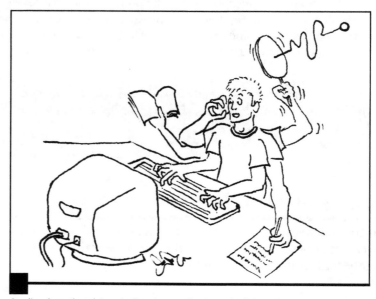

Studies show that doing challenging academic work while multitasking divides up attention and drives down comprehension and retention.

Studies show that when people multitask they don't pay equal attention to all tasks at the same time. Instead, they divide their attention by shifting it back and forth between tasks (Howard, 2000) and their performance on the task that demands the most concentration or deepest thinking suffers the most (Crawford & Strapp, 1994). When performing complex mental tasks that cannot be done automatically or mindlessly, other tasks and sources of external stimulation interfere with the quiet, internal reflection time needed for permanent connections to form between brain cells—which is what must happen if deep, long-lasting learning is to take place (Jensen, 2000).

Make meaningful associations between what you're learning and what you already know. Deep learning doesn't take place by passively absorbing information like a sponge—e.g., memorizing it in the same, prepackaged form as it appeared in the textbook or a professor's lecture. Instead, deep learning involves actively transforming the information we receive into a form that's meaningful to us (Feldman

& Paulsen, 1994; Mayer, 2002). This transforms short-term, surface-level learning (memorization of information) into meaningful long-term learning (acquisition of knowledge). So, instead of immediately trying to learn something by repeatedly pounding it into our brains like a hammer, our first strategy should be to try hooking or hanging it onto something that's already stored in our brains—something we already know that is meaningful to us. For instance, suppose you're taking a biology course and studying the autonomic nervous system—the part of the nervous system that operates without your conscious awareness or voluntary control (e.g., your heart beating and lungs breathing). The meaning of the phrase is found in its prefix *auto*, meaning self-controlling or "automatic" (e.g., automatic transmission).

Another way students can make meaningful associations is by comparing and contrasting what they're learning with what they already know. Suggest to students that when they're studying something new, they should get in the habit of asking themselves the following questions:

1. Is this idea similar or comparable to something that I've already learned? (Compare)
2. How is this idea different from what I've already learned? (Contrast)

Research indicates that this simple strategy is one of the most powerful ways to promote learning of academic information (Marzano, Pickering, & Pollock, 2001). When students ask themselves, "How is this similar to and different from concepts that I already know?" it makes learning more personally meaningful because they're relating what they're trying to learn to what they already know.

Note well! *Deep learning is not a transmission of knowledge from teacher to learner: it's a transformation of knowledge into a form that's meaningful to the learner.*

Integrate material from class notes and assigned readings that relate to the same concept by organizing them into the same category. Encourage students to get ideas related to the same point in the same place by recording them on the same index card under the same category heading. Index cards are a good tool for such purposes. Each card can be used like a miniature file cabinet for different categories of information. The category heading on each card functions like the hub of a wheel, around which individual pieces of related information are attached like spokes. Integrating information related to the same topic in the same place and studying it at the same time divides the total material to be learned into identifiable and manageable parts. In contrast, when ideas pertaining to the same point or concept are spread all over the place, they're more likely to take that form in the student's mind—leaving them mentally disconnected and leaving the student more confused (as well as more stressed and overwhelmed).

Note well! *Deep learners ask questions like, "How can this specific piece of information be categorized or classified into a larger concept? How does this particular idea relate to or 'fit into' something bigger?"*

Rather than jamming (cramming) study time into one long session, distribute it across several shorter sessions. Deep learning depends not only on *how* you learn (your method), but also on *when* you learn (your timing). Although cramming just before exams is better than not studying at all, it's far less effective than studying that's spread out across time. Instead of cramming total study time into one long session ("massed practice"), encourage students to use *distributed practice*—"distribute" or spread out their study time over several shorter sessions. Research consistently shows that short, periodic practice sessions are more effective than a single marathon session.

Distributed practice improves your learning and memory by:

1. Reducing loss of attention due to fatigue or boredom; and
2. Reducing mental interference by giving the brain some downtime to cool down and lock in information it has received before it's interrupted by the need to deal with additional information (Malmberg & Murnane, 2002; Murname & Shiffrin, 1991). If the brain's downtime is interfered with by the arrival of additional information, it gets overloaded and its capacity for handling information becomes impaired. This is what cramming does—it overloads the brain with lots of information in a limited period of time. In contrast, distributed study does just the opposite; it uses shorter sessions with downtime between sessions, which gives the brain time to slow down and retain the information it has previously received and processed (studied).

Another major advantage of distributed study is that it's less stressful and more motivating than cramming. Shorter sessions are more likely to motivate students to avoid procrastination and get their studying started because they know they won't have to do it for a long stretch of time (or lose any sleep doing it). It's much easier to maintain motivation and attention for any task that's done for a shorter rather than a longer period.

Use the part-to-whole study method. The part-to-whole method of studying is a natural extension of the distributed practice just discussed. With the part-to-whole method, you break up the material you need to learn into smaller parts and study those parts in separate sessions in advance of the exam; then you use your last study session just before the exam to review (restudy) all the parts you previously studied in separate sessions. Thus, your last session is not a cram session or even a study session; it's a review session.

Research shows that students of all ability levels learn material in college courses more effectively when it's studied in small units and when progression to the next unit takes place only after the previous unit has been mastered or understood (Pascarella & Terenzini, 1991, 2005).

Reflection 6.5

Are you more likely to study in advance of exams or cram just before exams?

How do you think most students would answer this question?

_____

Don't let students buy into the myth that studying in advance is a waste of time because they'll forget it all by test time. Procrastinators often use this myth to rationalize their habit of putting off studying until the very last moment, which forces them to cram frantically the night before exams. Students shouldn't underestimate the power of breaking material to be learned into smaller parts and studying those parts in advance of major exams. Even if they aren't able to recall what they previously studied when they look at it again closer to test time, once they start reviewing it, they'll discover that they can relearn it in a fraction of the

Consuming large doses of caffeine or other stimulants to stay awake for all-night cram sessions is likely to maximize anxiety and minimize memory.

time it took the first time. This proves that studying in advance is not a waste of time; it takes less time to relearn the material because the brain still has a memory trace for information studied in the earlier sessions (Kintsch, 1994).

Learn with and through as many sensory channels as possible. Research shows that information received through multiple sensory modalities is remembered better because it creates multiple interconnections in long-term memory areas of the brain (Bjork, 1994; Shams & Seitz, 2011; Zull, 2002). When a memory is formed in the brain, different sensory aspects of it are stored in different areas. For example, when your brain receives visual, auditory (hearing), and motor (movement) input while learning, each of these forms of sensory input is stored as a memory trace in a different part of the brain. **Figure 6.3** shows a map of the outer surface of the human brain; you can see how different parts of the brain are specialized to receive input from different sensory modalities. When multiple sensory modalities are used while studying, multiple memory traces of what you're studying are recorded in different parts of your brain, resulting in deeper learning and stronger memory for what's been studied.

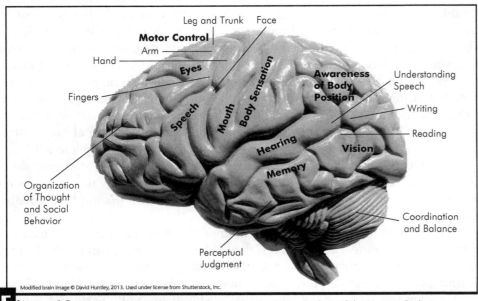

Modified brain image © David Huntley, 2013. Used under license from Shutterstock, Inc.

Figure 6.3   A Map of the Functions Performed by the Outer Surface of the Human Brain

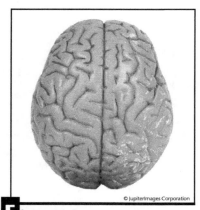

© JupiterImages Corporation

Figure 6.4 The Human Brain Consists of the Left Hemisphere (which processes words) and the Right Hemisphere (which processes images)

Capitalize on the power of visual learning. The human brain consists of two hemispheres (half spheres)—left and right. (See **Figure 6.4.**) Each of these hemispheres of the brain specializes in a different type of learning. For the vast majority of people, the left hemisphere specializes in verbal learning; it deals primarily with words. In contrast, the right hemisphere specializes in visual-spatial learning; it deals primarily with perceiving images, patterns, and things that occupy a physical place or space. If both hemispheres are used while studying, two different memory traces are recorded—one in each major hemisphere (half) of the brain. This process of laying down dual memory traces (verbal and visual) is referred to as *dual coding* (Paivio, 1990). When dual coding takes place, memory for what's been learned is substantially strengthened, primarily because two memory traces are better than one.

Note well! Drawing and other forms of visual illustration are not just artistic exercises; they're also powerful learning tools for strengthening learning and memory—i.e., we can draw to learn! Drawing increases active involvement in the learning process, and when we represent what's being learned in visual form, the information being studied is dual-coded, which doubles the number of memory traces recorded in the brain. As the old saying goes, "A picture is worth a thousand words."

Reflection 6.6

Would you say that you're more of a visual learner or a verbal learner?

How do you think most students would answer this question?

_____

Learn with passion. Information reaches the brain through the sensory input and is stored in the brain as memory traces; the same is true of emotional input. There are neural connections running between the emotional and memory centers (Zull, 1998). For instance, when we're emotionally excited about we're learning, adrenaline is released and is carried through the bloodstream to the brain. Once adrenaline reaches the brain, it increases blood flow and glucose production, which stimulates learning and strengthens memory (LeDoux, 1998; Rosenfield, 1988).

What does this emotion-memory link have to do with helping students remember academic information they're studying? Research indicates that emotional intensity, excitement, and enthusiasm strengthen memories of academic information just as they do for memories of life events and personal experiences. If students get psyched up about what they're learning, they have a much better chance of learning and remembering it. By becoming passionate or intense about what they're learning, and adopting the attitude that what they're learning is really important to know, they're more likely to remember it (Howard, 2000; Minninger, 1984).

One way to do this is by keeping in mind the importance or significance of what they're learning. For instance, if they're learning about photosynthesis, they should be mindful that they're not just learning a chemical reaction, they're learning about the driving force that underlies all plant life on the planet! If your students are not aware of the importance or significance of a particular concept they're studying, encourage them to ask their instructor, a student majoring in that field, or a graduate student in the field.

> *Note well!* *Enthusiasm is contagious; when students catch it while learning, they learn with more emotional intensity and more deeply.*

Learn collaboratively. Many college students approach learning as something that's to be done individually and in isolation, yet research indicates that learning is more effective when it's done collectively through collaboration (Cross, Barkley, & Major, 2005; Cuseo, 1996; Johnson, Johnson, & Smith, 1998).

> *TEAM = Together Everyone Achieves More*
> —Author unknown

To fully capitalize on the power of study teams, each team member should study individually before studying with the group. This paves the way for productive study groups because each member of the group is prepared to bring something to the table; it ensures that all team members are individually accountable and equally responsible for their own learning and for contributing to the learning of their teammates.

All members of a study group should come prepared with specific information or answers to share with teammates and specific questions or points of confusion about which they hope to receive help from the team. Research on study groups indicates that they are effective only if each member has done required course work in advance of the team meeting, such as completing required reading and other course assignments (Light, 2001).

In addition to the ground-floor prerequisite of individual students coming to study groups prepared for group work, study groups can also be far more productive when they implement effective group processes, such as establishing norms about (1) how they will be individually accountable to the group—e.g., no slacking or freeloading—and (2) how they will interact collectively as a group—e.g., civilly, collaboratively, and sharing leadership responsibilities. (For more detailed information on facilitating groups and promoting teamwork, see Chapter 8.)

Author's Experience What I realized fairly early in my college career was that I had a lot of questions about everything I read. Thus, I started having a sheet of paper and a writing tool next to me every time I sat down to read my textbooks. This helped me to think critically about my readings and also helped me to understand them at a deeper level. But since I am a verbal guy, I needed to have someone to bounce questions and answers off of to see if my thoughts were on or off target. So I decided I would ask some classmates at the beginning of the semester to set up a study team. We'd meet in the reading room in the library or in the lounge of the residence halls once a week and bring our notes, books, and questions to discuss. This was an absolutely wonderful way to learn. Plus, we had pizzas to round off the evening with a little sustenance.

— *Aaron Thompson*

> *Note well!* *Remember that team learning goes beyond late-night study groups. Students could and should form learning teams in advance of exams to help each other with other academic tasks, such as note-taking, reading, writing, and learning from test results. (See Chapter 4 for specific recommendations.)*

Reflect on what you're learning and whether you're learning deeply. Effective learners are *reflective* learners—they are self-aware and remain mindful of how well they're learning while they're learning. They just don't put in study time; they reflect, check, and self-assess whether they're really getting what they're attempting to learn. They monitor their comprehension by asking questions such as, "Am I following this?" and "Do I really know it?"

How do you know if you really know it? Probably the best answer to this question is "I find *meaning* in it—I can relate to it personally or put it in terms that make sense to me" (Ramsden, 2003). Listed below are some strategies for checking whether you're truly (deeply) understanding what you're learning. These strategies can be used as indicators or checkpoints for determining whether students are just memorizing or learning at a deeper level, helping them answer the question, "How do I know if I really know it?"

- **Can you paraphrase (restate or translate) what you're learning in your own words?** When you can paraphrase what you're learning, you're able to complete the following sentence: "In other words . . .". If you can complete that sentence in your own words, this is a good indication that you've moved beyond memorization to comprehension because you've transformed what you're learning into a form that's meaningful to you. You know you know it if you're not stating it the same way your instructor or textbook stated it, but restating it in words that are your own.

- **Can you explain what you're learning to someone who is unfamiliar with it?** One of the best ways to become aware of how well we know or don't know something is when we have to explain it to someone who's never heard it before (just ask any teacher). Simply put, if you can't explain it to someone else, you probably don't really understand yourself. However, if you can explain it to someone else who's unfamiliar with it, that's a good sign you've moved beyond shallow memorization to deeper comprehension, because you're able to translate it into language that's understandable to anyone. Studies show that students gain a deeper level of understanding for what they're learning when they're asked to explain it to someone else (Chi et al., 1994). If you cannot find someone else to explain it to, then explain it aloud as if you were talking to an imaginary friend.

- **Can you think of an example of what you've learned?** If you can come up with an instance or illustration of what you're learning that's your own—not one given by your instructor or textbook—this is a good sign that you truly understand it. It shows you've taken an abstract academic concept and applied it to a concrete personal experience (Bligh, 2000).

- **Can you apply what you're learning to solve a new problem that you haven't previously seen?** The ability to use knowledge by applying it in a different situation is a good indicator of deep learning (Erickson & Strommer, 2005). Learning specialists refer to this mental process as *decontextualization*—taking what you learned in one context (situation) and applying it to another (Bransford, Brown, & Cocking, 1999). For instance, you know that you've learned a mathematical concept deeply when you can use that concept to solve math problems that are different from the ones used by your instructor or your textbook. This is why math instructors rarely include on exams the exact problems that they solved in class or that were solved in your textbook. They're not trying to "trick" students at test time; they're trying to see whether they've learned the concept or principle deeply.

Reflection 6.7

If you were to ask a student preparing for an upcoming exam if he knew that material and the student responded, "I think I know it," what would be the first strategy you'd suggest to help that student determine if he really knows it (or if he needs to do more studying)?

Help Students to Think Critically

The term *critical thinking* refers to a higher level of thought than that used for learning basic skills and acquiring factual knowledge. It's a form of thinking that involves reflecting on the knowledge you've acquired and taking additional mental action on it, such as evaluating its validity, integrating it with something else you've learned, or creating new ideas.

As its name implies, higher-level thinking involves raising the bar and jacking up your thinking to levels that go beyond merely remembering, reproducing, or regurgitating factual information. Studies show that students' memory for factual information acquired in college fades quickly with the passage of time. However, higher-level thinking is a *skill* that's more likely to be retained and used for an entire lifetime (Pascarella & Terenzini, 1991, 2005).

In national surveys of college professors teaching freshman-level through senior-level courses in various fields, more than 95% of them report that the most important goal of a college education is to develop students' ability to think critically (Gardiner, 2005; Milton, 1982). Similarly, college professors teaching introductory courses to freshmen and sophomores indicate that the primary educational purpose of their courses is to develop students' critical thinking skills (Higher Education Institute, 2009; Stark et al., 1990). Simply stated, college professors are often more concerned with teaching you how to think than with teaching you what to think (i.e., what facts to remember).

This is not to say that acquiring knowledge and basic comprehension are unimportant; they supply students with the raw material needed to manufacture higher-level thinking. Deep learning and a broad base of knowledge provide the stepping stones students need to climb to higher levels of thinking—as illustrated in **Figure 6.5**.

> *The manager asks how and when; the leader asks what and why.*
>
> —Warren Bennis, former president of the University of Cincinnati, founding chairman of the Leadership Institute at the University of Southern California, and a pioneer of the contemporary field of leadership studies

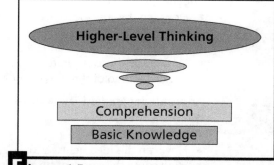

Figure 6.5 The Relationship between Knowledge, Comprehension, and Higher-Level Thinking

> *College professors expect students to do more than just retain or reproduce information: they want students to demonstrate higher levels of thinking with respect to what they've learned (e.g., analyze it, evaluate it, apply it, or connect it with other concepts that you've learned).*

Defining and Describing the Major Forms of Higher-Level Thinking

When college professors ask students to "think critically," they're usually asking them to use one or more of the eight forms of thinking listed in **Box 6.3**. One simple but powerful way to help students reflect on their thinking is through self-questioning. Since thinking often involves talking to ourselves silently, if we ask

If you do not ask the right questions, you do not get the right answers.

—Edward Hodnett, British poet

ourselves good questions, we can train our minds to think at a higher level. A thought-provoking question can serve as a springboard that launches us to higher levels of thinking in our quest to answer it. Thus, if students can get in the habit of asking themselves higher-level thinking questions while learning, they're likely to display a higher level of thinking in class discussions and on college exams and written assignments, and they'll earn higher grades in their courses.

Box 6.3 contains key questions designed to stimulate different forms of higher-level thinking. The questions are constructed as incomplete sentence so students can fill in the blank with any topic or concept they're studying in any course they may be taking. Research indicates that when students get in the habit of using question stems such as these, they demonstrate higher levels of thinking in different subject areas (King, 1990, 1995, 2002).

Box 6.3 Forms of Higher-Level Thinking and Question Prompts for Triggering Them

1. **Analysis (Analytical Thinking)**—breaking down information into its essential elements or parts.
   Trigger Questions
   - What are the main ideas contained in _____?
   - What are the important aspects of _____?
   - What are the issues raised by _____?
   - What are the major purposes of _____?
   - What hidden concepts are embedded within _____?
   - What are the reasons behind _____?

2. **Synthesis**—integrating separate pieces of information to form a more complete, coherent product or pattern.
   Trigger Questions
   - How can this idea be joined or connected with _____ to create a more complete or comprehensive understanding of _____?
   - How could these different _____ be grouped together into a more general class or category?
   - How could these separate _____ be reorganized or rearranged to produce a more comprehensive understanding of the big picture?

3. **Application (Applied Thinking)**—using knowledge for practical purposes to solve problems and resolve issues.
   Trigger Questions
   - How can this idea be used to _____?
   - How could this concept be implemented to _____?
   - How can this theory be put into practice to _____?
   - What could be done to prevent or reduce _____?

4. **Evaluation**—making critical judgments or assumptions.
   Trigger Questions for Evaluating Validity (truthfulness)
   - Is _____ true or accurate?
   - Is there sufficient evidence to support the conclusion that _____?
   - Is the reasoning behind_____ strong or weak?

   Trigger Questions for Evaluating Morality (ethics)
   - Is _____ fair?
   - Is _____ just?
   - Is this action consistent with the professed or stated values of _____?

   Trigger Questions for Evaluating Beauty (aesthetics)
   - What is the artistic merit of _____?
   - Does _____ have any aesthetic value?
   - Does _____ contribute to the beauty of _____?

Trigger Questions for Evaluating Practicality (usefulness)

- Will _____ work?
- How can _____ be put to good use?
- What practical benefit would result from _____?

Trigger Questions for Evaluating Priority (order of importance or effectiveness)

- Which one of these _____ is the most important?
- Is this _____ the best option or choice available?
- How should these _____ be ranked from first to last (best to worst) in terms of their effectiveness?

5. **Inferential Reasoning**—making an argument by inferring (stepping to) a conclusion that's supported by empirical (observable) evidence or logical consistency.

Trigger Questions for Seeking Empirical Evidence

- What examples support the argument that _____?
- What research evidence is there for _____?
- What statistical data document that this _____ is true?

Trigger Questions for Logical Consistency

- If _____ is true, doesn't it follow that _____ must also be true?
- If I believe in _____, shouldn't I practice _____?
- To draw the conclusion that _____, aren't I assuming _____?

6. **Balanced Thinking**—carefully considering reasons for and against a particular position or viewpoint.

Trigger Questions

- Have I considered both sides of _____?
- What are the strengths (advantages) and weaknesses (disadvantages) of _____?
- What evidence supports and contradicts _____?
- What are arguments for and counterarguments against _____?

Trigger Questions for Adduction (arguing for a particular idea or position by supplying supporting evidence)

- What proof is there for _____?
- What are logical arguments for _____?
- What research evidence supports _____?

Trigger Questions for Refutation (arguing against a particular idea or position by supplying contradictory evidence)

- What proof is there against _____?
- What logical arguments indicate that _____ is false?
- What research evidence contradicts _____?
- What counterarguments would provide an effective rebuttal to _____?

7. **Multidimensional Thinking**—thinking that involves viewing yourself and the world around you from different angles or vantage points.

Trigger Questions

- How would _____ affect different dimensions of myself (emotional, physical, etc.)?
- What broader impact would _____ have on the social and physical world around me?
- How might people living in different times (e.g., past and future) view _____?
- How would people from different cultural backgrounds interpret or react to _____?
- Have I taken into consideration all factors that could influence _____ or be influenced by _____?

8. **Creative Thinking**—generating ideas that are unique, original, or distinctively different.

Trigger Questions

- What could be invented to _____?
- Imagine what would happen if _____?
- What might be a different way to _____?
- How would this change if _____?
- What would be an ingenious way to _____?

(continued)

Note: Encourage your students to save these higher-level thinking questions so they can use them when completing different academic tasks required in their courses (e.g., preparing for exams, writing papers or reports, and participating in class discussions or study group sessions). Remind them to get in the habit of periodically stepping back to reflect on their thinking process and ask themselves what form of thinking they're engaging in (analysis, synthesis, application, etc.). They could even keep a "thinking log" or "thinking journal" to increase self-awareness of the thinking strategies they're using and developing. This strategy will not only help students acquire higher-level thinking skills, but also help them describe the thinking skills they have acquired during job interviews and in letters of application for career positions.

Reflection 6.8

Look back at the eight forms of thinking described in Box 6.3. Which of these forms of thinking had you heard of before? Have you used, or do you anticipate using, any of these forms of thinking in your leadership roles and activities?

Encouraging Students to Use Writing as a Tool to Learn Deeply and Think Critically

We learn most effectively from an experience when we're actively involved in the learning experience and when we reflect on the experience after it's taken place. Writing can help students learn from any experience—either inside or outside the classroom—by increasing both active involvement and personal reflection. The phrase *writing to learn* has been coined by scholars to capture the idea that writing is not only a communication skill learned in English composition classes; it's also a learning skill that deepens learning of any academic subject or any learning experience that takes place outside the classroom (Applebee, 1981; Elbow, 1973; Murray, 1984). Just as students can learn to write better, they can write to learn better and think critically.

Writing deepens learning because it requires physical action, which implements the effective learning principle of active involvement. Writing also essentially "forces" us to focus attention on our own thoughts and activate our thinking. In addition, writing slows down the thinking process, requiring us to think in a more deliberate, systematic fashion that makes us more consciously aware of the specific details of our thoughts and arguments. Lastly, the act of writing results in a visible product we can review and use as feedback to improve the quality of our thoughts (Applebee, 1984; Langer & Applebee, 1987). In other words, writing allows us to "think out loud on paper" (Bean, 2003, p. 102).

Students can use writing to improve their learning and thinking on a wide variety of learning tasks and purposes in college, such as those listed below.

Writing to listen. Writing can be used to increase attention and active listening during classroom lectures, study group sessions, and office visits with instructors. For instance, immediately after each class session, students could write a "one-minute paper" that takes a minute or less to complete, yet enables them to assess whether they've heard and grasped the most important message delivered in class

> *How can I know what I think 'til I see what I say?*
> —Graham Wallas, *The Art of Thought*

that day. For example, students could write a one-minute response to the following questions: "What was the most significant concept I learned in class today?" or "What was the most confusing thing that I experienced in today's class that I should ask my instructor to clarify?"

Writing to read. Just as writing can promote active listening, it can also promote active reading. Writing notes on what we're reading while we're reading implements the effective learning principle of active involvement because it requires more mental and physical energy than merely reading and highlighting sentences.

Writing to discuss. Prior to participating in class discussions or small-group work, students can gather their thoughts in writing before expressing them orally. This will ensure that they've carefully reflected on their ideas, which, in turn, should improve the quality of ideas they contribute. Gathering their thoughts in writing before speaking should also make students less anxious, more confident speakers because they have a better idea about what they're going to say before they start to say it. Their written notes also give them a script to build on and fall back on, which should reduce their speech anxiety while speaking.

Writing to remember. Writing lists or memos of things to remember, such as ideas generated at a group meeting, definitions, terms, or key concepts, is an old-fashioned but surefire way not to forget them. When we've recorded an idea in print, we've created a permanent record of it that will enable us to access it and review it at any time. Furthermore, the act of writing itself creates motor (muscle) memory for the information we're writing, which enables us to better retain and retrieve information that's been written. Writing also improves memory by allowing us to see the information we're trying to remember, which registers it in our brains as a visual memory trace.

> *I would advise you to read with a pen in your hand, and enter in a little book of short hints of what you find that is curious, or that might be useful; for this will be the best method of imprinting such particulars in your memory, where they will be ready.*
>
> —Benjamin Franklin, 18th-century inventor, politician, and signer of the *Declaration of Independence*

Author's Experience Whenever I have trouble remembering the spelling of a word, I take a pen or pencil and start to write the word out. I'm surprised at how many times the correct spelling comes back to my mind once I begin to write the word. However, the more I think about this, it's not surprising that my ability to remember the spelling immediately returns when I start writing it. This memory "flashback" is probably due to the fact that when I start using the muscles in my hand to write the word, it activates the "muscle memories" in my brain that were previously formed when I first learned to spell the word correctly.

— *Joe Cuseo*

Writing to organize. Constructing summaries and outlines, or writing ideas on different index cards that relate to the same category or concept, are effective ways of organizing and learning information. This type of organizational writing deepens learning because it requires synthesis of different ideas and restatement of ideas in our own words, both of which are deep-learning strategies.

Writing to study. Writing study guides or practice answers to potential test questions is an effective strategy that can be used when studying alone or when preparing for study groups. This is particularly effective preparation for essay tests because it enables students to study in a way that closely matches what they'll be expected to do on an essay test, which is to write out answers on their own; not pick out answers that have been provided to them as they would on a multiple-choice test.

Writing to understand. Paraphrasing or restating what we're attempting to learn by writing it in our own words is an effective way to provide ourselves with feedback about whether we've truly understood it (not just memorized it) because it transforms what we're learning into words that are meaningful to us.

Writing for creativity. Writing can stimulate discovery of new ideas because the very act or process of writing can trigger the creation of new ideas. Writing is not just an end result or final product of thinking; it's also a means or process for stimulating thinking.

You can generate creative ideas through a process called *freewriting*—quickly jotting down free-flowing thoughts on paper without worrying about spelling and grammar. Freewriting can be used as a warm-up exercise to generate ideas for a research topic, to keep track of original ideas you may happen to discover while brainstorming, or to note creative ideas that can suddenly come to your mind at the most unexpected times (and can just as quickly leave your mind unless you make note of them).

Writing for problem solving. Students can write to improve their thinking while solving math and science problems. By writing down the thoughts going through their minds at each major step in the problem-solving process, they can increase awareness of how they're thinking while they're thinking and produce a written record of their trains of thought. Students can review this written record later to help them retrieve the path of thought they took to solve the problem successfully so that they can use the same path or process of thinking to solve similar problems in the future.

This arsenal of writing strategies can be a powerful way to deepen and enrich learning, but they do take a commitment of time and effort. So, be sure to encourage students to build these writing strategies into their daily time-management and task-management plans.

> *I write to understand as much as to be understood.*
>
> —Elie Wiesel, world-famous American novelist, Nobel Prize winner, and Holocaust survivor

> *There is in writing the constant joy of sudden discovery, of happy accident.*
>
> —H. L. Mencken, 20th-century American journalist and social critic

> *There are some kinds of writing that you have to do very fast, like riding a bicycle on a tightrope.*
>
> —William Faulkner, Nobel Prize-winning author

Reflection 6.9

Which of the writing-to-learn strategies listed above do you think would be particularly helpful to you in your leadership role? Why?

Using Results of Tests and Assignments as Feedback to Improve Academic Performance

Often, when students get a test back, they check to see what grade they got on it, then stuff it in a binder or toss it into the nearest wastebasket. As a learning coach, try to break students of this unproductive habit by strongly encouraging them to reflect on their academic performances, examine what transpired (and why), assess what went well and what needs improvement, and make strategic changes to improve their next performance. Suggest to students that they STOP and ask themselves questions like the following:

- Were these the results you expected?
- What do the results suggest about how effective your approach was to learning the material?
- What can you do with this information to improve your next performance?

Following are additional strategies you can share with students to help them use their test results as performance-enhancing feedback to improve their future academic performance and final course grades:

> *People can't learn without feedback. It's not teaching that causes learning. Attempts by the learner to perform cause learning, dependent upon the quality of the feedback and opportunities to use it.*
> —Grant Wiggins, author of *Feedback: How Learning Occurs*

1. **Look at your test results with an eye toward learning from your mistakes and repeating your successes.** A test score is not just an end result; it can be used as a means to an end—a higher score on the next test. When you get tests back, examine them carefully, making special note of any written comments from your instructor and any answer key that may be provided.

   Advise students to use their results as a diagnostic—to troubleshoot what went wrong so they don't repeat the same mistake, and to pinpoint what went right so they can do it again. Encourage them not to let a bad test grade get them mad, sad, or down, particularly if it occurs early in the course when they're still learning the rules of the game. Tell them not to be bitter, but to get better—by viewing their mistakes in terms of what they can do *for* them, rather than to them. A poor test performance can be turned into a productive learning experience if students use their test results as a source of feedback for improving their future performance.

> *When you make a mistake, there are only three things you should do about it: admit it; learn from it; and don't repeat it.*
> —Paul "Bear" Bryant, legendary college football coach

Note well! Mistakes should be neither ignored nor neglected; they should be detected and corrected so that they're not replayed in the future.

Listed below are some strategies you can suggest to students for identifying sources of lost points on exams. They can use these strategies to pinpoint the particular stage in the learning process where the breakdown occurred that caused them to miss the answer and lose points.

- **Did you have the information you needed to answer the question correctly?** If you didn't have the information, where should you have acquired it in the first place? Was it information presented in class that didn't get into your notes? If so, consider strategies for improving your classroom listening and note-taking (such as those on p. 145). If the missing information was contained in your assigned reading, check whether you're using effective reading strategies (such as those on pp. 148–149).
- **Did you have the information but not study it because you didn't think it was important?** If you didn't realize the information would be on the test, review the study strategies for finding and focusing on the most important information in class lectures and reading assignments. (See p. 150.)
- **Did you study it, but not retain it?** Not remembering information you studied may mean one of three things:
  a. You didn't learn it deeply and didn't lay down a strong enough memory trace in your brain for you to recall it at test time. This suggests that more study time needs to be spent on making meaningful associations with what you're learning. (See pp. 150–151 for specific strategies.)

b. You may have tried to cram in too much information in too little time just before the exam and may have not given your brain time enough to "digest" (consolidate) it and store it in long-term memory. The solution may be to distribute your study time more evenly in advance of the next exam and take advantage of the part-to-whole study method. (See p. 152.)

c. You put in enough study time and didn't cram, but you need to use more effective study strategies. (See pp. 162–163.)

■ **Did you study the material but not really understand it or learn it deeply?** This suggests you may need to self-monitor your comprehension more carefully while studying to track whether you truly understand the material. (See p. 163.)

■ **Did you know the answer but just make a careless test-taking mistake?** If your mistake was careless, the solution may simply be to take more time to review your test once you've completed it and check for absentminded errors before turning it in. Or, your careless errors may be the result of test anxiety that's interfering with your ability to concentrate during exams. (For help with test anxiety, see the Learning Center or Counseling Center.)

2. **Seek feedback from others.** In addition to students using their own results as a source of feedback, recommend that they ask for feedback from others whose judgment they trust and value. Three key social resources students can use to obtain feedback on how to improve their performance are their instructors, professionals in the Learning or Academic Support Center, and their classmates.

   Encourage students to make appointments with their instructors during office hours for feedback on how they might be able to improve their next performance. It's likely that students will find it easier to get access to their instructors after tests and assignments have been returned because most students attempt to get last-minute help before work is due, but fail to take advantage of the fact that instructors can provide valuable feedback about their work when it is completed. Tutors and other learning support professionals on campus can also be excellent sources of feedback about what adjustments to make in their study habits or test-taking strategies to improve their future performance.

3. **Lastly, remind students that classmates can provide another valuable source of information on how to improve their academic performance.** They can review tests and assignments with other students in the course, particularly with students who did exceptionally well. Their outstanding work can provide a valuable model of what type of work their instructor expects. Encourage your students to seek out successful students and ask them what they did to be successful—for example, what general approach they took and what specific strategies they used.

Summary and Conclusion

Students must be able to meet higher expectations for deep learning and critical thinking set by college faculty. However, learning doesn't end at college graduation; it's a lifelong process that critical for success in the 21st century. The ongoing information technology revolution and increasing global interdependence have created great demand for humans to develop effective learning skills that they will use throughout life and to apply those skills in diverse cultural and occupational contexts.

This chapter identifies key principles of human learning and supplies specific strategies that you can share with students to empower them to learn more effectively in college and throughout life.

Deep learning goes deeper than surface-level memorization. It's connecting new ideas to ideas that are already stored in the brain. Deep learners build mental bridges between what they're trying to learn and what they already know. They dive below the surface of shallow memorization to reflect, evaluate, and apply what they've learned. Numerous studies suggest that college students do not engage in deep learning; thus, change is needed in the culture of learning on college campuses. Peer leaders can be key catalysts in this change process. They can assume the role of a *learning coach* by inspiring, modeling, and enabling students to develop the attributes of deep, lifelong learners. They can do this by modeling and equipping students with effective learning strategies at the following key stages in the learning process: (1) acquiring knowledge through effective note-taking in the classroom and effective reading outside the classroom, (2) retaining knowledge through effective study strategies, (3) demonstrating critical thinking on college exams and assignments, and (4) using their test results as feedback to improve their future performance.

Internet Resources

For additional information related to the ideas discussed in this chapter, we recommend the following websites:

Learning Strategies and Study Skills
www.dartmouth.edu/~acskills/videos/index.html
http://research.uc.iupui.edu/EvaluationReports/BedkoLearningCenter.aspx

Brain-Based Learning
www.brainrules.net/the-rules

Critical Thinking
www.criticalthinking.org

Creative Thinking
www.amcreativityassoc.org

Exercise 6.1 *Note Taking Strategies Scale*

Rate yourself in terms of how frequently you use these note-taking strategies according to the following scale:

4 = always; 3 = sometimes; 2 = rarely; 1 = never

1.   I take notes aggressively in class.   4   3   2   1

2.   I sit near the front of the room during class.   4   3   2   1

3.   I sit upright and lean forward while in class.   4   3   2   1

4.   I take notes on what my instructors say, not just what they write on the board.   4   3   2   1

5.   I pay special attention to information presented at the start and end of class.   4   3   2   1

6.   I take notes in paragraph form.   4   3   2   1

7.   I review my notes immediately after class to check that they are complete and accurate.   4   3   2   1

Go back and rate these items as you think your students would rate them.

Exercise 6.2 *Study Skills Strategies Scale*

Rate yourself in terms of how frequently you use these study strategies according to the following scale:

4 = always; 3 = sometimes; 2 = rarely; 1 = never

1. I block out all distracting sources of outside stimulation when I study.   4   3   2   1

2. I try to find meaning in technical terms by looking at their prefixes or suffixes or by looking up their word roots in the dictionary.   4   3   2   1

3. I compare and contrast what I'm currently studying with what I've already learned.   4   3   2   1

4. I organize the information I'm studying into categories or classes.   4   3   2   1

5. I integrate or pull together information from my class notes and readings that relates to the same concept or general category.   4   3   2   1

6. I distribute or spread out my study time over several short sessions in advance of the exam, and I use my last study session before the test to review the information I previously studied.   4   3   2   1

7. I participate in study groups with my classmates.   4   3   2   1

Go back and rate these items as you think your students would rate them.

Exercise 6.3 *Critical Thinking Scenario*

Trick or Treat: Confusing or Challenging Test?

Students in Professor Plato's philosophy course just got their first exam back and they're going over the test together in class. Some students are angry because they feel that Professor Plato deliberately included "trick questions" to confuse them. Professor Plato responds by saying that his test questions were not designed to trick the class but to "challenge them to think."

Reflection and Discussion Questions

1. Why do you think that some students thought Professor Plato was trying to trick or confuse them?

2. What do you think the professor meant when he told his students that his test questions were designed to "challenge them to think"?

3. On future tests, what might the students do to reduce the likelihood that they will feel tricked again?

4. On future tests, what might Professor Plato do to reduce the likelihood that students will complain about being asked "trick questions"?

Exercise 6.4 *Midterm Self-Evaluation*

Near the midpoint of their first term in college, new students will be receiving the results of their first wave of college tests and assignments. This may be a good time to step back and reflect on their academic progress.

Using the form below, ask your students to list the courses they're taking and the grades they're currently receiving in each of these courses. If they don't know what their grade is, ask them to add up the scores on their completed tests and assignments and check their syllabus for the instructor's grading policy; this should give them at least a rough idea of where they stand in the course. If they're still having difficulty determining their grade in a course, even after checking their course syllabus and returned tests or assignments, ask them to consult with their instructor to get an estimate of their current grade.

Course No.	Course Title	Instructor	Grade
1.			
2.			
3.			
4.			
5.			

Ask your students the following self-assessment questions about their midterm grades:

1. Were these the grades you were hoping for? Are you pleased or disappointed by them?

2. Were these the grades you expected? If not, were they better or worse than you anticipated?

3. Do you see any patterns in your performance that suggest things you're doing well or things you need to improve?

4. If you had to pinpoint one action you could take immediately to improve your lowest course grades, what would it be?

chapter 7

Holistic Leadership
Leading and Developing the Whole Person

Reflection 7.1

What does being a "well-rounded" person and leading a "well-balanced" life mean to you?

Mentoring involves providing support and guidance that goes beyond academic development to support holistic development—i.e., development of the "whole person" (Bordes & Arredondo, 2005; Gould & Lomax, 1993; Harmon, 2006; Sanft, Jensen, & McMurray, 2008).

College success depends on factors that aren't strictly academic in nature. Research shows that the vast majority of students who withdraw from college are in good academic standing at the time of their withdrawal; they're not forced to withdraw because they've "flunked out" or have been academically dismissed (Gardiner, 1994; Tinto, 1993; Cuseo, Fecas, & Thompson, 2010). Even in cases where students are experiencing academic difficulty at the time of their withdrawal, their poor grades may be the result of personal issues that are interfering with or suppressing their academic performance. The first year of college, in particular, can be a very stressful stage of the college experience because it involves a major life transition, requiring not only academic adjustments, but also significant changes in social relationships, emotional experiences, and personal identity. Thus, peer support programs designed to promote new students' success must address students as whole persons.

Key Dimensions of Holistic Development

One primary goal of a college education is self-awareness or knowledge of oneself. In addition to expanding students' knowledge of the world around them, the college experience is designed to expand their knowledge of the world within them. To "know thyself" requires knowledge and development of the *whole* self. As illustrated in **Figure 7.1**, the human self is comprised of diverse dimensions that join together to form the "whole person."

I want to see how all the pieces of me come together to make me, physically and mentally.

College sophomore

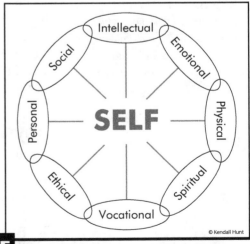

Figure 7.1 Key Elements of Holistic (Whole-Person) Development

Development of the "Whole Person": Key Components

1. *Intellectual* development–acquiring knowledge, learning how to learn and to think at a higher level.
2. *Emotional* development–strengthening the ability to understand, control, and express one's emotions.
3. *Social* development–enhancing the quality and depth of your interpersonal relationships.
4. *Ethical* development–building moral character (the ability to make and act on ethical judgments), developing a clear value system for guiding personal decisions, and demonstrating consistency between one's convictions (beliefs) and one's commitments (actions).
5. *Physical* development–applying knowledge about the human body to prevent disease, preserve wellness, and promote peak performance.
6. *Spiritual* development–sensitivity to the "big questions," such as the meaning or purpose of life and death, and issues that transcend human life and the physical or material world.
7. *Vocational* development–exploring occupational options, making wise choices, and developing skills needed for lifelong career success.
8. *Personal* development–developing positive self-beliefs, attitudes, and self-management habits.

Each of the above elements of self plays an influential role in ensuring health, success, and happiness. Research strongly suggests that quality of life depends on attention to and development of all key elements of the self. For instance, it's been found that people who are healthy (physically and mentally) and successful (personally and professionally) are those who attend to and integrate different dimensions of the self, enabling them to lead well-rounded and well-balanced lives (Covey, 1990; Goleman, 1995; Heath, 1977). As a peer leader, you can play an important role in helping students achieve this balance by sharing effective strategies and modeling balance in your own life.

> *Being successful is being balanced in every aspect of your life.*
>
> —First-year college student's response to the question "What does being successful mean to you?"

> *Wellness is an integrated method of functioning, which is oriented toward maximizing the potential of the individual.*
>
> —H. Joseph Dunn, originator of the term *wellness*

What Is Wellness?

Wellness may be described as a state of high-quality health and personal well-being that promotes peak physical and mental performance. Wellness and wholeness are interrelated; they require balanced attention to both physical and mental well-being. Each of these key components of wellness (body and mind) is described in the following sections, along with the roles that peer leaders can play in fostering their development.

Physical Wellness

A healthy physical lifestyle includes three key elements:

1. Supplying our bodies with effective fuel (nutrition);
2. Giving our bodies adequate rest (sleep) so that they can recover and replenish the energy they have expended; and
3. Avoiding risky substances (abuse of alcohol and drugs) and risky behaviors that can threaten our health and safety.

Promoting Nutritional Self-Awareness and Healthy Eating Habits

Like high-performance gasoline in a car, a high-quality (nutritious) diet improves the performance of the human body and mind, allowing each to operate at peak capacity. Unfortunately, people frequently pay more attention to the quality of fuel they put in their cars than to the quality of food they put into their bodies. They often eat without any intentional planning about what they eat. They eat at places where they can get access to food fast, where they can pick up food conveniently while they're on the go, and where they can consume it without having to step out of their cars (or off their butts) to consume it. America has become a "fast food nation" and Americans have grown accustomed to consuming food that can be accessed quickly, conveniently, cheaply, and in large (super-sized) portions (Schlosser, 2005). National surveys reveal that less than 40% of Americans report that they maintain a healthy diet (Sax et al., 2004).

Tell me what you eat and I'll tell you what you are.

—Anthelme Brillat-Savarin, French lawyer, gastronomist, and founder of the low-carbohydrate diet

If we are what we eat, then I'm cheap, fast, and easy.

—Steven Wright, award-winning comedian

Reflection 7.2

Have your eating habits changed since you've begun college? If yes, in what ways have they changed?

Figure 7.2 depicts the MyPlate graph, which is the new version of the former Food Guide Pyramid created by the American Dietetic Association. Since foods vary in terms of the nutrients they provide (carbohydrates, protein, and fat), no single food group can supply all the nutrients your body needs. Therefore, our diets should be balanced and include all of these food groups, but in different proportions or percentages.

To help students find the daily amount of food they should consume from each of these major food groups (based on age and gender), refer them to www.ChooseMyPlate.gov or www.cnpp.usda.gov/dietaryguidelines.htm. They can use these guidelines to create a personal dietary plan that ensures they consume each of these food groups every day, resulting in a balanced diet that minimizes their risk of nutritional deficiencies and disorders.

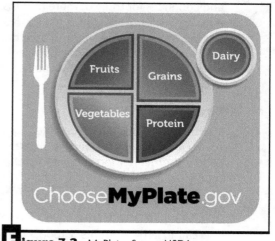

Figure 7.2   MyPlate. *Source:* USDA.

Eating Disorders

While some students experience the "freshman 15," a 15-pound weight gain during the first year of college (Brody, 2003), others experience eating disorders related to weight loss and loss of control of their eating habits. These disorders are more common among females (National Institute of Mental Health, 2001), largely because Western cultures place more emphasis and pressure on females than males to maintain lighter body weight and body size. Studies show that approximately one of every three college women indicates that she worries about her weight, body image, or eating habits (Leavy, Gnong, & Ross, 2009).

Box 7.1 provides a short summary of the major eating disorders experienced by college students. These disorders are often accompanied by emotional issues (e.g., depression and anxiety) that are serious enough to require professional treatment (National Institute of Mental Health, 2011). The earlier these disorders are identified and treated, the better the prognosis or probability of complete and permanent recovery. Keep your eye out for students who may be experiencing these disorders and be ready to reach out and help them seek support from the Counseling Center or Student Health Center on campus.

Box 7.1

Major Eating Disorders

Anorexia Nervosa

Students experiencing anorexia nervosa see themselves as overweight and have an intense fear of gaining weight, even though they're dangerously thin. Anorexics typically deny that they're severely underweight, and even if their weight drops to the point where they may look like walking skeletons, they may continue to be obsessed with losing weight, eating infrequently, and eating in extremely small portions. Anorexics may also use other methods to lose weight, such as compulsive exercise, diet pills, laxatives, diuretics, or enemas.

Bulimia Nervosa

This eating disorder is characterized by repeated episodes of "binge eating"—consuming excessive amounts of food within a limited period of time. Bulimics tend to lose all sense of self-control during their binges, and then they try to compensate for overeating by engaging in behavior to purge their guilt and prevent weight gain. They may purge themselves by self-induced vomiting, consuming excessive amounts of laxatives or diuretics, using enemas, or fasting. The binge-purge pattern typically takes place at least twice a week and continues for three or more months.

Bulimics are harder to detect than anorexics because their binges and purges typically take place secretly and their body weight looks about normal for their age and height. However, similar to anorexics, bulimics fear gaining weight, aren't happy with their bodies, and have an intense desire to lose weight.

> *I had a friend who took pride in her ability to lose 30 lbs. in one summer by not eating and working out excessively. I know girls that find pleasure in getting ill so that they throw up, can't eat, and lose weight.*
>
> —Comments written in a first-year student's journal

Binge-Eating Disorder

Like bulimia, binge-eating disorder involves repeated, out-of-control episodes of consuming large quantities of food. However, unlike bulimics, binge eaters don't purge after binging episodes. Those who suffer from binge-eating disorder demonstrate at least three of the following symptoms, two or more times per week, for several months:

1. Eating at an extremely rapid rate.
2. Eating until becoming uncomfortably full.
3. Eating large amounts of food when not physically hungry.
4. Eating alone because of embarrassment about others seeing how much they eat.
5. Feeling guilty, disgusted, or depressed after overeating.

Sources: American Psychiatric Association (2000); National Institute of Mental Health (2011).

Rest and Sleep

Sleep experts agree that humans in today's information-loaded, multitasking world aren't getting the quantity and quality of sleep needed to perform at peak levels (Mitler, Dinges, & Dement, 1994). We often underestimate the power of sleep and think we can cheat on sleep without compromising the quality of our lives.

College students, in particular, tend to have poor sleep habits and experience more sleep problems. Heavier academic workloads, more opportunities for late-night socializing, and more frequent late-night (or all-night) study sessions often lead to more irregular sleep schedules and more sleep deprivation among college students.

Reflection 7.3

How many hours of sleep per night do you think you need to perform at a peak mental and physical level?

How many nights per week do you typically get this amount of sleep?

If you're not getting this optimal amount of sleep each night, what's preventing you from getting it?

First of all, you should probably know that your body will not function without sleep. I learned that the hard way.

—Words written by a first-year student in a letter of advice to incoming college students

Strategies for Improving Sleep Quality

If you can improve the quality of your sleep, you can improve your physical and mental well-being. Listed here is a series of strategies for improving sleep quality that should improve your health and performance. Consider adopting them for your own benefit and suggest them to the students you lead and mentor.

1. **Become more aware of your sleep habits by keeping a sleep log or sleep journal.** Make note of what you did before going to bed on nights when you slept well or poorly. Tracking your sleep experiences in a journal may enable you to detect patterns that reveal relationships between certain things you do (or don't do) during the day and sleeping well. If you find a pattern, you may have found yourself a routine you can follow to ensure that you consistently get a good night's sleep.

2. **Try to get into a regular sleep schedule by going to sleep and getting up at about the same time each day.** The human body functions best on biological rhythms of set cycles, so if you can get your body on a regular sleep schedule or cycle, you're more likely to establish a biological rhythm that makes it easier for you to fall asleep, stay asleep, and wake up naturally from sleep according to your own "internal alarm clock."

   Establishing a stable sleep schedule is particularly important around midterms and finals. Unfortunately, these are the times during the term when students do just the opposite by cramming in last-minute studying, staying up later, and getting up earlier (or pulling all-nighters and not going to sleep at all). Sleep research shows that if students want to be at their physical and mental best for upcoming exams, they should get themselves on a regular sleep schedule of going to bed at about the same time and getting up at about the same time for at least one week before their exams are to be taken (Dement & Vaughan, 1999).

3. **Attempt to get into a relaxing pre-bedtime ritual each night.** Taking a hot bath or shower, consuming a hot (non-caffeinated) beverage, or listening to relaxing music are bedtime rituals that can get you into a worry-free state and help you fall asleep sooner. Making a list of things you intend to do the next day before going to bed may create peace of mind and help you relax

I 'binge' sleep. I don't sleep often and then I hibernate for like a day or two.

—First-year student

and fall asleep, since you know that you're organized and ready to handle the following day's tasks.

A light review of class notes or reading highlights at bedtime can also be a good ritual to adopt because sleep helps you retain what you experienced just before going to sleep. Many years of studies show that the best thing you can do after attempting to learn information is to "sleep on it," probably because your brain can focus on processing and sorting that information without interference from outside distractions (Jenkins & Dallenbach, 1924; Kuriyama et al., 2008).

Reflection 7.4

What do you do on most nights immediately before going to bed? Do you think this helps or hinders the quality of your sleep?

_____

4. **Avoid intense mental activity just before going to bed.** Light mental work may serve as a relaxing pre-sleep ritual, but cramming intensely for a difficult exam or doing intensive writing before bedtime is likely to generate a state of mental arousal, which can interfere with your ability to wind down and fall asleep.

5. **Avoid intense physical exercise before bedtime.** Physical exercise generates an increase in muscle tension and mental energy (by increasing oxygen flow to the brain) that can energize you and prevent you from falling asleep. If you like to exercise in the evening, it should be done at least three hours before bedtime (Epstein & Mardon, 2007).

6. **Avoid consuming sleep-interfering foods, beverages, or drugs in the late afternoon or evening.** In particular, avoid the following substances near bedtime:

    - **Caffeine.** It works as a stimulant drug, so it's likely to stimulate your nervous system and keep you awake.
    - **Nicotine.** This is a stimulant drug that's also likely to reduce the depth and quality of your sleep. (Note: Smoking hookah through a water pipe delivers the same amount of nicotine as a cigarette.)
    - **Alcohol.** It's a drug that will make you feel sleepy in larger doses; however, in smaller doses, it can have a stimulating effect. Furthermore, alcohol in any amount disrupts the quality of sleep by reducing the amount of time you spend in dream-stage sleep. (Marijuana does the same.)
    - **High-fat foods.** Eating just before bedtime isn't a good idea because your stomach has to increase its activity to digest the food, which is likely to interfere with the soundness of your sleep. Peanuts, beans, fruits, raw vegetables, and high-fat snacks should especially be avoided because these are harder-to-digest foods.

Note well! _Substances that may make you feel sleepy or cause you to fall asleep (e.g., alcohol and marijuana) actually reduce the quality of your sleep by interfering with dream sleep._

Alcohol, Drugs, and Risky Behavior

In addition to putting healthy nutrients into our bodies, wellness also depends on keeping risky substances out of our bodies and keeping away from risky behaviors that endanger our bodies. Students are often confronted with new choices to make about what risks to take, or not to take, after they enter college, one of which is whether to consume alcohol and to what degree.

Alcohol Use among College Students

In the United States, alcohol is a legal beverage (drug) for people 21 years of age and older. However, whether or not students are of legal age to drink, alcohol is likely to be readily available to them while they're in college.

If your students choose to drink, remind them that it should be *their* choice, not a choice imposed on them through social pressure or the need to conform. Research indicates that first-year college students drink more than they did in high school (Johnston et al., 2005) and that alcohol abuse is higher among first-year college students than among students at more advanced stages of their college experience (Bergen-Cico, 2000). The most common reason why students drink is to "fit in" or to feel socially accepted (Meilman & Presley, 2005). However, college students overestimate the number of their peers who drink and the amount they drink. This overestimation can lead them to believe that if they don't conform to this "norm," they're not "normal" (DeJong & Linkenback, 1999).

The fact is that the number-one drug problem on college campuses is *binge drinking*: periodic drinking episodes during which a large amount of alcohol (four or five drinks) are consumed in a short period of time, resulting in an acute state of intoxication—i.e., a drunken state (Marczinski, Estee, & Grant, 2009). Although binge drinking is not alcoholism, it's still a form of alcohol abuse because it has direct, negative effects on the drinker's:

- Behavior—e.g., resulting in drunk driving accidents and deaths, and increased risk of date rape;
- Body—e.g., producing acute alcohol withdrawal syndrome (better known as a "hangover"); and
- Mind—e.g., triggering total memory loss ("blackouts") or partial memory loss ("gray-outs").

Furthermore, binge drinking can have indirect negative effects on health and safety by reducing the drinker's inhibitions about engaging in risk-taking behavior, which, in turn, increases the risk of personal accidents, injuries, and illnesses. Arguably, no other drug reduces a person's inhibitions as dramatically as alcohol. After consuming a significant amount of alcohol, people often become much less cautious about doing things they normally wouldn't do (e.g., fighting or destroying property). This chemically induced sense of courage (sometimes referred to as "liquid courage") can override the process of logical thinking and decision making, increasing the drinker's willingness to engage in irrational risk-taking behavior (e.g., reckless stunts). Typically, binge drinkers become less inhibited about engaging in reckless driving, increasing the risk of accidental injury or death, and less cautious about engaging in reckless (unprotected) sex, increasing the risk of accidental pregnancy or contracting sexually transmitted infections (STIs). It could be said that students who binge-drink think they've suddenly become invincible, immortal, and infertile.

> *If you drink, don't park.*
> *Accidents cause people.*
> —Steven Wright, American comedian

Since alcohol is commonly accessible at college parties and social gatherings, students will be confronted with two sets of decisions about drinking:

1. To drink or not to drink, and
2. To drink responsibly or irresponsibly—i.e., drinking to get drunk or escape problems.

If the students you lead or mentor decide to drink, here are some quick tips to share with them about drinking safely and responsibly.

1. **Don't let yourself be pressured into drinking.** Keep in mind that college students tend to overestimate how much their peers drink, so don't feel you're "uncool," unusual, or abnormal if you prefer not to drink.
2. **Don't drink with the intention of getting intoxicated; set a limit about how much you will drink.** Use alcohol as a beverage, not as a mind-altering drug.
3. **Maintain awareness of how much you're drinking while you're drinking by monitoring your physical and mental state.** Don't continue to drink after you've reached a state of moderate relaxation or a mild loss of inhibition. Drinking to the point where you're drunk or bordering on intoxication doesn't improve your physical health or your social life. If you're slurring your speech, nodding out, or vomiting in the restroom, you're not exactly the life of the party.
4. **Drink slowly.** Sip, don't gulp, and avoid "shotgunning" or "chug-a-lugging" drinks.

    Space out your drinks over time. (This gives the body time to metabolize the alcohol and keeps its blood-alcohol level manageable.)
5. **Eat well before drinking and snack while drinking.** This will help lower the peak level of alcohol in the bloodstream.

Lastly, remind students that alcohol is costly, in terms of both money and calories. Thus, reducing or eliminating drinking is not only a good way to manage their health, but also a good money-management and weight-management strategy.

Reflection 7.5

Do you drink alcohol? If yes, why? If no, why not?

How do you think the students you're working with would answer the above questions?

Risky (Unhealthy) Relationships

If students are involved in relationships that leave them feeling disrespected, controlled, or concerned for their safety, it's essential that they acknowledge and act upon these threats to their well-being. Relationship abuse—whether emotional, psychological, physical, or sexual—is *never* appropriate or acceptable. See Box 7.2 for a summary of the major types of relationship abuse and violence, along with recommendations you can share with students on how to deal with them.

Behaviors that characterize relationship abuse include, but are not limited to, degrading language, dominating or dictating a partner's actions, and physical and/or sexual assault (Murray & Kardatzke, 2007). Often, victims and perpetrators don't recognize that they are in fact in a violent relationship because they don't recognize the behaviors as abusive. Without such recognition, victims and perpetrators are likely to remain in their current relationship or have other such relationships that are more violent in the future (Miller, 2011).

Unfortunately, this type of relationship abuse is highly common among college-aged women and men. In fact, recent studies have reported data that 13% to 42% of college students have experienced and/or perpetrated physical relationship violence (Beyers et al., 2000; Luthra & Gidycz, 2006; Miller, 2011).

Since victims of relationship violence often experience distress and perhaps even trauma, it's critical that they seek help quickly. Unfortunately, victims tend to be reluctant to do so, for fear of embarrassment or retribution. If your leadership and mentoring work bring you in contact with students who are involved in such relationships, urge them to talk about it and get immediate support. Even just talking about it with a trusted friend is a good place to start. Also, remind students that the Counseling Center is staffed with professionals who have experience working with victims (and perpetrators) of relationship violence and will explain their rights as a victim. If the Counseling Center on your campus isn't staffed with such professionals, they can refer students to counseling centers in the community that do.

Box 7.2 — Relationship Abuse and Violence

This list explains various forms of abuse and violence experienced by both men and women. Note that these examples are not just physical or sexual in nature; emotional and psychological violence can be just as harmful to victims.

An abusive relationship may be defined as one in which one partner abuses the other physically, verbally, or emotionally. Abusers are often dependent on their partners for their sense of self-worth; they commonly have low self-esteem and fear their partners will abandon them, so they attempt to prevent this abandonment by over-controlling their partners. Frequently, abusers feel powerless or weak in other areas of their lives and overcompensate by attempting to exert power and personal strength over their partners.

Abusive Relationships

Potential signs of abuse:

- The abuser is possessive and tries to dominate or control all aspects of the partner's life (e.g., discourages the partner from having contact with friends or family members).
- The abuser frequently yells, shouts, intimidates, or makes physical threats toward the partner.
- The abuser constantly puts down the partner and damages the partner's self-esteem.
- The abuser displays intense and irrational jealousy (e.g., accusing the partner of infidelity without evidence).
- The abuser demands affection or sex when the partner is not interested.
- The abuser often appears charming to others in public settings, but is abusive toward the partner in private.
- The abused partner behaves differently and is more inhibited when the abuser is around.
- The abused partner fears the abuser.

Strategies for avoiding or escaping abusive relationships:

- Avoid relationship isolation by continuing to maintain social ties with friends outside of the relationship.
- Don't make excuses for or rationalize the abuser's behavior (e.g., he was under stress or he was drinking).
- Get an objective third-party perspective by asking close friends for their views on your relationship (love can be "blind," so it's possible to be in denial about an abusive relationship and not "see" what's really going on).
- Speak with a professional counselor on campus to help you see your relationships more objectively and help you cope or escape from any relationship that you sense is becoming abusive.

(continued)

Sexual Assault, a.k.a. Sexual Violence

Sexual assault refers to nonconsensual (unwanted or unwilling) sexual contact, which includes rape, attempted rape, and any other type of sexual contact that a person forces on another person without their consent. *Rape* is an extreme form of sexual assault or sexual violence that involves forced sexual penetration (intercourse), which takes place through physical force, by threat of bodily harm, or when the victim is incapable of giving consent due to alcohol or drug intoxication. Rape takes place in two major forms:

1. **Stranger rape**—when a total stranger forces sexual intercourse on the victim.
2. **Acquaintance rape or date rape**—when the victim knows, or is dating, the person who forces unwanted sexual intercourse. It's estimated that about 85% of reported rapes are committed by an acquaintance. Alcohol is frequently associated with acquaintance rapes because it lowers the rapist's inhibitions and reduces the victim's ability to judge whether she is in a potentially dangerous situation. Since the victim is familiar with the offender, she may feel at fault or conclude that what happened is not sexual assault. The bottom line: even though the partners know each other, acquaintance rape is still rape and still a crime because it's nonconsensual sex.

Recommendations for women to reduce the risk of experiencing sexual assault:

- Don't drink to excess or associate with others who drink to excess.
- Go to parties with at least one other friend so you can keep an eye out for each other.
- Clearly and assertively communicate your sexual limits. Use "I" messages to firmly resist unwanted sexual advances by rejecting the behavior rather than the person (e.g., "I'm not comfortable with your touching me like that").
- Remain mindful of the difference between lust and love. If you just met someone who makes sexual advances toward you, that person lusts for you but doesn't love you.
- Take a self-defense class.
- Carry mace or pepper spray.

Recommendations for men to reduce the risk of committing sexual assault:

- Don't assume a woman wants to have sex just because she's:
  a. very friendly or flirtatious,
  b. dressed in a provocative way, or
  c. uninhibited from drinking alcohol.

- If a woman says "no," don't interpret that to mean she's really saying "yes."
- Don't think that just because you're "the man," you have to be the sexual initiator or aggressor.
- Don't interpret sexual rejection as personal rejection or a blow to your masculinity.

Sexual Harassment

Sexual harassment in a college setting includes any unwanted and unwelcome sexual behavior, whether it's committed by a peer or an employee of the college, that significantly interferes with a student's access to education opportunities. Harassment can take the following forms:

1. **Verbal**—e.g., making sexual comments about someone's body or clothes; sexual jokes or teasing, which includes spreading rumors about a person's sexual activity or orientation; requesting sexual favors in exchange for a better grade, job, or promotion.
2. **Nonverbal**—e.g., staring or glaring at another person's body; making erotic or obscene gestures at the person; sending unsolicited pornographic material or obscene messages.
3. **Physical**—e.g., contact by touching, grabbing, pinching, or brushing up against another person's body.

Recommendations for dealing with sexual harassment:

- Make your objections clear and firm. Tell the harasser directly that you are offended by the unwanted behavior and that you know it constitutes sexual harassment.
- Keep a written record of any harassment. Record the date, place, and specific details about the harassing behavior.

- Become aware of the sexual harassment policy at your school. (Your school's policy is likely to be found in the *Student Handbook* or may be available from the Office of Human Resources on campus.)
- If you're unsure about whether you're experiencing sexual harassment, or what to do about it, seek help from the Counseling Center or Office of Human Resources.

Note: Title IX of the Education Amendment of 1972 is a federal civil rights law that prohibits discrimination on the basis of sex, which includes sexual harassment, rape, and sexual assault. A college or university may be held legally responsible when it knows about and ignores sexual harassment or assault in its programs or activities, whether the harassment is committed by a faculty member, staff, or a student. If you have been sexually harassed and believe that your campus has not responded effectively to your concern, you can contact or file a complaint with the Department of Education's Office for Civil Rights (http://www2.ed.gov/about/offices/list/ocr/complaintintro.html).

Sources: ETR Associates (2000); ETR Associates (2001); Karjane, Fisher, & Cullen (2002); National Center for Victims of Crime (2008); Ottens & Hotelling (2001); Penfold (2006).

Reflection 7.6

Have you ever witnessed or experienced an abusive relationship?

How common do you think abusive relationships are among college students?

Illegal Drugs

In addition to alcohol, other substances are likely to be encountered on college campuses that are illegal for anyone to use at any age. Following is a list of the major types of illegal drugs that may be available to college students, accompanied by a short description of their effects.

It's true that the college years are a time for exploring and experimenting with different ideas, feelings, and experiences. However, doing illegal drugs just isn't worth the risk. Even if we know how an illegal drug affects people in general, we don't know how it will affect the individual because each person has a unique genetic makeup. Furthermore, unlike legal drugs that have to pass through rigorous testing by the Food and Drug Administration before they're approved for public consumption, we can't be sure how an illegal drug has been produced and packaged from one time to the next, and we don't know if it may have been "cut" (mixed) with other substances during the production process. Thus, students are not just taking a criminal risk when using illegal drugs; they're also taking a health risk by consuming an unregulated substance whose effects on their bodies and minds may be unpredictable and potentially dangerous. For students who find themselves in a situation where an illegal drug is available to them, your bottom-line recommendation should be, "When in doubt, keep it out. Don't put anything into your body that's illegal and unregulated."

- **Marijuana (weed, pot).** Primarily a depressant or sedative drug that slows down the nervous system and induces feelings of relaxation.
- **Ecstasy (X).** A stimulant typically taken in pill form that speeds up the nervous system and reduces social inhibitions.
- **Cocaine (coke, crack).** A stimulant that's typically snorted or smoked and produces a strong "rush" (an intense feeling of euphoria).

- **Amphetamines (speed, meth).** A strong stimulant that increases energy and general arousal; it's usually taken in pill form but may also be smoked or injected.
- **Hallucinogens (psychedelics).** Drugs that alter or distort perception and are typically swallowed—e.g., LSD ("acid") and hallucinogenic mushrooms ("shrooms").
- **Narcotics (e.g., heroin and prescription pain pills).** Sedative drugs that slow the nervous system and produce feelings of relaxation. (Heroin is a particularly powerful narcotic, which can either be injected or smoked, producing an intense rush of euphoria.)
- **Date-rape drugs.** Depressant (sedative) drugs that induce sleepiness, memory loss, and possible loss of consciousness; they are typically colorless, tasteless, and odorless, so they can be easily mixed into a drink without the drinker noticing it, rendering the drinker vulnerable to rape or other forms of sexual assault. The most common date-rape drugs are Rohypnol ("roofies") and GHB ("liquid E"). If you're a woman who drinks, or who frequents places where others drink, remain aware of the possibility of date-rape drugs being dropped into your drink. To guard against this risk, don't let others give you drinks, and hold onto your drink at all times (e.g., don't leave it, go to the restroom, and come back to drink it again).

Reflection 7.7

What drugs (if any) have you seen being used on your campus?

How would the type and frequency of drug use on your campus compare to what you saw in high school?

Motivation for Drug Use among College Students

Students use drugs for a variety of reasons, the most common of which are listed below. As a peer leader and mentor, if you're aware of these motives, it should help you raise students' awareness of their motives for using or considering, and reduce the risk that they'll do drugs for unconscious or subconscious reasons.

1. **Social pressure.** To "fit in" or be socially accepted (e.g., drinking alcohol because lots of other college students seem to be doing it).
2. **Recreational (party) use.** For fun, stimulation, or pleasure (e.g., smoking marijuana at parties to relax, loosen inhibitions, and have a "good time").
3. **Experimental use.** Doing drugs out of curiosity—to test out their effects (e.g., experimenting with LSD to see what it's like to have a psychedelic or hallucinogenic experience).
4. **Therapeutic use.** Using prescription or over-the-counter drug for medical purposes (e.g., taking Prozac for depression or Ritalin to treat attention deficit disorder).
5. **Performance enhancement.** To improve physical or mental performance (e.g., taking steroids to improve athletic performance or stimulants to stay awake all night and cram for an exam).
6. **Escapism.** To temporarily escape a personal problem or an unpleasant emotional state (e.g., taking ecstasy to escape depression or boredom).
7. **Addiction.** Physical or psychological dependence resulting from habitual use of a drug (e.g., continuing to use nicotine or cocaine because stopping triggers withdrawal symptoms such as anxiety or depression).

> 'For fun.' 'To party.' 'To fit in.' 'To become more talkative, outgoing, and flirtatious.' 'To try anything once.' 'To become numb.' 'To forget problems.' 'Being bored.'
>
> —Responses of freshmen and sophomores to the question "Why do college students take drugs?"

Reflection 7.8

What motives for drug use would you say are most common on your campus?

Any drug has the potential to be addictive (habit-forming), especially if it's injected intravenously (directly into a vein) or smoked (inhaled into the lungs). These routes of drug delivery are particularly dangerous because they allow the drug to reach the brain faster and with more intense impact, resulting in the drug producing a rapid, higher peak effect that's immediately followed by a rapid and sharp drop (crash) (see **Figure 7.3**). This peak-to-valley, roller-coaster effect creates a greater risk for craving and desire to use the drug again, thereby increasing the user's risk of dependency (addiction).

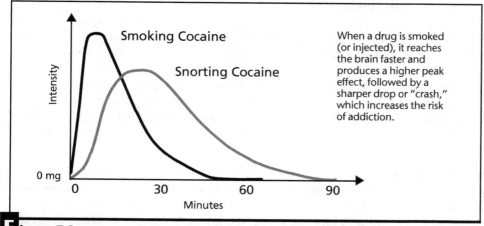

Figure 7.3   Drugs Smoked Produce a Higher and More Rapid Peak Effect

Listed here are common signs that use of any drug (including alcohol) is moving in the direction of *dependency* (*addiction*):

- Steadily increasing the amount (dose) of the drug and/or using it more often;
- Difficulty cutting back (e.g., unable to use the drug less frequently or in smaller amounts);
- Difficulty controlling or limiting the amount taken after starting;
- Keeping a steady supply of the drug on hand;
- Spending more on the drug than the person can afford;
- Using the drug alone;
- Hiding or hoarding the drug;
- Lying about drug use to family and friends;
- Reacting angrily or defensively when questioned about drug use;
- Being in denial about abusing the drug (e.g., "I don't have a problem");
- Rationalizing drug abuse (e.g., "It's no big deal; it's just part of the college experience"); and
- When continuing use of the drug matters more to the user than the personal and interpersonal problems caused by its use.

Helping others overcome drug dependency or other psychological problems (e.g., eating disorders and abusive relationships) can be challenging because the people experiencing them are often in *denial*—i.e., they don't "see" their problem because they've pushed it out of conscious awareness. Denial is not simply lying; it's a defense mechanism that's used unconsciously to protect one's self-image or self-esteem. Thus, the first step to helping a student overcome drug abuse or other psychological disorders involves helping that student overcome denial. Guidelines for doing so are provided in **Box 7.3**.

Box 7.3 — Guidelines for Helping Students Overcome Denial

1. Make your purpose and motives clear—that you care and want to help or support, not criticize or condemn.
2. Avoid heavy "guilt trips." Don't accuse the person; instead, share your perceptions by using "I" messages (e.g., "What I'm seeing is . . .").
3. Don't focus on the individual's character or personal traits. Instead, focus on objective evidence—the student's observable behavior (e.g., how frequently it's occurring) and its negative consequences for the student and others affected by the student's behavior.
4. Point out other people who see the student's situation as you do (e.g., the student's closest friends) and anyone who may have once been through the same type of denial and overcame it. This will help assure the student that it's not just your perception (or misperception) of the situation, and that positive change can be made.
5. If possible, when you approach the student in denial, try to bring with you his/her close friends or family members. (This will assure the person that it's not just your personal "crusade" or "rescue mission.")
6. Be patient and persistent; it's likely to take more than one attempt to make a breakthrough.

Reflection 7.9

Are you familiar with the concept of an intervention—a planned attempt by a group of people (usually family and friends) to intervene with someone in denial and persuade that person to seek professional help?

If you have taken part in an intervention, what was the problem and how well did the intervention work?

Mental Health and Emotional Wellness

In addition to physical health, mental health is the other "twin tower" of personal wellness. Studies show that students entering college today are reporting record levels of stress (Astin, Parrot, Korn, & Sax, 1997; Sax et al., 2000) and mental health issues such as anxiety, depression, eating disorders, and suicidal thoughts (Archer & Cooper, 1998; Drum, 2008; Kadison & DiGeronimo, 2004). Studies also reveal that college students report higher levels of stress and lower levels of emotional health at the end of their first year of college than they did before beginning college (Bartlett, 2002; Sax, Bryant, & Gilmartin, 2004). Students who experience emotional problems in college that remain untreated are more likely to withdraw from college (Schuh, 2005; Wilson, Mason, & Ewing, 1997).

Discussed below are the key signs (symptoms) associated with two major emotional problems that can interfere with student success in college: stress (anxiety) and depression. Research-based strategies are also provided that you can use to help students manage these emotions.

Stress and Anxiety

Among the most common emotions that humans must monitor, manage, and regulate is stress. Students report experiencing higher levels of stress in college than they did in high school (Bartlett, 2002; Sax, 2003). If stress can be kept at a moderate level and not reach a level where it results in anxiety, it can be a productive emotion that promotes learning and personal development. Moderate stress can improve:

- Physical performance (e.g., strength and speed),
- Mental performance (e.g., attention and memory), and
- Mood (e.g., hope and optimism).

> *It's not stress that kills us, it is our reaction to it.*
> —Hans Selye, Canadian endocrinologist and author of *Stress Without Distress*

Reflection 7.10

Can you think of a situation in which you performed at a higher level because you were slightly nervous or experienced a moderate amount of stress?

If stress becomes extreme and continues for a prolonged period, it moves from being productive to destructive. **Box 7.4** provides a short summary of the signs or symptoms of stress that has climbed to a level where it's creating distress or anxiety. If these symptoms are experienced for an extended period (e.g., longer than a week), encourage students to take immediate action to reduce them.

Box 7.4 — High Anxiety: Recognizing the Symptoms (Signs) of Distress

- Jitteriness or shaking, especially in the hands;
- Accelerated heart rate or heart palpitations (irregular heartbeat);
- Muscle tension—tightness in the chest or upper shoulders or a tight feeling (lump) in the throat (the expressions *uptight* and *choking* derive from these symptoms of upper-body tension);
- Body aches—heightened muscle tension leading to tension headaches, backaches, or chest pain (in extreme cases, it can feel as if a heart attack is taking place);
- Sweating, especially sweaty (clammy) palms;
- Cold, pale hands or feet—these symptoms have led to the expressions *white knuckles* and *cold feet* to describe someone who's highly anxious;
- Dry mouth—decreased production of saliva (accounting for the expression *cotton mouth* and the need for very nervous people to repeatedly sip water);
- Stomach discomfort or indigestion, due to increased secretion of stomach acid (the expression *feeling butterflies in my stomach* relates to this symptom);
- Gastrointestinal discomfort, e.g., stomach cramps, constipation, or diarrhea;
- Feeling faint or dizzy, due to constriction of blood vessels that decreases oxygen flow to the brain;
- Weakness and fatigue—a sustained (chronic) state of arousal and prolonged muscle tension becomes tiring;
- Menstrual changes—missing or irregular menstrual periods;
- Difficulty sleeping—insomnia or interrupted (fitful) sleep; and
- Increased susceptibility to colds, flu, and other infections, due to suppression of the body's immune system.

> *My stress has caused me to lose a lot of weight; my appetite is cut in half. My sleep pattern is off; I have trouble falling/staying asleep. No matter how stressed I was in high school, this never happened [before]. What can I do to de-stress?*
> —First-term college student

Reflection 7.11

What strategies do you use to cope with stress?

Would you say that these strategies have worked well for you and would be worth sharing with your students?

Studies also show that students experiencing high levels of academic stress and performance anxiety are more likely to use ineffective surface approaches to learning that rely on memorization, rather than effective deep-learning strategies that involve seeking meaning and understanding (Biggs & Tang, 2007; Ramsden, 2003). Also, high levels of test anxiety interfere with students' ability to recall information that's been studied and increase their risk of making careless concentration errors on exams—e.g., overlooking key words in test questions (Tobias, 1985, 1993).

Effective Methods for Managing Stress

If you perceive your students' level of stress to be reaching a point where it interferes with the quality of their academic performance or personal life, here are three simple but effective stress-management methods that are well-supported by research in psychology and biology (Benson & Klipper, 1990; Lehrer et al., 2007).

> There are thousands of causes for stress, and one antidote to stress is self-expression. That's what happens to me every day. My thoughts get off my chest, down my sleeves, and onto my pad.
>
> —Garson Kanin, American writer, actor, and film director

1. **Exercise.** Exercise reduces stress by increasing release of serotonin—a mellowing brain chemical that reduces feelings of tension (anxiety) and depression. Studies show that people who exercise regularly tend to report feeling happier (Myers, 1993). Exercise also elevates mood by improving people's sense of self-esteem that comes from experiencing a sense of accomplishment and improving their physical self-image. It is for these reasons that counselors and psychotherapists recommend exercise for patients experiencing milder forms of anxiety or depression (Johnsgard, 2004).

2. **Keep a journal of feelings and emotions.** Writing about our feelings in a personal journal helps us identify the emotions we're experiencing (a form of emotional intelligence) and provides a safe outlet for releasing stress (Seaward, 2011). Writing about our emotions reduces the risk that we'll deny or repress them—i.e., push them out of our conscious awareness.

Author's Experience I'm the kind of person who carries the worries of the day with me, and it really affects my sleep. I'm also the type of person who juggles many balls during the day, which also adds to my stress level. By chance I discovered a great strategy for managing my stress. I was doing a conflict-resolution workshop about 15 years ago and I asked the participants to write down in a journal all the conflicts they encountered during the day for 30 consecutive days. We would then come together as a group at the end of the 30 days to review those conflicts, the strategies they learned in my workshop to resolve those conflicts, and how well those strategies worked. What they found was that many of their conflicts fell into a few categories, and they were soon able to recognize what created the conflicts and what strategies worked best to resolve them. I decided to try this experiment on my stressors. So, every night before I went to bed (I still do this most of the time), I wrote down the categories or sources of stress that I experienced during the day. After 30 days, I was able to recognize patterns in the causes of my stress and what strategies I could use to combat them. The other thing I noticed was that over the 30 days, my stress level decreased and the quality of my sleep increased.

— *Aaron Thompson*

3. **Take time for humor and laughter.** Research on the benefits of humor for reducing tension is clear and convincing. In one study, college students were suddenly told they had to deliver an impromptu (off the top of their head) speech. This unexpected assignment caused the students' heart rates to elevate to an average of 110 beats per minute during delivery of the speeches. However, students who watched humorous episodes of sitcoms before delivering their impromptu speeches had an average heart rate during the speeches that was significantly lower (80–85 beats per minute)—indicating that the humor they experienced reduced their level of anxiety (O'Brien, as cited in Howard, 2000). Research also shows that humor strengthens the immune system by blocking the body's production of the stress hormone cortisol—a biochemical that suppresses our immune system when we're under stress (Berk, as cited in Liebertz, 2005b).

> *The arrival of a good clown exercises a more beneficial influence upon the health of a town than the arrival of twenty asses laden with drugs.*
>
> —Thomas Sydenham, 17th-century physician

Reflection 7.12

In your leadership role, what do you anticipate will be your most common source(s) of stress?

What strategies will you likely use to cope with these sources of stress?

Depression

Along with anxiety, depression is the other major emotional problem that needs to be managed. Research indicates that depression is a significant predictor of lower college GPA and greater risk of withdrawing from college, even among highly motivated and academically well-prepared students (Eisenberg, Golberstein, & Hunt, 2009). **Box 7.5** provides a summary of symptoms or signs of depression. If these symptoms continue to occur for two or more weeks, students should take action to relieve them.

Depression may be succinctly described as an emotional state characterized by loss of optimism, hope, and energy. As the term implies, when we're depressed, our mood is lowered or pushed down. In contrast to anxiety, which typically involves worrying about something that is currently happening or is about to happen (e.g., test anxiety before or during an exam), depression more often relates to something that has already happened, particularly after a loss, such as a lost relationship (e.g., departed friend, broken romance, or death of a family member) or a lost opportunity (e.g., losing a job, failing a course, or failing to be accepted into a major) (Bowlby, 1980; Price, Choi, & Vinokur, 2002). It's natural and normal to feel dejected after losses such as these. However, if dejection reaches a point where a student can't concentrate and complete day-to-day tasks, and if this continues for an extended period of time, that student may be experiencing what psychologists call *clinical depression*—i.e., depression so serious that he or she should receive immediate professional help.

Box 7.5

Recognizing the Symptoms (Signs) of Depression

- Feeling low, down, dejected, sad, or blue;
- Pessimistic feelings about the future (e.g., expecting failure or feeling helpless or hopeless);
- Decreased sense of humor;
- Difficulty finding pleasure, joy, or fun in anything;
- Lack of concentration;
- Loss of motivation or interest in things previously found to be exciting or stimulating (e.g., loss of interest in school, sudden drop in rate of class attendance or completion of course assignments);
- Stooped posture (e.g., hung head or drawn face);
- Slower and softer speech rate;
- Decreased animation and slower bodily movements;
- Loss of energy;
- Changes in sleeping patterns (e.g., sleeping more or less than usual);
- Changes in eating patterns (e.g., eating more or less than usual);
- Social withdrawal;
- Neglect of physical appearance;
- Consistently low self-esteem (e.g., thinking "I'm a loser");
- Strong feelings of worthlessness or guilt (e.g., thinking "I'm a failure"); and
- Suicidal thoughts (e.g., thoughts such as "I can't take it anymore," "People would be better off without me," or "I don't deserve to live").

It is especially important to be observant and ready to reach out to students who you think may be experiencing the foregoing symptoms, because depression and suicidal thoughts occur at alarmingly high rates among college students. In one national study of more than 26,000 students at 70 campuses, 15% of the students surveyed reported they had "seriously considered" suicide and more than 5% reported having actually attempted suicide; however, only half the students who had suicidal thoughts sought counseling or treatment (Drum et al., 2009). If you suspect that a student needs help, express your concern in a nonthreatening way (e.g., "You don't seem like yourself today," or "You seem kind of down, are you okay?"). If your initial concern proves to be accurate, connect the student to a personal counselor by using the referral strategies described in Chapter 4.

Reflection 7.13

Have you, or has a member of your family, ever experienced clinical depression?

What do you think was the primary cause or factor that triggered it?

Strategies for Coping with Depression

Depression can vary widely in intensity. Moderate and severe forms of depression often require professional counseling or psychotherapy, and their cause often lies in genetic factors that involve inherited imbalances in brain chemistry. The following strategies are offered primarily for milder cases of depression that are manageable through self-help and self-control. Students may use these strategies in conjunction with professional help or psychiatric medication to reduce the intensity and frequency of depression.

1. **Focus on the present and the future, not the past.** Consciously fight the tendency to dwell on past losses or failures, because you can no longer change or control them. Instead, focus on things you can still control, which are occurring now and will occur in the future.

2. **Increase your effort to engage in positive or emotionally uplifting behavior.** If our behavior is upbeat, our mind (mood) often follows suit. "Put on a happy face" can be an effective depression-reduction strategy because smiling induces certain changes in our facial muscles that trigger changes in brain chemistry and improve our mood (Liebertz, 2005a). In contrast, frowning activates a different set of facial muscles that tend to reduce production of mood-elevating brain chemicals (Myers, 1993).

3. **Continue to engage in activities that are fun and enjoyable.** Falling into the downward spiral of withdrawing from doing things that bring you joy because you're too down to do them will bring you even lower by taking away the very things that bring you up. We should continue to socialize with friends and engage in our usual recreational activities. Interestingly, the root of the word *recreation* means "to re-create" (create again), which suggests that recreation can revive, restore, and renew us physically and emotionally.

4. **Continue trying to get things done.** Staying busy and getting things done when we're feeling down helps boost our mood because we experience a sense of accomplishment that elevates our self-esteem. Doing things for others less fortunate than ourselves can be a particularly effective way to boost our mood, because it helps us realize that our issues are often far more manageable than the more serious problems faced by others.

5. **Intentionally seek out humor and opportunities to laugh.** In addition to reducing anxiety, laughter can lighten and brighten a dark mood. Furthermore, humor improves memory (Nielson, as cited in Liebertz, 2005a), which can combat the memory interference typically caused by depression.

6. **Make a conscious effort to focus on personal strengths and accomplishments.** Another way to drive away the blues is by keeping track of the positive developments in our lives. We can do this by keeping a "positive events journal" in which we note the good things that happen to us and for us, such as the fortunate experiences in our lives, the things we're grateful for, and our personal accomplishments or achievements. Positive journal entries leave us with a visible uplifting record that we can review anytime we're feeling down.

7. **If you're unable to overcome depression on your own, seek help from others.** In some cases, individuals may be able to help themselves overcome emotional problems through personal effort and effective coping strategies. This is particularly true if they experience depression or anxiety in milder forms and for shorter periods of time. However, overcoming more serious and long-lasting episodes of depression or anxiety isn't as simple as people make it out to be when they glibly and insensitively say, "Just deal with it," "Get over it," or "Snap out of it." More serious cases of depression (and anxiety) can be strongly associated with genetic factors, which are not completely within the person's control.

> *The best way to cheer yourself up is to try to cheer somebody else up.*
>
> —Samuel Clemens, a.k.a. Mark Twain, writer, lecturer, and humorist

> *If you can laugh at it, you can survive it.*
>
> —Bill Cosby, American comedian, actor, and activist

Reflection 7.14

If you thought you were experiencing a serious episode of anxiety or depression, would you feel comfortable seeking help from a professional? If yes, why? If no, why not?

How do you think your students would respond to the above question?

Summary and Conclusion

Peer leadership and mentoring involve providing support and guidance that go beyond academic development to support students' holistic development—i.e., development of the "whole person." Student success in college depends on factors that aren't strictly academic in nature. Even in cases where students experience academic difficulties, their poor grades may just be a byproduct of personal issues that are interfering with and suppressing their academic performance. Thus, peer support programs designed to promote new students' success must address the student as a "whole person," which includes the following key dimensions of human development: *intellectual, emotional, social, ethical, physical, spiritual, vocational,* and *personal* (e.g., developing positive self-beliefs, attitudes, and self-management habits). Each of these elements of self plays an influential role in promoting success and wellness.

Wellness may be described as a state of high-quality health and personal well-being that promotes peak physical and mental performance. Physical wellness includes four key elements of a healthy lifestyle: (1) supplying our bodies with effective fuel (nutrition) for optimal energy, (2) giving our bodies adequate rest (sleep) so that they can recover and replenish the energy they have expended, (3) avoiding risky substances (alcohol and drugs) and risky behaviors that can threaten our health and safety, and (4) avoiding risky (unhealthy) relationships that are abusive or violent.

Emotional well-being is also an essential element of wellness. Two major emotional problems that can interfere with student success in college are stress (anxiety) and depression. By becoming aware of the signs or symptoms of anxiety and depression, and being ready to reach out and support students who are experiencing these emotions, peer mentors can play a key role in promoting students' personal well-being and college success.

Internet Resources

For additional information related to the ideas discussed in this chapter, we recommend the following websites:

Nutrition
www.eatright.org

Fitness
www.fitness.gov/resource-center

Sleep
www.sleepfoundation.org

Alcohol and Drugs
www.nida.nih.gov

Sexual Harassment, Assault, and Abuse
www.princeton.edu/uhs/healthy-living/hot-topics/sexual-harassment-assault

Exercise 7.1 *Self-Assessment of Holistic Development*

Since wholeness is essential for wellness, success, and happiness, take the time to read through the following descriptions and specific skills associated with each of the eight elements of holistic development. As you read the specific skills and qualities listed beneath each of the eight elements, place an asterisk (*) beside those that you think are particularly important for your development as a *person* and a checkmark (✓) next to those that you believe are important for your development as a *peer leader.*

1. **Intellectual Development**—acquiring knowledge and learning how to learn and how to think at a higher level.

   Specific Skills and Qualities

   _____ Becoming aware of your intellectual abilities, interests, and learning styles.

   _____ Maintaining attention and concentration.

   _____ Improving your ability to retain knowledge (long-term memory).

   _____ Acquiring effective research skills for finding information from a variety of sources and systems.

   _____ Viewing issues from multiple angles or viewpoints (psychological, social, political, economic, etc.) in order to attain a balanced, comprehensive perspective.

   > *Intellectual growth should commence at birth and cease only at death.*
   > —Albert Einstein, Nobel Prize-winning physicist

   _____ Responding constructively to differing viewpoints or opposing arguments.

   _____ Critically evaluating ideas in terms of their truth and value.

   _____ Thinking creatively or imaginatively.

   _____ Detecting and rejecting persuasion tactics that appeal to emotion rather than reason.

2. **Emotional Development**—strengthening your ability to understand, control, and express your emotions.

   Specific Skills and Qualities

   _____ Maintaining a healthy balance between emotional control and emotional expression.

   _____ Responding with empathy and sensitivity to emotions experienced by others.

   _____ Using effective stress-management strategies to control anxiety and tension.

   _____ Dealing effectively with depression.

   _____ Dealing effectively with anger.

   _____ Responding constructively to frustrations and setbacks.

   _____ Dealing effectively with fear of failure and poor performance.

   _____ Accepting feedback in a constructive, non-defensive manner.

   _____ Maintaining optimism and enthusiasm.

   > *The best leaders are careful not to let their feelings manage them. Instead, they manage their feelings.*
   > —Kouzes & Posner, *Student Leadership Planner: An Action Guide to Your Personal Best*

3. **Social** Development—enhancing the quality and depth of your interpersonal relationships.

Specific Skills and Qualities

_____ Developing effective conversational skills.

_____ Becoming an effective listener.

_____ Relating effectively to others in one-to-one, small-group, and large-group situations.

_____ Collaborating effectively with others when working in groups or teams.

_____ Overcoming shyness.

_____ Developing meaningful and intimate relationships.

_____ Dealing with interpersonal conflicts assertively, rather than aggressively or passively.

_____ Providing feedback to others in a constructive and considerate manner.

_____ Relating effectively to others from different cultural backgrounds and lifestyles.

_____ Developing leadership skills.

> *Chi rispetta sara rippetato. (Respect others and you will be respected.)*
> —Italian proverb

4. **Ethical** Development—building moral character (the ability to make and act on ethical judgments), developing a clear value system for guiding personal decisions, and demonstrating consistency between your convictions (beliefs) and your commitments (actions).

Specific Skills and Qualities

_____ Gaining deeper self-awareness of your values and ethical assumptions.

_____ Making personal choices and life decisions based on a meaningful value system.

_____ Developing the capacity to think and act with personal integrity and authenticity.

_____ Using electronic technology in an ethical and civil manner.

_____ Resisting social pressure to act in ways that are inconsistent with your values.

_____ Treating others in an ethically responsible manner.

_____ Exercising individual freedom without infringing on the rights of others.

_____ Developing concern and commitment for human rights and social justice.

_____ Developing the courage to challenge or confront others who violate human rights and social justice.

_____ Becoming a morally responsible citizen.

> *If you don't stand for something you will fall for anything.*
> —Malcolm X, African-American Muslim minister, public speaker, and human rights activist

5. *Physical* **Development**—applying knowledge about the human body to prevent disease, preserve wellness, and promote peak performance.

Specific Skills and Qualities

_____ Developing awareness of your physical condition and state of health.

_____ Applying knowledge about exercise and fitness training to improve your physical and mental health.

_____ Understanding how sleep patterns affect health and performance.

_____ Maintaining a healthy balance between work, recreation, and relaxation.

_____ Acquiring knowledge about nutrition to reduce risk of illness and promote peak performance.

_____ Becoming knowledgeable about nutritional imbalances and eating disorders.

_____ Developing a positive body image.

_____ Becoming aware of the effects of drugs and their impact on physical and mental well-being.

_____ Acquiring knowledge about human sexuality, sexual relations, and sexually transmitted diseases.

_____ Understanding how biological differences affect male-female relationships and gender orientation.

> *To keep the body in good health is a duty, otherwise we shall not be able to keep our mind strong and clear.*
>
> —Buddha, founder of Buddhism

6. *Spiritual* **Development**—searching for answers to the "big questions," such as the meaning or purpose of life and death, and exploring issues that transcend human life and the physical or material world.

Specific Skills and Qualities

_____ Developing a philosophy of life or worldview about the meaning and purpose of human existence.

_____ Exploring the unknown or what cannot be completely understood scientifically.

_____ Exploring the mysteries associated with the origin of the universe.

_____ Searching for the connection between the self and the larger world or cosmos.

_____ Searching for the mystical or supernatural—that which transcends the boundaries of the natural world.

_____ Being open to examining questions relating to death and life after death.

_____ Being open to examining questions about the possible existence of a supreme being or higher power.

_____ Acquiring knowledge about different approaches to spirituality and their underlying beliefs or assumptions.

_____ Understanding the difference and relationship between faith and reason.

_____ Becoming aware and accepting of different religious beliefs and practices.

> *You may think I'm here, living for the 'now' . . . but I'm not. Half of my life revolves around the invisible and immaterial. At some point, every one of us has asked the Big Questions surrounding our existence: What is the meaning of life? Is my life inherently purposeful and valuable?*
>
> —College student, quoted in Dalton et al. (2006)

> *Everyone is a house with four rooms: a physical, a mental, an emotional, and a spiritual. Most of us tend to live in one room most of the time but unless we go into every room every day, even if only to keep it aired, we are not complete.*
>
> —Native American proverb

7. **Vocational** Development—exploring occupational options, making career choices wisely, and developing skills needed for lifelong career success.

Specific Skills and Qualities

_____ Understanding the relationship between college majors and future careers.

_____ Using effective strategies for exploring and identifying potential careers.

_____ Identifying career options that are compatible with your personal values, interests, and talents.

_____ Acquiring work experience in fields that relate to your career interests.

_____ Developing an effective resume and portfolio.

_____ Adopting effective strategies for identifying personal references and sources for letters of recommendation.

_____ Acquiring effective job-search strategies.

_____ Using effective strategies for writing letters of inquiry and application to potential employers.

_____ Developing strategies for performing successfully in personal interviews.

_____ Acquiring networking skills for connecting with potential employers.

> "Students may be pushed into careers by their families, while others have picked one just to relieve their anxiety about not having a career choice. Still others may have picked popular or lucrative careers, knowing nothing of what they're really like or what it takes to prepare for them."
>
> —Lee Upcraft, Joni Finney, and Peter Garland, student development specialists

8. **Personal** Development—developing positive self-beliefs, attitudes, and self-management habits.

Specific Skills and Qualities

_____ Developing a strong sense of personal identity and a coherent self-concept. (Answering the question "Who am I?")

_____ Finding a sense of purpose and direction in life. (Answering the question "Whom will I become?")

_____ Developing self-respect and self-esteem.

_____ Increasing self-confidence.

_____ Developing self-efficacy—belief that the outcomes of your life are within your control and determined largely by personal initiative and effort.

_____ Setting realistic personal goals and priorities.

_____ Becoming self-motivated and self-disciplined.

_____ Developing the persistence and perseverance to reach long-range goals.

_____ Acquiring practical skills for managing personal resources (e.g., time and money).

_____ Becoming independent, self-directed, and self-reliant.

> "Remember, no one can make you feel inferior without your consent."
>
> —Eleanor Roosevelt, human rights activist, author, and diplomat

> "I'm a great believer in luck and I find the harder I work, the more I have of it."
>
> —Thomas Jefferson, third president of the United States and founder of the University of Virginia

Look back at the asterisks and checkmarks you've placed by each of the eight general areas of self-development. Did you place about the same number in all eight areas, or were there large differences across areas?

Based on the distribution of asterisks and checkmarks in each area, what qualities did you rate as important for both personal development and peer leadership development?

Exercise 7.2 *Wellness Self-Assessment and Self-Improvement*

For each aspect of wellness listed here, rate yourself in terms of how close you are to doing what you should be doing (1 = farthest from the ideal; 5 = closest to the ideal). Circle the number that most closely matches your rating.

	Nowhere Close to What I Should Be Doing 1	2	Not Bad but Should Be Better 3	4	Right Where I Should Be 5
Nutrition	1	2	3	4	5
Exercise	1	2	3	4	5
Sleep	1	2	3	4	5
Alcohol and Drugs	1	2	3	4	5

For each area in which there's a gap between where you are now and where you should be, identify the best action you could take to reduce or eliminate this gap.

CASE STUDY: "Drinking to Death—College Partying Gone Wild"

At least 50 college students nationwide die each year as a result of drinking incidents on or near campus. During one 30-day stretch of time, three college students died as a result of binge drinking at college parties. One involved an 18-year-old first-year student at a private university who collapsed after drinking a mixture of beer and rum, fell into a coma at his fraternity house, and died three days later. He had a blood-alcohol level of more than .40, which is about equal to gulping down 20 shots of liquor in one hour.

The second incident involved a student from a public university in the South who died of alcohol poisoning (overdose). The third student died at another public university in the Northeast, where after an evening of partying and heavy drinking, he accidentally fell off a building in the middle of the night and fell through the roof of a greenhouse. Some colleges in the Northeast now have student volunteers roaming the campus on cold winter nights to make sure that no students freeze to death after passing out from an intense bout of binge drinking.

Listed below are some strategies that have been suggested by politicians to stop or reduce the problem of dangerous binge drinking:

1. A state governor announced that he was going to launch a series of radio ads designed to discourage underage drinking.

2. A senator filed bills to toughen penalties for those who violate underage drinking laws, such as producing and using fake identification cards.

3. A group of city council members was going to look into stiffening penalties for liquor stores that deliver directly to fraternity houses.

Source: Los Angeles Times (2000).

Reflection and Discussion Questions

1. Rank the potential effectiveness of these three strategies for stopping or reducing the problem of binge drinking mentioned above (1 = the most effective strategy; 3 = the least effective).

2. Comparing your highest-ranked and lowest-ranked choices:

   a. Why did you rank the first one as most effective?

   b. Why did you rank the last one as least effective?

3. What other strategies do you think would be effective for reducing the frequency of dangerous binge drinking on college campuses?

Leading Groups
Understanding Group Dynamics and Facilitating Teamwork

Reflection 8.1

Think of a situation in which you were a member of a group headed by an effective leader.

1. How did the leader act?

2. How did the leader's actions affect the group's behavior?

3. How did the leader make you feel personally?

Leadership can produce positive change in an individual (e.g., personal mentoring) or a group (e.g., student club). The focus of this chapter is effective leadership in group situations, whether the group is an athletic team, a campus club, or a learning community. The ultimate goal of this chapter is to develop your group leadership skills by (1) strengthening your understanding of group dynamics and group development, and (2) enhancing your ability to manage groups and facilitate group work.

Establishing a Common Vision and Shared Purpose

"If you build it, they will come." You may be familiar with this quote from the movie *Field of Dreams*. In this movie, an Iowa farmer (played by Kevin Costner) builds a beautiful baseball diamond in the middle of his farm hoping to attract great (but long dead) baseball players. Of course, nobody believes they will come, but they do! The ghosts from 1919 come to a 1980s farm. Why? Because they have a *passion* for baseball. The farmer offers a place and a space in which their passion can be played out. In leadership terms, the farmer established a vision that attracted followers and enabled them to fulfill this vision. He carefully prepared the field, attracted participants, reassured skeptics, and persevered in the face of setbacks. And not only did the players come, but fans came as well! Although the movie is obviously fictional, it dramatically highlights the importance of creating a common vision.

When a sense of shared purpose is effectively established in a group, its members will be far more likely to invest their time, energy, and effort to make the group's vision a reality. The best group leaders inspire, encourage, and challenge

> *A dream you dream alone is only a dream. A dream you dream together is reality.*
>
> —John Lennon, founding member of the Beatles

their group to fulfill its intended purpose. In the words of an old spiritual that became prominent during the U.S. civil rights movement, they empower the group to "keep its eyes on the prize."

Establishing a shared sense of purpose is particularly vital during the initial stages of a group's development. As the group's leader, you will play a major role in introducing a purpose and vision to your group, planning activities, and modeling accountability. However, even though your group members may not initially know what they need and want, you should still make every effort to consult with them and include them in the process of defining the group's purpose and direction. One way to provide the group with some sense of structure and direction—while still allowing its members some opportunity for input—is to initiate the process by supplying them with a list or menu of possible group goals, have members rank them, and allow them to add their own ideas to the list.

Although it's especially important to get group members' input early on, don't stop there: continue to seek their feedback as the group develops. Group members are much more likely to buy into a vision that's been shaped by them, rather than imposed on them.

Once input from group members has been sought and considered, work with your group to create a *vision statement*. What's a vision statement? It's a powerful statement of:

- The group's primary purpose (What are we here for?);
- The group's most deeply held principles (What do we stand for?);
- The end point of the group's actions (Where are we going?); and
- The essential actions the group will engage in to achieve its purpose (How will we get there?).

If the group's vision is to come alive in everyday practices, it should be "owned" by its members and incorporate their interests, needs, priorities, and values. To do so requires that you learn about each group member as an individual and identify goals and aspirations that group members share in common (Kouzes & Posner, 2012). This represents the critical first step in the process of transforming your group into a team with a common vision and common goals. (To facilitate this process, you could use the personal information questions listed in Exercise 1.2 at the end of Chapter 1, pp. 17–22).

As a peer leader, you can help groups develop a common vision by implementing the following practices:

- Asking group members to submit goals to you in writing about what they'd like to accomplish.
- Asking members to identify specific tasks and action steps they'd be willing to take to reach these goals.
- Creating a draft version of a vision statement that synthesizes the group's common aspirations, purposes, and commitments.
- Distributing the draft and asking for feedback (e.g., inviting the group to edit it on a discussion board).
- Constructing a final draft of the vision statement and requesting the group's approval. (The vision statement doesn't have to be perfect; it can always be revised and refined later. What's most important is that it be authentic and serve as a living document that the group can refer to and reflect on as it proceeds with its work.)

> *People support what they helped create.*
> —Komives, Lucas, & McMahon

> *The real key to a successful team is having a firm understanding of the goal of the group, and then knowing how each individual can most effectively contribute to the achievement of this goal.*
> —Senior peer leader, quoted in Shankman & Allen (2008)

- Placing the vision statement in a place where your group regularly meets, or posting it on an electronic site that it frequently uses (e.g., Blackboard or Facebook).
- Reminding the group to periodically review its vision statement and assess how well it's living it.

Once the group's vision has been established, the next step is to translate that vision into specific goals and action steps that align with the vision. Like individuals, groups need focused goals to strive for and work toward. Encourage your group to engage in the process of goal setting described in Chapter 5, pp. 115–119. After a final "group goals" document is created, distribute a copy to all group members, post it at all group meetings, and continually refer to it to keep the group on course and moving toward its stated goals.

Reflection 8.2

Think of a successful group experience you once had. How did the leader establish purpose and keep the group focused on achieving its primary goal?

Stages of Group Development

Leadership will test your confidence, patience, and perseverance. Despite your best intentions and most heartfelt efforts, not every member of the group you lead will immediately jump on board and stay on board for the entire trip. A group's development is prone to ebbs and flows. Similar to personal development, group development is a maturational process that takes time and typically evolves gradually through different stages.

Research suggests that groups typically pass through the successive stages of development listed in Box 8.1 (Tuckman, 1965; Tuckman & Jensen, 1977). The time taken to progress through these stages will vary across different groups, but most all groups tend to proceed through the same sequence of development. Some groups move through these stages in a spiral path, where they move ahead and then slip back to a previous stage before moving forward again. Other groups make sudden movements forward and then have periods with no change.

As a group leader, becoming familiar with the following stages of group development will enable you to understand how groups develop and monitor whether your group is moving in the right direction. Share your knowledge of these stages with the groups you lead so they can become more aware of what they're experiencing and monitor their progress toward higher levels of group performance.

Stage 1. Forming

When a group is first formed, participants typically feel a bit anxious because they don't know each other, how well they're going to work together, or what exactly will be required of them. As group members progress through this first stage of development, they begin to grow more comfortable relating to each other and develop a better understanding of the group's purpose and goals.

Stage 2. Storming

As the word suggests, this is the stage when things can get difficult. Results don't come as easily as was first thought. Conflicts emerge, differences of opinion are expressed, the leader's role may be challenged, and the value of the group's work may be questioned. The group may also begin to perceive gaps between its initial expectations and its current reality.

This is a make-or-break stage in the group's development because its initial enthusiasm may be dampened or destroyed by early frustrations and setbacks. It's at this time that you, as the group leader, should (1) maintain and model optimism, (2) help the group assess what's happening and remind them that this is a normal stage of group development, and (3) make necessary changes to ensure that the group continues to maintain optimism and make progress.

Note well! When your group appears to be going nowhere or its members are arguing so much that no work can be started, remember that this is normal! Remind yourself and your teams that thunderstorms do occur, but the skies will eventually clear.

Stage 3. Norming

This stage represents the calm after the storm. The group weathers the tumult of the previous stage by addressing its issues and modifying its approach; it begins to make significant progress toward its goals. Group members work more harmoniously and collaboratively, provide each other with mutual support, and reach agreement on the methods they'll use to accomplish the group's goal as well as the specific roles each of them will play in the process.

Stage 4. Performing

At this stage, the group begins to function in a highly effective and efficient manner. Communication is honest, open, and respectful. Individual members take on specific roles, personal responsibility is equally distributed, and a wide variety of group members become actively involved. It's at this stage that co-leaders often emerge to help facilitate the group process and help keep the group on course.

Stage 5. Retiring/Adjourning

Following completion of group tasks, members continue to chat informally and confer with each other about the group's performance. They may spend time together socializing and discussing the group's work in a more relaxed setting. As group leader, you can capitalize on this stage by arranging optional and informal get-togethers after official meetings. These follow-up activities may just serve the purpose of helping members bond together as a team. However, they may also be used to encourage group reflection by posing the simple question: "Did we accomplish what we set out to do?" If the answer is yes, then this group accomplishment should be formally acknowledged. Research suggests that high-performing groups tend to have regular rituals through which accomplishments and milestones are celebrated (Kouzes & Posner, 2012). These celebratory events reinforce the group's vision and further solidify its relationships. You can celebrate group successes by arranging for the group to periodically share meals together or drinks at a local coffeehouse. Even a short congratulatory e-mail or Facebook post following a successful meeting can be a very effective way to provide personal validation to group members for their efforts.

6. Grieving/Mourning

When a group officially dismantles or disbands after being together for an extended period of time, its members often go through a stage of mourning or grieving; they may feel empty or sad that the group's energy and camaraderie has come to an end. As group leader, you can help combat this feeling of loss by planning a final group celebration activity. This doesn't have to be an expensive or labor-intensive event; it could simply be a modest awards get-together at which all group members are personally recognized for their contributions. Such rituals remind people that their efforts mattered, are worthy of public recognition, and are worth doing again in the future.

Facilitating Group Interaction

Facilitation may be defined as the act of assisting or improving the progress of improving something. Effective group facilitation requires knowledge and practice of skills that serve to increase group interaction, collaboration, and productivity. Groups typically do not facilitate themselves; don't assume that groups will run smoothly without attention to group dynamics and strategic use of effective group-facilitation skills, such as those discussed below.

Team Building

This is a critical first step in the group-facilitation process. Outstanding leaders are able to transform a group into a *team* that is characterized by (1) a common goal, (2) interdependent (mutually supportive) roles performed by group members, and (3) a strong sense of collective identity (Hughes, Ginnett, & Curphy, 1993). As a peer leader, you can begin to convert group work into teamwork by intentionally implementing specific procedures that build a genuine feeling of team identity. Team-building activities help to build an *esprit de corps* ("spirit of a body")—a team spirit and a sense of interconnectedness that allows the group to express their personal viewpoints openly, disagree with each other respectfully, and make decisions collaboratively. The benefits of small-group learning are more likely to be realized in a social context that has been carefully crafted to promote team cohesiveness, mutual trust, and emotional security.

Team-building activities that you can use to create this sense of group identity and social cohesiveness include the following:

- Taking team photos.
- Creating team names.
- Engaging group members in "icebreakers" or "community-building" activities (e.g., the "Personal Scavenger Hunt" exercise on p. 231). The Office of Student Affairs or Student Activities on campus should be able to provide you with a variety of such activities you could use with your group.

Taking the time needed to build a sense of community in a group acknowledges that relationships are central to effective leadership [and] builds a strong organization with committed participants who know they matter.

—Susan Komives, Nance Lucas, & Timothy McMahon, *Exploring Leadership for College Students Who Want to Make a Difference*

Setting Ground Rules and Establishing Group Norms

Once a sense of team identity has been built, the next step in the group-facilitation process is to provide specific suggestions and concrete illustrations for promoting cooperation and teamwork.

Social-interaction guidelines and ground rules that are established "up front" lay the initial groundwork needed for subsequent group work to run smoothly. It's much easier to build a group that functions effectively and efficiently right from the start than it is to go back and try to fix it later, after it's broken.

Group norms are clear, mutually agreed-upon guidelines for group interaction that specify how individuals should communicate and how group members should treat each other during group meetings and discussions. Group norms work most effectively when team members collaborate to create the norms and enforce them. Here are some strategies for making this happen.

- Ask the group for behaviors they would like to see all members of the group display. For example:
    a. How would you like to be treated by members of our group?
    b. What do you expect from other members of our group?
    c. What would really bother you if a group member was to _____?
- Discuss these questions with the group. If your group is larger than 10, you may want to start with small-group discussions (in groups of three to five), followed by larger group sharing.
- Ask the group to identify shared viewpoints that emerged during the discussions.
- Generate a first draft of group norms that reflect these shared viewpoints and distribute the draft to the group for comment.
- Based on the group's feedback, revise the draft and construct an official list of group norms.
- Once the group's norms have been agreed upon, send them around to all of the group members via e-mail or whatever electronic communication mode they tend to use. Also print them out on a poster board, bring it to group meetings, and place it in a position where it can be easily seen by all group members.
- Periodically ask the group to reflect on and discuss how well it's adhering to the norms. Be specific—go from norm to norm and ask group members for a precise analysis, e.g., have members rate the group's performance on each norm on a scale of 1–10 and provide an explanation for each of their ratings.

See **Box 8.1** for a sample list of group norms.

When group norms are well defined and effectively implemented, group members become more comfortable about expressing their ideas openly and are more likely to focus more on the group's agenda than their personal agendas.

Box 8.1

Group Norms: A Sample

1. Come prepared for group meetings by:
   a. Reviewing notes from the previous meeting;
   b. Being ready to report on tasks that you were to complete from the previous meetings; and
   c. Bringing questions and ideas for the upcoming meeting.
2. Arrive at meetings on time, or ahead of time, because all meetings will start on time.
3. During meetings:
   a. Share air time—don't dominate conversation;
   b. Only one person speaks at a time while others listen actively;
   c. No "sidebars"—side conversations while someone else is speaking; and
   d. No texting or checking e-mail or Facebook posts.
4. Don't introduce a new topic until discussion of the current topic is complete. (Any issue raised that does not directly relate to the topic under discussion will be put in a "parking lot"—i.e., put on hold and not discussed until discussion of the current topic is finished.)
5. When others are expressing ideas you disagree with:
   a. Respectfully allow them to express their point of view (e.g., no head shaking while the person is speaking and no interruptions until the person is finished speaking).
   b. First look for and acknowledge areas of agreement before launching into points of disagreement.
   c. Focus disagreements on ideas, not people—i.e., on *what* is being said, not *who* is saying it.

Reflection 8.3

Do you think it's difficult for peer groups to establish and follow group norms? Why or why not?

Planning Group Meetings and Activities

When group meetings and activities are planned in a thoughtful manner, group members are more apt to become engaged, and group goals are more likely to be achieved. By taking the time and effort to carefully plan group meetings, you demonstrate commitment to the group and respect for its members' time and effort. An effective meeting plan should include the following components:

- Communication prior to the meeting that answers the following questions:
  a. When are we meeting?
  b. What are the goals of the meeting?
  c. What preparation is expected for the meeting?
  d. What do we need to bring to the meeting?
  e. What will we be expected to do during the meeting?

- If possible, use an assortment of modalities to communicate with group members before the meeting—e.g., face-to-face communication, e-mail, Facebook, Blackboard discussion board, etc.—to deliver information about the meeting, post questions to be addressed at the meeting, and provide resources to help them prepare for the meeting.
- Deciding on the building, room, and seating configuration that would work best for the meeting's purpose or goal.

- A short social "warm-up" at the outset of the meeting before group work is begun. For instance, starting the session with a "check-in"—a short question or prompt that each group member quickly responds to, such as "What's the best thing that's happened to you since our last meeting?"

Note well!   People come first; paper and PowerPoint come later.

- Identifying the meeting's primary purpose. Always be sure to take time to explain why the meeting is being held and how it relates to the group's goals; group members are unlikely to become fully engaged if they aren't clear about why they're being asked to do it.
- Including a "hook" at the start of the meeting to grab attention and spark interest (e.g., short video, quick game, or provocative story).
- "Tying it all together" at the end of the meeting. For instance, before members leave, the following questions should be asked and answered to bring some sense of closure to the meeting:
  a. What did we accomplish during this meeting? (This question could be answered by providing members with an index card and requesting written feedback.)
  b. When will we meet next?
  c. What should we do individually and collectively to prepare for the next meeting?
- Assuring equal input from all group members by setting aside one minute of input time for each member at the end of the meeting (e.g., if your group includes 10 members, set aside 10 minutes). Members could elect to pass if they have no input or if they feel their input has already been expressed.
- Ending meetings with a real "ending." For example, sum up what was accomplished and set up what will be accomplished next time. This practice not only provides a nice "wrap-up" for the meeting, but also serves to "psych up" members about what they did and what they will do.
- Following up after the meeting with correspondence (e.g., e-mail requests for feedback about the meeting, thank-you notes for contributions to the meeting, or reminders of tasks to complete prior to the next meeting).

Monitoring Group Members' Engagement during Meetings

During group meetings, pay attention to group members' nonverbal signals. Be on the lookout for social cues that suggest that certain group members may not be on board. Are students visibly disengaged? Are they tuning out? Are they engaging in side conversations unrelated to the task at hand? Privately and sensitively approach those individuals who seem to be disengaged by using "I" messages to express your concern (e.g., "I'm sensing that you're not really into what we're doing") and ask for their feedback. In some cases, student engagement may be restored or re-ignited by simply taking the time to check in with the student. There may be times when the student's disengagement may have nothing to do with you as group leader or the group itself. Instead, it may be a reflection or symptom of something else going on in the student's life that you may be able to help with, or connect the student to someone who can.

If the group as a whole is visibly disengaged, bring it to their attention—not in a judgmental or accusatory manner, but as a topic for discussion. For example, pose questions such as "Why is this not working well? What can I do, or what can we do together, to make it work better?"

Making Presentations to Groups

While much of what you do as a group leader may involve facilitating groups, there will be occasions where you need to deliver presentations. Your ability to present ideas to groups in a clear, concise, and confident manner will strengthen your leadership performance in college and beyond. Listed below are top tips to keep in mind when making presentations as a group leader.

Establish the purpose of your presentation. A presentation usually falls into one of the following two categories, depending on its purpose or objective:

1. *Informative* presentations—intended to provide the audience with accurate information and explanations, or
2. *Persuasive* **(expository) presentations**—intended to persuade (convince) the audience to agree with a certain position or buy into a particular course of action. Be sure you're clear about what you intend to accomplish and keep that objective in mind as you develop your presentation by asking yourself, "Is this particular piece of information or idea relevant to the intended purpose of my presentation?"

Outline your presentation before making your presentation. Get your major points down on index cards or PowerPoint slides and arrange them in an order that provides the best sequence or flow of your ideas from start to finish. The major points you've recorded on separate index cards or slides can serve as memory "cue cards" to trigger your recall of specific details relating to each of your major points.

Rehearse and revise. Just as you should write several drafts of a paper before turning it in, your oral presentation should be rehearsed and revised before delivering it. Rehearsal will improve your memory and increase the clarity of your presentation by reducing long pauses, stops and starts, and use of distracting "fillers" (e.g., *uh, um, like, you know*). Rehearsal will also help reduce your level of speech anxiety. Studies show that fear of public speaking is often really a fear of failure—fear of being negatively evaluated by the audience. So, if your oral presentation is well prepared and well rehearsed, your fear of receiving a negative evaluation should decrease along with your level of speech anxiety.

When rehearsing your presentation, pay special attention to the following parts:

1. The *introduction.* This part should be rehearsed carefully because it sets the stage and creates a powerful first impression. As in a written report, your introduction should include a thesis statement—a statement of what you propose to accomplish by the end of your presentation.
2. **Statements that signal your** *transition* **from one major idea to another.** These statements serve to highlight your presentation's organization, showing how its separate parts are connected.

Begin with the end in mind.
—Stephen Covey, *The Seven Habits of Highly Effective People*

> *First, I tell 'em what I'm gonna tell 'em; then I tell 'em; then I tell 'em what I told 'em.*
>
> —Anonymous country preacher's formula for successful sermons

3. **Your *conclusion.*** This is your chance to finish strong and create a powerful last impression that drives home your presentation's most important point or most memorable idea. Your conclusion should include a statement that refers back to and reinforces your original thesis statement, thereby connecting your ending with your beginning.

During your speech, minimize reading time and maximize face-to-face time. You can occasionally look at your notes or slides during your presentation and use them as cue cards to help you recall the key points you intend to make; however, they shouldn't be used as a script that's read verbatim. This is the major danger associated with PowerPoint presentations: the speaker ends up looking at and reading from the slides rather than speaking to an audience. (See **Box 8.2** for tips on how to use, not abuse, PowerPoint.)

A presentation should not be something that's written out entirely in advance and read (or memorized) word for word (Luotto, Stoll, & Hoglund-Kettmann, 2001), nor should it be an impromptu speech—something spontaneously delivered off the top of your head. Instead, it should be an *extemporaneous* presentation—something in between a formal reading and an impromptu speech that includes advanced preparation and use of notes or slides as memory-retrieval cues. Extemporaneous speaking is not reading because it allows you some freedom to ad-lib or improvise. For instance, if you forget the exact words you intended to use, some improvising can prevent you from getting struck by silence and prevent your audience from even noticing that you forgot anything.

Box 8.2   Tips for Using (Not Abusing) PowerPoint

- List information on your slides as bulleted points, not as complete sentences. Wordiness will result in your audience spending more time reading your slides than listening to you. You can further focus group members' eye contact on you (not your slides) by showing only one point on your slide at a time. This will keep the audience members focused on the point you're discussing and prevent them from reading ahead.
- Avoid reading your slides. Keep eye contact primarily with your audience.

Note well! The words or images on your PowerPoint slides are not your entire presentation: they're merely cue cards that trigger your additional ideas relating to each point on the slide.

- List only three to five points on each slide. Research indicates that humans can hold only about four points or bits of information in their short-term memory (Cowan, 2001).
- Use the title of the slide as a general heading for organizing or grouping the bulleted points on the slide.
- Use a font size of at least 18 points, or else people in the back of the room will have difficulty reading what's printed on the slide.
- Color should be not be used for decoration or distraction, but as a visual aid to highlight the organization of points included on the slide. For example, a dark or bold blue heading could be used to highlight each major category, and the subcategories could be distinguished by presenting them in a lighter (but still visible) shade of blue.
- Use slides to deliver pictures or visual images that relate to and reinforce the points you're making verbally. (The projection of visual images may be the true power of PowerPoint.)

> *A presentation is about explaining things to people that go above and beyond what they get in the slides. If it weren't, they might just as well get your slides and read them in the comfort of their own office, home, boat, or bathroom.*
>
> —Jesper Johansson, senior security strategist for Microsoft and author of *Death by PowerPoint* (personal blog) (2005)

> **Note well!** *Probably the most powerful advantage of PowerPoint is its ability to enhance your verbal presentation with visual images that complement and augment your spoken words.*

- If you include words or an image on a slide that are not your own work, acknowledge the source at the bottom of the slide.
- Before going public with your slides, proofread them with the same care as you would a written paper.

Sources: Johansson (2005); *Ten Commandments of PowerPoint Presentations* (2005); University of Wisconsin, La Crosse (2001).

Prepare questions to stimulate interaction and discussion. You don't want your presentation to turn into a lecture where the group sits passively for prolonged periods of time. Rather than speaking *at* them, speak *with* them by modifying your presentation so that group members have some degree of interaction with you and with each other. The following formats may be used to infuse interaction into your presentation.

> *I think [peer mentor's name] really tried too hard. She talked so much she didn't give us a chance. It was like another lecture.*
>
> —First-year student, quoted in Wasburn (2008)

1. **"*Shared* Presentation" Format.** Before presenting your ideas on the topic, have group members share their ideas first and record their ideas on the board or a flip chart. You could do this quickly by using a strategy known as the *whip,* where you ask each group to quickly share one word or phrase that comes to mind about the presentation topic in rapid-fire fashion. Or, you could employ a procedure called *background interest probes,* in which you ask each group member to jot down what they already know, or would like to know, about the topic you're presenting.

   After group members have shared their ideas, you share the ideas you were going to present by first noting which of your ideas the group already mentioned (e.g., by underlining or highlighting them). Then you add any of your ideas that were not mentioned by the group to create a jointly produced composite or "master list," which represents the *shared* efforts of both the group and the group leader.

2. **"*Punctuated* Presentation" Format.** During your presentation, periodically stop and have students do something with the information you've just presented. This strategy serves to punctuate or break up your presentation and prevent "attention drift" that typically takes place when students do nothing but listen for more than 10 minutes at a time (Bligh, 2000). You can help maintain your group's attention by periodically pausing to ask members to react to or act on the information you've just presented (e.g., what they agree or disagree with, or how they may be able to use it).

3. **"*Post-Presentation* Reflection" Format.** Following completion of your presentation, ask group members to reflect on the major ideas you presented. They could do so by completing a *one-minute paper* (a short paragraph that takes one minute or less to complete) in response to a question that asks them to reflect on the meaning or personal significance of your presentation. For example, any of the following questions may serve as prompts for a one-minute paper at the end of a presentation.

   - What do you think was the major purpose or objective of today's presentation?
   - What do you think was the most important point or central concept communicated in today's presentation?

- What was the most surprising and/or unexpected idea presented?
- Were there any puzzling, confusing, or disturbing ideas that surfaced in your mind during the presentation?
- Was there a particular idea presented that struck you as something that our group should immediately implement or put into practice?

Reflection 8.4

Think about an instructor you've had in college or high school who was particularly good at presenting ideas and engaging students in discussion of those ideas. Did the instructor use any specific strategies that you might be able to use as a peer leader when making group presentations or leading group discussions?

Leading and Facilitating Group Discussions

Effective group leaders are able to draw out members and engage them in discussion of their ideas. Described below are research-based strategies you can use to increase your students' level of involvement and participation in group discussions.

Asking Discussion-Stimulating Questions

The way in which a discussion question is framed or posed can affect whether you receive many (or any) responses from the group. All questions are not created equally; some are more effective at stimulating involvement than others. Careful forethought should be given to the art of questioning, because studies show that how a question is framed or phrased will affect whether or not it triggers discussion. Research indicates that the following types of questions are most likely to trigger student responses (Cuseo, 2005):

- *Open-ended* questions. These are questions that open up the floor to a variety of different responses and encourage *divergent* thinking—i.e., thinking that goes off in different directions rather than converging on one (and only one) "correct" answer. Open-ended questions contain a plural noun that sends the message that a variety of answers are welcomed and expected: for example, "What options (plural) do we have for reaching our goal?"
- *Focused* questions. These are questions that are tied to a particular concept or issue. Here's an example of a focused question: "What do you think accounts for the fact that there are consistently more females than males participating in our student clubs and campus organizations?" In contrast, here's an unfocused question: "Does anybody have any questions or comments at this time?"
- *Conditionally phrased* questions (e.g., "What *might* be . . ." "What *could* be . . .?" "What *may* be . . .?"). Such tentative phrasing sends a signal to group members that a diversity of answers is possible, encourages their creativity, and reduces their fear or embarrassment about not providing "the" correct answer you're "looking for."

Questions that call for *nonverbal responses.* Questions that ask students to respond with body language rather than spoken language can generate responses from all group members simultaneously. For example, students can respond by a show of hands to a question like "How many of you agree with the following statement . . . ?" or "How many of you had an experience similar to . . . ?"

Other ways in which students can become engaged nonverbally are by (1) having them take a position represented by one of four corners in the room with each corner representing one of four choices: strongly agree, agree, disagree, strongly disagree; or (2) asking them to move to either side of the room depending on where they stand on an issue or debate. For example, "The center aisle represents middle ground, the far right side of the room represents extreme agreement, and the far left side represents extreme disagreement. Where do you stand (literally) on the issue of _____?"

Questions that call for such nonverbal responses involve all students, not just those who are the most verbally assertive or outspoken. Nonverbal responses can also be used as a stepping stone to subsequent verbal discussion. For instance, students could be asked why they chose to occupy their particular position (the space they occupied). Or, they could be given the opportunity to change places after hearing other members' ideas and then asked why they decided to change.

In addition to intentionally designing and delivering effective questions, you can elevate student involvement in group discussions by using the following strategies:

Prior to the discussion, arrange chairs in a way that will maximize eye contact among group members. Instead of having chairs arranged in rows and columns, place them in a circle, semicircle, or horseshoe so that group members make greater eye contact with each other. This increased eye contact is likely to lead to more interpersonal interaction and discussion.

Before officially beginning the discussion, take a moment to express to the group that you really value (and need) their participation in the upcoming discussion. Start off by making a sincere statement about how their viewpoints will be respected and valued. First impressions can be lasting impressions. Making such a welcoming statement at the very outset of the session capitalizes on the power of first impressions and establishes a very warm, inviting atmosphere that sets the stage for high levels of subsequent involvement.

After asking a question, be sure to wait long enough to give group members a chance to respond. If you don't get an immediate response and you start to speak again, it may send a signal to students that your question is merely rhetorical, or that you're more concerned about moving on and covering the point yourself. Another advantage of patiently waiting for a response is that it creates time for those reflective members of the group who need more time to think before responding.

If your question fails to elicit any response—even after waiting for a considerable period—rephrase the question in a different way. It's possible that the lack of response to the question isn't a reflection of disinterest or disengagement, but may have to do with the question itself. The question may not have been worded in a way that group members could relate to, or it may not have contained enough background information for them to feel comfortable about risking a response.

If dead silence continues for a significant period of time, use a little humor to lighten the moment and make a plea for involvement. For instance, you might say in a humorous tone, "Can someone, anyone, help me out here? I feel like I'm flying solo without any copilots or passengers!"

Encourage further involvement from students who respond by asking a probing follow-up question that encourages them to elaborate on their original response. Some effective follow-up questions might be (1) "Can you provide us with a few more details?", (2) "Can you connect or piggyback your idea onto an idea that's been previously suggested?", or (3) "What do you think might be some action steps we could take with respect to your idea?"

Acknowledge the name of the student who responds. This serves to affirm the student's individuality and shows everyone that you remembered the student's name. Moreover, when you refer to group members by name, it reinforces your memory of their names and helps group members remember each other's names.

Record the ideas expressed by group members on the board or a flip chart. This practice serves to reinforce the contributions of individual students and provides a cumulative record of all members' contributions. This record can be later reviewed and used as a springboard for further student involvement (e.g., by asking the group to identify any recurrent themes or patterns of variation among the responses).

Whenever possible, deflect and redirect questions directed to you to other members of the group by asking for volunteers to respond. This practice has the following advantages (1) it increases overall group participation, (2) it encourages group members to become co-leaders with you, and (3) it shows the questioning student how other students can be a valuable resource.

If a student's response to your discussion question is off-base or inaccurate, try to praise some aspect of the student's response (e.g., its creativity). If nothing about the student's response can be praised without appearing patronizing, then at least praise the effort (e.g., "Thanks for taking a stab at it."). This practice serves to reinforce the student's willingness to take the risk of speaking up, which should increase the probability that the student will contribute again.

If the discussion goes off track and in a direction that's irrelevant to the question you asked, use "I" and "we" messages to bring the discussion back on track. For instance, you could say, "I think we've strayed from the original question, haven't we?" This strategy gently reminds the whole group to keep the discussion focused on one point at a time, and it does so without simultaneously singling out or embarrassing the student who derailed the discussion (which could make that student reluctant to participate again).

Encourage the participation of students who have not yet responded by asking for their reaction to the ideas of other students who have just responded. For instance, you could say, "Let's hear from some of you who haven't spoken yet." You could also ask questions such as "Does anyone else agree with what has already been said?" or "Does anyone else want to express an opposing point of view?"

Keep an eye out for students who have not been involved verbally, but who display nonverbal signals of involvement. Looks for students whose body language indicates they are reacting to what's being discussed (e.g., by nodding their heads, raising their eyebrows, or other facial expressions). Using their first names, mention that you noticed their nonverbal response and gently invite them to respond verbally (e.g., "Donna, I think this point under discussion has triggered your interest—would you like to share your thoughts about it?").

Author's Experience I've been able to involve students in class discussions by using information I obtain from them early in the course through a series of questions (see Exercise 1.2, pp. 17–22). I save their responses to these questions and use them throughout the term to involve them in class discussions. For instance, if we're discussing a topic or issue that relates to a student's interest or past experience, I introduce the topic by mentioning the student's name when I introduce the topic. Students really perk up when I mention their names in association with their interests; it provides them with personal validation and encourages them to become more involved in class. (Students are also amazed by my apparent ability to remember interests they shared with me on the very first day of class at times much later in the term; they don't realize I've saved their responses to the questions and review them periodically.)

I also use the information students provide me about themselves to intentionally make personal connections with students who are not participating or seem "detached." For example, before class, I'll take a moment to review the information provided by a non-participating student and use that information to strike up a short conversation with the student before class starts, or when the student is leaving the room I've found that this little bit of personal attention often increases non-participating students' personal connection with me and increases their level of subsequent participation in class.

I've shared this strategy with peer leaders on my campus. Many of them decided to try it with groups they led and reported that it helped increase their personal connection with group members and raised the level of student participation in group discussions.

— *Joe Cuseo*

Make eye contact with students who have been reluctant to participate and, if possible, move closer to them when delivering questions. Making eye contact and moving a little closer to someone when posing a question can send a subtle but powerful nonverbal signal to that person that you're really interested in hearing their response. There is an art to effective questioning and much of it is created through nonverbal channels. A warm demeanor, an inviting smile, and inviting body language can spell the difference between a question that evokes an enthusiastic response or dead silence.

If you run out of questions and there's still time remaining in your discussion session, allow group members to take control of the agenda. Ask them a question like "What's on your mind that you'd like to talk about?" or "Is there anything you're curious about or concerned about that we should spend some time discussing as a group?" (Using back-up questions like these at the end of a group session is sometimes referred to as a "sponge activity" because it "soaks up" the session's remaining time in a productive way.)

Reflection 8.5

What do you think are your strengths, or potential strengths, as a discussion leader?

What aspect(s) of leading discussion groups do you think will be most challenging?

If you're facilitating a large group (e.g., more than six people), break it into smaller groups to increase each member's level of involvement. Certainly, there are times when large-group discussions and meetings must be held, but relying exclusively on them may result in some students becoming disengaged—particularly those who are shy and less verbally assertive. As you might expect, there is an inverse relationship between the size of the group and the percentage of group members who become actively involved in the group's discussion; as one goes up, the other goes down (Karau & Williams, 1993). Smaller group size allows more individuals to participate, gives them a greater sense of ownership of the group process, and provides them with more opportunities to become co-leaders.

You can get more members of a large group actively engaged by subdividing it into smaller groups and using the following small group formats developed by educational and social psychologists (Aronson et al., 2009; Cuseo, 2002; Kagan, 1994).

1. **Pairs-share.** This format involves a group of two. One partner shares his or her ideas while the other listens; then the members switch roles. Pair work ensures that both members of the group are involved equally and simultaneously—either as speaker or listener. (It's hard to hide or get lost in a group of two.)

2. **Pairs-square.** Students first share their ideas in pairs, then they join another pair of students to form a "square" (four-member team) that integrates the ideas they previously shared while working in pairs.

3. **Corners.** This is a four-member group process that involves the following steps:
   - Each corner of the room is designated for a different task (e.g., a different component of a general topic to be discussed, or a different aspect of an event to be planned).
   - The larger group is divided into four smaller groups, each of which occupies one corner of the room and completes the task designated for that corner. (The peer leader floats among the groups, observing the dynamics and providing encouragement, but without interrupting or interfering with their independent work.)
   - Each group selects a recorder to compile the ideas generated by the group and a spokesperson to share the group's ideas with the other groups.
   - The four small groups reconvene as a large group and the spokesperson from each small group shares the group's ideas with the whole group.

4. **Jigsaw.** In this small-group format, each member of the team assumes responsibility for becoming an "expert" on one part or piece of a task; then they reconvene as a team to piece together their separate parts to complete the whole, as if they were completing a jigsaw puzzle. Listed below is each major step in the process.
   - Break the large group into three- or four-member "home teams" and ask these teams to have each member take responsibility for becoming an expert on one component of a task or topic. For example, if you're planning an event, members of the group assume different roles, such as organizational expert, public relations expert, financial expert, etc. Encourage group members to assume roles that capitalize on their personal talents, interests, or perspectives.
   - Members leave their home teams to form teams with other students who chose to be experts on the same subtopic (e.g., all the public relations ex-

perts and financial experts come together in separate groups to share ideas relating to their particular area of expertise).

- After meeting in their separate "expert groups," students return to their home teams to share what they learned with members of their home teams and "piece together" their separate parts into an integrated whole.
- This jigsaw method works particularly well when group members are working on a complex task that has multiple parts or components. It can also be used to keep things fresh by introducing a unique group-interaction format that allows members of a large group to work in a more intimate small-group context, giving each of them an opportunity to play an active co-leadership role in their small groups.

Note well! When a group has a common goal and its members have interdependent roles, group work is transformed into teamwork.

Another advantage of the jigsaw method is that provides a format for integrating the separate work of small groups in a way that generates cross-group synergy and a stronger sense of community. It does so by reconstructing the large group after it's been deconstructed into small, segregated groups and enabling their separate work to be integrated into a unified whole. Connecting the work of different groups is important because it creates (1) a final product that's more comprehensive and complete than that produced by each small group, and (2) a sense of whole-group solidarity by reuniting the separated groups in a single community.

In addition to the jigsaw method, you can use the following practices to reconnect a large group after it's been subdivided into small groups:

> *All of us are smarter than any of us.*
> —Douglas Merrill, former chief information officer and vice president of engineering at Google

- **Plenary reporters.** After completing a small-group task, one student from each small group plays the role of "plenary reporter" whose role is to share the group's main ideas with the large group. You can use a flip chart or some other very visible place to write down the main ideas reported from each group. This serves to validate their contributions and helps you track recurrent themes and variations across different groups.
- **Roving reporters.** After small groups complete their work, one "roving reporter" from each small group visits the other groups to share her team's ideas. Remaining members of each small group stay "home" to listen to the ideas presented by roving reporters from the other small groups and their role is to integrate these ideas with the ideas generated by their own group.
- **Group rotation.** After small groups complete their work, they rotate clockwise and merge with another small group to share and synthesize their separate work. This "share-and-synthesize" process continues until each group has interacted with all other groups. The final step in the process is for each group to create a final product that integrates their ideas with the ideas of other groups.

All of the above group-interaction strategies have the following advantages (1) they enable groups to piggyback on each other's ideas, which creates synthesis and synergy, and (2) they enable students in small groups to interact with members of other small groups, which creates a sense of large-group solidarity and community.

Developing Co-Leaders

Another indicator that your group has been transformed into a team is when its members begin to become co-leaders with you. You can encourage co-leadership by voicing your belief in your group members' abilities and by distributing leadership responsibility among group members (Kouzes, 2002). Students will often rise to your beliefs and expectations about what they can do.

You can facilitate the development of co-leaders by intentionally sharing leadership responsibilities with group members for tasks such as choosing and organizing activities, designing implementation strategies, and encouraging individual participation. While you cannot turn over leadership before group members are prepared to assume it, there are ways to begin sharing authority by stepping aside and "off stage." Here are some strategies for doing so:

- Use the jigsaw or corners format (see pp. 218–219) to break down big tasks into component parts—or, better yet, ask your group to do so. Ask for volunteers to become experts on each particular component and let them know you are available to answer questions, provide direction, etc. As the process evolves, ask how it's going and share your perspective about what's going well and what the group could do more effectively; however, give the group space to make its own corrections and solve its own problems.
- Involve group members in making decisions about *what* the group will do and *how* it will do it—i.e., the processes or methods they'll use to get the job done.
- Occasionally ask different students to help you co-facilitate group discussions.
- Recognize the group's accomplishments and credit its members—not yourself as leader—for the group's success.

> *Good leaders grow team members . . . their key job is not doing programs but growing others.*
>
> —Tim Elmore, founder and president of Growing Leaders, a nonprofit organization

> *I'm trying to teach every one of them [my players] to lead. Leadership is about everybody else, not yourself. We've won a lot more games when it has been about everybody else and not about me. When it's about the players first, they play for you.*
>
> —John Calipari, head basketball coach, University of Kentucky, 2012 national champions

Note well! Effective leadership is a "we" thing, not a "me" thing.

> *A leader is best when people barely know he exists, when his work is done, his aim fulfilled, they will say: we did it ourselves.*
>
> —Lao Tzu

Effective leaders know when to take charge directly and when to get out of the way and let others lead the charge. There may be times when you will have to take a central role in setting the group's goals and directing its activities. Students want you to be out in front, but not so far out in front that they don't feel consulted, involved, or respected. As the group evolves and matures, your role should become less directive and more facilitative. Great leaders eventually do a Houdini act—they disappear!

Managing Unproductive or Disruptive Behavior in Groups

Reflection 8.6

What negative or disruptive behaviors have you seen students display in groups?

Have you observed a group leader who was particularly adept at handling these behaviors effectively? If yes, what did the leader do that you might be able to apply to the group(s) you are leading?

The following strategies, based on research in the fields of human relations and conflict resolution, may be used to handle conflict with group members in a sensitive and constructive manner. As a group leader, you can use these strategies to address behavioral problems you may encounter with a group member, and you can share them with groups you lead so that their members can better handle problems that may emerge with other members of their group.

1. **Focus on the specific behavior causing the conflict, not the person's character.** Avoid negative terms that refer to the person's traits (e.g., you're "inconsiderate" or "self-centered."). For instance, if you're upset with a group member for not carrying his fair share of the workload, refrain from using aggressive labels like "You're a slacker!" Labeling others with broad statements like this is likely to make them feel they're under attack or being verbally assaulted, which is likely to put them on the defensive and perhaps cause them to launch a counterattack on you.

   Rather than focusing on the person's general character, focus on the particular behavior that's causing the problem (e.g., not showing up or not completing tasks). This will enable the student to know exactly what action needs to be modified to take care of the problem. It's much easier for a person to change a behavior than it is to change a personality trait.

2. **Use "I" messages to focus on how the other person's behavior is affecting you and others members of the other group.** An "I" message centers on you—what you're perceiving and feeling, rather than targeting the other person (McKay, Davis, & Fanning, 2009). By saying, "I feel angry when . . ." (as opposed to "you make me angry when . . ."), you're taking responsibility for the way you feel, rather than guilt-tripping the individual for making you feel that way. In contrast, a "you" message (e.g., "You are . . .") is more likely to make the other person feel resentful and defensive (Bippus & Young, 2005).

Reflection 8.7

One member of your group isn't carrying his weight on a group project. What might be an "I" message you could use to communicate your concern in a non-threatening way?

---

3. **Focus on solving the problem, not winning the argument.** Don't approach conflict with the attitude that you're the leader and you're going to "show them who's boss" or "prove that you're right." Instead, approach the conflict with the attitude that it's a problem to be solved, and that both parties can "win"—i.e., both of you can end up with a better relationship in the long run if the issue is resolved.

4. **Conclude your discussion of the conflict on a warm, constructive note.** Thank the person for hearing you out and express your confidence that things can be worked out. By ending on a positive and optimistic note, you let the student know that there are no hard feelings, that you're confident the conflict can be resolved, and that you will work well together in the future.

5. **If after discussing the problem, the person makes a change in behavior to resolve the conflict, recognize the person's effort and express your appreciation.** Even if your complaint was legitimate and your request justified, the person's effort to accommodate your request shouldn't be taken for granted. The very last thing you want to do is ignore that effort or punish it with "rubbing it in" comments like "That's more like it" or "It's about time!"

   Expressing appreciation is not only the socially sensitive thing to do: it's also the smart thing to do, because by recognizing the person's changed behavior, you socially reinforce it and increase the likelihood that the behavior will continue.

Reflection 8.8

How hard do you think it is to walk the line between being a trusted friend and a peer leader? How can you best provide guidance and direction without being overbearing or hypercritical?

Acquiring and Utilizing Group Feedback

To learn how to do something well, you need to know how well you're doing it. To know how well you're doing as a group leader, you need to get feedback from the group you're leading. By seeking ongoing and timely input from the group, you stay ahead of the game by anticipating and intercepting problems before they mushroom into full-blown crises. Feedback gathered "after the fact"—after a problem or crisis has emerged—may come too late to restore the group's energy and enthusiasm. Seeking feedback on an ongoing basis also shows your group members that their ideas matter to you and enables you to continuously improve your leadership performance.

Another way to begin collecting feedback from the groups you lead is by asking open-ended questions such as:

- What have been the most effective or productive things we've done thus far? Why?
- What activities haven't worked very well? Why?
- What are some specific things I can do to improve as a group leader?
- What are some specific things we can do to improve as a group?
- Is there anything else on your mind you'd like to share?

You can also get a sense of the pulse of the group at any given time by using more formal procedures, such as (1) conducting a quick debriefing session at the end of group meetings or activities where members provide feedback orally or by writing on index cards, (2) posting feedback prompts on an electronic site shared by group members (e.g., "I thought that today's meeting was . . ."), (3) arranging one-on-one sessions with individual members of the group, and (4) distributing short surveys such as the following:

<table>
<tr><td>1</td><td>10</td></tr>
<tr><td>strongly disagree</td><td>strongly agree</td></tr>
</table>

My leader:
- Is organized,
- Is approachable,
- Is available and accessible,
- Is interested in the group's ideas,
- Effectively involves different members of the group,
- Conducts productive meetings,
- Involves students in decisions and responsibilities, and
- Effectively leads group activities.

When students provide you with feedback, whether it be positive or negative, express your appreciation and let them know that you'll take their feedback seriously. Take time to reflect on any feedback you've received and share your reflections with the group by noting what you've learned from it and pointing out how you intend to use it to make positive changes.

When you show the group you're open to feedback, your group will become more open to feedback from you. Feedback is a two-way street: it should flow from and to you.

Reflection 8.9

Think of a situation in which you have received critical (or even downright negative) feedback. How did you feel? How did you respond?

What can you do to respond to group feedback constructively rather than defensively?

In addition to seeking feedback about your work as group leader, encourage group members to reflect on and assess their own performance. The following questions may be posed to students to increase self-awareness and self-assessment of their performance in group situations.

1. For scheduled group meetings, did I:
   a. Attend regularly?
   b. Show up on time?
   c. Come prepared?
2. Did I participate as much as, more than, or less than other members of my group?
3. Did I do my fair share of the group's work? (Can I honestly say that I "carried my load" or "pulled my own weight"?)

4. Did I actively seek out ideas or information from other members of the group?
5. Did I encourage quiet or reluctant teammates to participate?
6. Did I help keep the group on track and moving toward its goal?
7. The strongest skill or greatest contribution I brought to the group was _____.
8. What I could do differently in the future to improve my performance or as a group member is to _____.

Asking questions that encourage group members to reflect on and assess their role in the group process serves to increase their social self-awareness, their sense of personal responsibility, and their ability to learn from the group experience.

Summary and Conclusion

Effective leadership can take place in one-to-one relationships (e.g., personal mentoring) or in the context of a group. High-impact leaders often are able to work well with groups and transform them into teams by helping the group define its vision, mobilizing its members around that vision, and continuously encouraging members to work together in pursuit of a common goal. More specifically, effective group leadership involves:

- Engaging group members individually and collectively to create a shared vision.
- Defining and clarifying the group's purpose, establishing its goals, and tracking and tuning its efforts.
- Establishing group-interaction guidelines and ground rules up front to ensure that the group functions harmoniously and productively.
- Understanding principles of group dynamics and stages of group development.
- Facilitating group discussions.
- Enabling a wide variety of group members to share ideas and provide input.
- Developing co-leaders by sharing leadership responsibilities with other group members.
- Encouraging the group to assess its progress through honest self-evaluation.
- Recognizing and celebrating the accomplishments of the group and its individual members.
- Seeking ongoing and timely feedback from group members and reflecting on that feedback to continually improve leadership performance.

In short, effective group leadership involves creating a unified vision, creating common goals, and transforming a group of independent individuals into interdependent teammates.

Internet Resources

For additional information related to the ideas discussed in this chapter, we recommend the following websites:

Understanding Group Dynamics
facultystaff.richmond.edu/~dforsyth/gd

Facilitating Group Discussions
www.oucom.ohiou.edu/fd/facilitatorresources.htm

Making Presentations to Groups
socserv2.mcmaster.ca/Inquiry/presentationsmaking.htm

Managing Group Conflict
ianrpubs.unl.edu/epublic/live/g2115/build/g2115.pdf

Exercise 8.1 *Journal Reflections*

What would be your top strategy for handling the following difficult group leadership situations?

1. Students aren't participating in planned activities because they're "too cool for school" or claim that the activities are "boring."

2. Students are questioning why they have to go to scheduled activities.

3. Students are not showing up for meetings or planned events.

4. Only a handful of students are participating in group discussions; not everyone is speaking up or getting involved.

5. Certain students are dominating group discussions.

6. A student is disrupting group discussions by joking around and making sarcastic comments.

7. Students are not responding to messages or staying in touch with their peer leader.

8. The peer leader is not viewed by students as a trusted peer, but more like an authority figure—i.e., a superior or supervisor.

9. The peer leader is viewed as just another student—i.e., someone without any special expertise, authority, or influence.

Exercise 8.2 *Group Goal Setting*

Choose a group that you're now leading or planning to lead and construct a SMART goal for your group. (See Chapter 5, p. 118 for key characteristics of a SMART goal.)

Exercise 8.3 *Team Building for Large Groups: The Personal Scavenger Hunt*

Use this team-building exercise to build an early sense of group trust and cohesiveness in any large group you're currently leading or will be leading. At your first group meeting, ask each group member to write down an interesting or distinctive piece of information about themselves on an index card. Collect the index cards and create a list of personal statements for all members of the group. Here's a sample of statements that were once collected from a group of students:

1. I'm a beach volleyball player who's good in math and would love to take a spontaneous trip to Ireland.

2. I'm a computer graphics major who's good at math, loves the arts, and would like to become a cartoonist.

3. I'm a former swim instructor, lifeguard, and peer mediator who wants to work with kids as a child psychologist or teacher.

Make copies of the list and bring it to the next group meeting so that each student has a copy. Have group members circulate around the room to find each group member whose personal statement appears on the list. (Be sure to include a personal statement of your own so that you can participate as well.) Instruct students to pair up with another group member and take turns trying to identify the personal statement on the list that belongs to the partner. The partners continue to alternate this question-asking role until a match is found for each partner, at which time the pair concludes their interaction and each member looks to pair up with another partner.

Listed below are specific steps for this personal scavenger-hunt procedure; print out and hand out the directions to your group, or project the directions on a screen while they engage in the exercise. Before having the group members actually engage in the exercise, role-play the exercise with a member of the group so that everyone can literally see what they're about to do.

Box 8.3

Steps in the Personal Scavenger–Hunt Exercise: A Community Building Exercise

1. Pair up with a classmate. One of you takes the role of questioner, who attempts to find the partner's description on the list, reading one description at a time until you find the correct match. The other person assumes the role or respondent, who answers either "yes" or "no" to each description read by the questioner.
2. Alternate roles (questioner becomes respondent and vice versa), and follow the same process described in step 1.
3. Continue alternating roles until both of you find the statement that describes your partner.
4. When you find the statement that matches your partner, ask for the person's name and record it next to his or her personal statement on your copy of the scavenger list.
5. After both of you find each other's matching description, move on to join another partner, and continue this pairing-up process until you have met all group members and written their names next to their correct self-descriptions.

Important reminders:

- When you're asked a question by your partner, you can only say "yes" or "no." Don't tell your partner the statement that describes you, or take your partner's copy of the list and sign your name to it, until your partner has discovered the statement that belongs to you.
- After your partner finds the statement that matches you, don't take your partner's sheet and write your name on it; instead, please say your name and have your partner record it.
- When trying to find your partner's personal statement, rather than just randomly going down the list, try to pick a statement that you *think* is associated with that person. See how good you are at guessing or predicting people's interests based on their appearance or behavior. Take a look at the list now to get an idea of the different descriptions you'll be looking for.

Exercise 8.4 *Assessing the Quality of Group Work*

Following is an assessment instrument that you can use to obtain feedback on key aspects of group work. Ask the group you're leading to complete the instrument, or ask a fellow peer leader to observe your group in action and evaluate the group's performance with this assessment tool. You can also complete the assessment instrument yourself and compare your responses to those provided by group members or to responses provided by a peer leader who has observed your group in action.

Encourage your group to discuss the results of this assessment and identify strategies for improving those areas that received the least positive ratings.

Directions: For each of the following pairs of statements, check the statement you think is the more accurate assessment of our group. (**Note:** Each pair of statements contains one statement that is considerably more positive than the other.)

Communication within the Group

_____ Group members displayed a positive attitude (e.g., their nonverbal behavior indicated interest and enthusiasm).

_____ Group members' nonverbal behavior suggested that they were bored or indifferent.

_____ Group members expressed their ideas freely and openly.

_____ Group members appeared to be afraid of "rocking the boat" or having their ideas rejected.

_____ Group members listened actively to each other.

_____ Group members were not fully attentive when other members spoke and often interrupted one another.

_____ Group members made sure they understood each other and connected what they said to what others previously said.

_____ When a group member spoke, other members appeared to be just waiting for their turn to speak and didn't relate what they said to what was said by other group members.

Interdependence and Teamwork

_____ All members of the group appeared to contribute equally.

_____ One or two members seemed to contribute most of the ideas or dominated the discussion.

_____ Group members encouraged each other to share ideas.

_____ Group members seemed unaware of, or oblivious to, members who were shy and silent.

_____ Leadership was displayed by different group members at different times.

_____ One member seemed to take charge of the whole group from start to finish.

_____ Group members worked together like a team.

_____ Group members worked separately or independently, rather than collaboratively.

Resolving Group Disagreements and Conflict

_____ Group members were willing to negotiate and modify their ideas after hearing the ideas of other members.

_____ Group members tended to cling to their own ideas and stubbornly resisted the ideas of others.

_____ Group members seemed to trust each other enough to express disagreement openly.

_____ Group members seemed to hold back and appeared uncomfortable about expressing disagreement or creating conflict.

Group Progress and Decision Making

_____ The group was usually able to stay on track and stick to the point being discussed.

_____ The group frequently got off track and went on tangents.

_____ The group was able to keep moving forward toward its goal and effectively handled disagreements that took place along the way.

_____ The group seemed to get repeatedly bogged down by disagreements and conflicts.

_____ The group was able to reach consensus and make decisions that incorporated the ideas of all group members.

_____ The group's decisions seemed to represent the ideas of just a few members, rather than the group as a whole.

Group Effectiveness

_____ The group was productive; it achieved its goal.

_____ The group failed to accomplish what it set out to do.

Overall Assessment

The group's greatest strength (what it did most effectively) was _____.

The group's greatest weakness (what it needed to improve the most) was _____.

chapter 9

Leadership for Diversity
Appreciating and Harnessing the Power of Human Differences

Reflection 9.1

When I hear the word *diversity*, the first thoughts that come to mind are . . .

Leadership is challenging under any circumstances; it's never easy to take students where they might not be initially inclined to go. But leadership in the context of diversity is especially challenging because most of us tend to feel more comfortable, capable, and confident when we mentor others whose backgrounds and prior experiences are similar to our own. Research indicates that we are more likely to associate and develop relationships with others similar to us in backgrounds, beliefs, and interests, which scholars refer to as the "self-similarity principle" (Uzzi & Dunlap, 2005). However, our nation is diverse and will continue to grow more diverse throughout the remainder of the 21st century (U.S. Census Bureau, 2008). Effective leaders will need to lead in this context of diversity; you not only want to exert positive impact on as *many* people as possible, but also on as many *different* kinds of people as possible.

An important goal of almost all American colleges and universities is to have students experience and appreciate diversity. Peer leaders can play a pivotal role in achieving this goal by facilitating interaction among students from diverse groups. The primary objective of this chapter is to increase your competence and confidence with respect to promoting this interaction among diverse groups and providing effective peer leadership for students from diverse backgrounds.

Understanding Diversity

The word *diversity* derives from the Latin root *diversus*, meaning "various." Thus, human diversity refers to the variety of differences that exist among people who comprise humanity (the human species). In this chapter, we use the term *diversity* to refer primarily to differences among the major groups of people who, collectively, comprise humanity.

The relationship between humanity and human diversity may be described as similar to the relationship between sunlight and the spectrum of colors. Similar to how sunlight passing through a prism is dispersed into all groups of colors that comprise the visual spectrum, the human species spread across planet earth is dispersed into all groups of people that comprise the human spectrum (humanity). This relationship between diversity and humanity is depicted in **Figure 9.1**.

> We are all brothers and sisters. Each face in the rainbow of color that populates our world is precious and special. Each adds to the rich treasure of humanity.
>
> —Morris Dees, civil rights leader and co-founder of the Southern Poverty Law Center

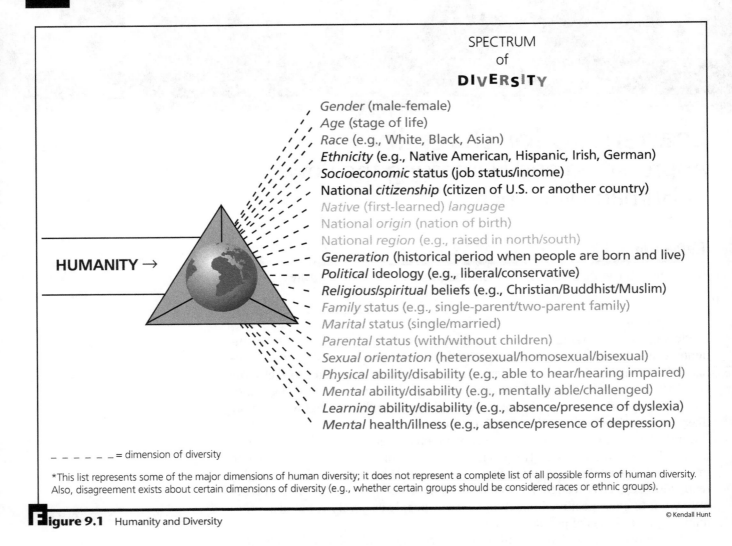

SPECTRUM
of
DIVERSITY

HUMANITY →

Gender (male-female)
Age (stage of life)
Race (e.g., White, Black, Asian)
Ethnicity (e.g., Native American, Hispanic, Irish, German)
Socioeconomic status (job status/income)
National *citizenship* (citizen of U.S. or another country)
Native (first-learned) *language*
National *origin* (nation of birth)
National *region* (e.g., raised in north/south)
Generation (historical period when people are born and live)
Political ideology (e.g., liberal/conservative)
Religious/spiritual beliefs (e.g., Christian/Buddhist/Muslim)
Family status (e.g., single-parent/two-parent family)
Marital status (single/married)
Parental status (with/without children)
Sexual orientation (heterosexual/homosexual/bisexual)
Physical ability/disability (e.g., able to hear/hearing impaired)
Mental ability/disability (e.g., mentally able/challenged)
Learning ability/disability (e.g., absence/presence of dyslexia)
Mental health/illness (e.g., absence/presence of depression)

_ _ _ _ _ _ = dimension of diversity

*This list represents some of the major dimensions of human diversity; it does not represent a complete list of all possible forms of human diversity. Also, disagreement exists about certain dimensions of diversity (e.g., whether certain groups should be considered races or ethnic groups).

Figure 9.1 Humanity and Diversity

© Kendall Hunt

As you can see in Figure 9.1, human diversity expresses itself in a multiplicity of ways, which include differences in external features, religious beliefs, mental and physical abilities, national origins, social backgrounds, gender, and sexual orientation. Some of these dimensions of diversity are obvious, others are subtle, and some are invisible.

Diversity and Humanity

It's important to realize that human variety and human similarity coexist and complement each other. Diversity involves appreciation of both similarities and differences (Public Service Enterprise Group, 2009). It includes appreciation of the unique perspectives of different groups of people, and appreciation of the universal aspects of the human experience that are common to all humans regardless of their particular cultural background. For example, despite our racial and cultural differences, all of us experience and express the same human emotions with the same facial expressions. (See **Figure 9.2.**)

Above all nations is humanity.
—Motto of the University of Hawaii

Humans all over the world display the same facial expressions when experiencing certain emotions. See if you can detect the emotions being expressed in the following faces. (To find the answers, turn your book upside down.)

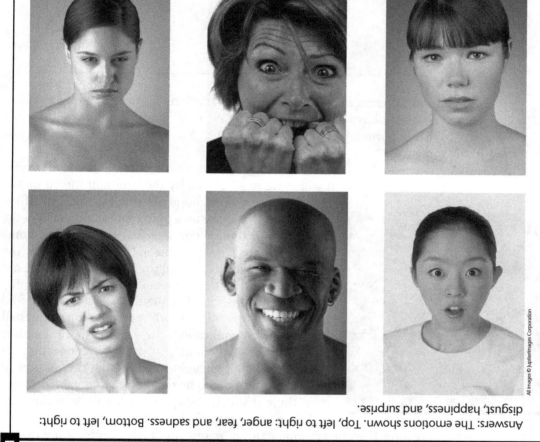

Answers: The emotions shown. Top, left to right: anger, fear, and sadness. Bottom, left to right: disgust, happiness, and surprise.

Figure 9.2

Other human characteristics that anthropologists have found to be shared by all groups of people in every corner of the world include storytelling, poetry, adornment of the body, dance, music, decoration of artifacts, families, socialization of children by elders, a sense of right and wrong, supernatural beliefs, and mourning of the dead (Pinker, 2000). Although different ethnic groups may express these shared experiences in different ways, these universal experiences are common to all humans.

Note well! *Diversity represents variations on the common theme of humanity. Although groups of humans may have different cultural backgrounds, they're still cultivated from the same soil—we're all grounded in the common experience of being human.*

Reflection 9.2

List three human experiences you think are universal—i.e., experienced by all humans in all cultures:

1.

2.

3.

> We are all the same, and we are all unique.
>
> —Georgia Dunston, African American biologist and research specialist in human genetics

Cultural differences may be viewed as variations on the same theme: being human. You may have heard the question "We're all human, aren't we?" The answer to this important question is "yes and no." Yes, we are all the same, but not in the same way.

A good metaphor for understanding this apparent contradiction is to visualize humanity as a quilt in which we're all united by the common thread of humanity—the universal bond of being human. The different patches that make up a quilt represent diversity—the distinctive or unique cultures that make up our common humanity. The quilt metaphor acknowledges the identity and beauty of all cultures. It differs from the old American "melting pot" metaphor, which viewed differences as something that should be melted down and eliminated, or the "salad bowl" metaphor that suggested America is a hodgepodge or mishmash of cultures thrown together without any common connection. In contrast, the quilt metaphor implies that the cultures of different groups are to be recognized and valued. However, these distinctive cultures can still be woven together to create a unified whole. This is captured in the Latin expression *E pluribus unum* ("Out of many, one")—the motto of the United States, which you'll find printed on all of its coins.

When we appreciate diversity in the context of humanity, we capitalize on the variety and beauty of our differences (diversity) while still preserving the power and strength of our unity (humanity).

© steven r. hendricks, 2013. Used under license of Shutterstock, Inc.

> We have become not a melting pot but a beautiful mosaic.
>
> —Jimmy Carter, 39th president of the United States and winner of the Nobel Peace Prize

Diversity and Individuality

It's important to keep in mind that the differences among individual groups are greater than the average differences between groups. For example, differences in physical attributes (e.g., height and weight) and behavior patterns (e.g., personality characteristics) across individuals within the same racial group are greater than any average differences that may exist between racial groups (Caplan & Caplan, 2009). We need to remain mindful of the fact that a great degree of individuality exists within any particular group and make a strong effort to know and treat others not as members of a group, but as unique individuals in their own right.

While it's valuable to learn about different cultures and common characteristics shared by members of the same culture, it shouldn't be done at the expense of ignoring individual differences among individuals who share the same culture. Don't assume that all individuals who share the same cultural background share the same personal characteristics.

As you proceed through this chapter, keep in mind the following distinctions among humanity, diversity, and individuality:

- **Diversity.** All humans are members of *different groups* (e.g., different gender and ethnic groups).
- **Humanity.** All humans are members of the *same group* (the human species).
- **Individuality.** All humans are *unique individuals* who differ from any other member of any group to which they may belong.

> *Every human is, at the same time, like all other humans, like some humans, and like no other human.*
> —Clyde Kluckholn, American anthropologist

Culture: Ties That Bind Us (and Sometimes Blind Us)

Culture may be defined as a distinctive pattern of beliefs and values learned by a group of people who share the same social heritage and traditions. In short, culture is the whole way in which a group of people has learned to live (Peoples & Bailey, 2008), including their style of speaking (language), fashion, food, art, music, values, and beliefs. Cultural differences can exist within the same society (multicultural society), within a single nation (domestic diversity), or across different nations (international diversity).

A major advantage of culture is that it helps bind us together into a supportive, tight-knit community. However, it can also blind us to other cultural perspectives. Since culture shapes the way people think, it can cause groups people from the same cultural groups to be *ethnocentric*—i.e., to view the world solely through their own cultural lens or frame of reference (Colombo, Cullen, & Lisle, 2010). Optical illusions are a good example of how cultural perspectives can blind us, or lead us to inaccurate perceptions. Compare the lengths of the two lines in **Figure 9.3**.

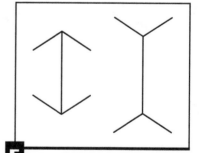

Figure 9.3   Optical Illusion

If you perceive the line on the right to be longer than the one on the left, your perception has been shaped by Western culture. Virtually all Americans and people from other Western cultures perceive the line on the right to be longer. However, both lines are actually equal in length. (If you don't believe it, take out a ruler and check it out.) Interestingly, this perceptual error isn't made by people from certain non-Western cultures whose architectural structures are primarily circular structures (e.g., huts or igloos), not the rectangular buildings with angled corners that characterize Western cultures (Segall, Campbell, & Herskovits, 1996).

The key point underlying this optical illusion is that cultural experiences shape and sometimes distort perceptions of reality. People think they are seeing things objectively or as they really are, but they're really seeing things subjectively from their particular cultural vantage point. Being open to the viewpoints of diverse people who perceive the world from different cultural vantage points widens our range of perception and helps us overcome our cultural blind spots. As a result, we tend to perceive the world around us with greater clarity and accuracy.

> *We see what is behind our eyes.*
> —Chinese proverb

The reality of our own culture is not the reality of other cultures. Our perceptions of the outside world are shaped (and sometime distorted) by our prior cultural experiences.

Effective leaders are open to reflection and critical examination of their own cultural perspective and are willing to commit themselves to exploring and understanding those of others. They open themselves and the students they lead to alternative perspectives, experiences, and possibilities.

Racial Diversity

A racial group (race) is a group of people who share distinctive physical traits, such as skin color or facial characteristics. The U.S. Census Bureau (2010) identifies four races: White, Black, Asian, and American Indian or Alaska Native. However, as Anderson and Fienberg (2000) caution, racial categories are social-political constructs (concepts) that are not based on scientific research but on classifications constructed by people. There continues to be disagreement among scholars about what groups of people constitute a human race or whether distinctive races exist (Wheelright, 2005). No identifiable set of genes distinguishes one race from another. In other words, you can't do a blood test or some type of internal genetic test to determine a person's race. Humans have simply decided to categorize people into races on the basis of certain external differences in physical appearance, particularly the color of their outer layer of skin. The U.S. Census Bureau could just as easily have divided people into categories based on such physical characteristics as eye color (blue, brown, and green) or hair texture (straight, wavy, curly, and frizzy).

The differences in skin color we now see among different human beings are largely due to biological adaptations that evolved over thousands of years among human groups living in different regions of the world under different climatic conditions. Darker skin tones developed among humans inhabiting and reproducing in hotter regions nearer the equator (e.g., Africans), where their darker skin color helped them adapt and survive by providing their bodies with better protection from the potentially damaging effects of the sun (Bridgeman, 2003). In contrast, lighter skin tones developed over time among humans inhabiting colder climates that were farther from the equator (e.g., Scandinavia), which enabled their bodies to absorb greater amounts of vitamin D supplied by sunlight that was in shorter supply in their region of the world (Jablonski & Chaplin, 2002).

While humans may display diversity in the color or tone of their outer layer of skin, the biological reality is that all members of the human species are remarkably similar. More than 98 percent of the genes that make up humans from different racial groups are exactly the same (Bridgeman, 2003; Molnar, 1991). This large amount of genetic overlap among humans accounts for the many similarities that exist among us, regardless of what differences in color appear on the surface of our skin. For example, all of us have similar external features that give us a "human" appearance and clearly distinguish us from other animal species; all humans have internal organs that are similar in structure and function; and whatever the color of our outer layer of skin, when it's cut, we all bleed in the same color.

Reflection 9.3

What race do you consider yourself to be? Would you say you identify strongly with your race, or are you rarely conscious of it?

Author's Experience My mother was from Alabama and was dark in skin color, with high cheek bones and long curly black hair. My father stood approximately six feet tall and had light brown straight hair. His skin color was that of a Western European with a slight suntan. If you didn't know that my father was of African American descent, you would not have thought of him as Black. All of my life I've thought of myself as African American, and all of the people who are familiar with me thought of me as African American. I've lived half of a century with that as my racial description. Several years ago, after carefully looking through records available on births and deaths in my family history, I discovered that fewer than 50 percent of my ancestors were of African lineage. Biologically, I'm not Black; socially and emotionally, I still am.

— *Aaron Thompson*

The old cliché is true: "You can't judge the book by its cover." However, books do come in different covers and there's different content between the covers. We need to look inside the cover to appreciate the unique content and character of each individual. However, we shouldn't ignore the cover and overlook the outside, because their outer appearance may have affected their personal experiences and may now be an integral element of their personal identity.

Ethnic Diversity

What is an ethnic group? It's simply a group of people who share the same culture. Thus, *culture* refers to what an ethnic group has in common and an *ethnic group* refers to people that share the same culture. Unlike members of a racial group, whose shared physical characteristics have been inherited, members of an ethnic group share similar cultural characteristics that have been learned through common social experiences. Thus, members of the same racial group may still be members of different ethnic groups. For instance, White Americans belong to the same racial group, but differ in terms of their ethnic group (e.g., French, German, Irish). However, members of ethnic minority groups who are White can more easily "blend into" or assimilate into the majority (dominant) culture because their minority status can't be visibly detected. When White minority immigrants of European ancestry came to America, a number of them even changed their last names to appear to be Americans of English descent—the majority group. In contrast, the immediately detectable minority status of African Americans, or darker-skinned Hispanics and Native Americans, doesn't allow them the option of presenting themselves as members of an already-assimilated majority group (National Council for the Social Sciences, 1991). Currently, the major cultural (ethnic) groups found within the United States include:

- Native Americans (American Indians)
  - Cherokee, Navajo, Hopi, Alaskan natives, Blackfoot, etc.

- European Americans (Whites)
  - Descendants from Western Europe (e.g., United Kingdom, Ireland, Netherlands), Eastern Europe (e.g., Hungary, Romania, Bulgaria), Southern Europe (e.g., Italy, Greece, Portugal), and Northern Europe or Scandinavia (e.g., Denmark, Sweden, Norway), etc.
- African Americans (Blacks)
  - Americans whose cultural roots lie in the continent of Africa (e.g., Ethiopia, Kenya, Nigeria) and the Caribbean Islands (e.g., Bahamas, Cuba, Jamaica), etc.
- Hispanic Americans (Latinos)
  - Americans with cultural roots in Mexico, Puerto Rico, Central America (e.g., El Salvador, Guatemala, Nicaragua), and South America (e.g., Brazil, Columbia, Venezuela), etc.
- Asian Americans
  - Americans who are cultural descendants of East Asia (e.g., Japan, China, Korea), Southeast Asia (e.g., Vietnam, Thailand, Cambodia), and South Asia (e.g., India, Pakistan, Bangladesh), etc.
- Middle Eastern Americans
  - Americans with cultural roots in Iraq, Iran, Israel, etc.

European Americans still are the majority ethnic group in the United States because they account for more than 50 percent of the American population. Native Americans, African Americans, Hispanic Americans, and Asian Americans are considered to be ethnic *minority groups* because each of these groups represents less than 50 percent of the American population.

Reflection 9.4

Which ethnic group(s) do you belong to or identify with?

What are the most common cultural values shared by your ethnic group(s)?

> *I'm the only person from my 'race' in class.*
>
> —Hispanic student commenting on why he felt uncomfortable being the only Latino in his class on Race, Ethnicity, and Gender

As with racial grouping, classifying humans into different ethnic groups can also be very arbitrary and subject to different interpretations. Currently, the U.S. Census Bureau classifies Hispanics as an ethnic group, not a race. However, among those who checked "some other race" in the 2000 Census, 97 percent were Hispanic. This finding suggests that Hispanic Americans consider themselves to be a racial group, probably because this is how they feel they're perceived and treated by non-Hispanics (Cianciotto, 2005). Supporting the Hispanic viewpoint that others perceive them as a race, rather than an ethnic group, is the recent use of the term *racial profiling* in the American media to describe Arizona's controversial 2010 law that allows police to target people who "look" like illegal aliens from Mexico, Central America, and South America. Again, this illustrates how race and ethnicity are subjective, socially constructed concepts that depend on how society perceives and treats certain social groups, which, in turn, affect how these groups perceive themselves.

This disagreement illustrates how difficult it is to conveniently categorize groups of people into particular racial or ethnic groups. The United States will continue to struggle with this issue because the ethnic and racial diversity of its population is growing and members of different ethnic and racial groups are forming cross-ethnic and interracial families. Thus, it is becoming progressively more difficult to place people into distinct categories based on their race or ethnicity. For example, by 2050, the number of people who will identify themselves as being of two or more races is projected to more than triple, growing from 5.2 million to 16.2 million (U.S. Census Bureau, 2008).

Author's Experience I am "White." I grew up in New Jersey in a predominantly "White" town. I am married to a "Black" woman and we have a racially "mixed" child (Lauren). The town we now live in is mostly, but not exclusively "White." I'm not sure how people perceive Lauren racially; I've never asked. Her best friend is "White." Her other good friend is "Latina." Another one of her friends is "Black." Who is Lauren Metz?

—*Greg Metz*

The ethnic and racial diversity of students in American colleges and universities is rapidly rising. In 1960, Whites made up almost 95 percent of the total college population; in 2005, that percentage had decreased to 69 percent. At the same time, the percentage of Asian, Hispanic, Black, and Native American students attending college increased (Chronicle of Higher Education, 2003).

International Diversity

Humans are members of a world that includes multiple nations. Communication and interaction across nations are now greater than at any other time in world history, largely because of rapid advances in electronic technology (Dryden & Vos, 1999). Economic boundaries between nations are also breaking down due to increasing international travel, international trading, and development of multinational corporations. The world of the 21st century is "flatter" (Friedman, 2005); it has become a "small world after all" and success in it requires an international perspective. By reaching out and learning from and about different nations, students become more than citizens of their own nation; they become cosmopolitan—citizens of the world. At the University of Oklahoma, domestic students adopt international students as their "cousins," welcome them to campus, and spend time with them during the academic year (Boren, 2008).

Gender Diversity

Gender traits and roles are reflective of social and cultural conventions, interests, and customs. While the characteristics associated with masculinity and femininity are socially ascribed, how rigidly we adhere to these definitions depends on the level at which we see these qualities in ourselves (Priest et al., 2012).

Gender characteristics are not exclusive to a single gender, nor are they set in stone. For example, would you consider a woman to be unfeminine if she were a semi-professional football player? Would you consider a man to be unmasculine if he were a nanny? These questions give us pause because certain behaviors and qualities socially define what's masculine and feminine, but these definitions are also open to our individual interpretation. A woman can be very feminine and also enjoy playing a sport that is typically played by men; a man can be very masculine and also enjoy fulfilling duties that are typically thought to be maternal (e.g., taking primary responsibility for child care). The characteristics we associate with gender also change over time and vary across cultures. Thus, be mindful, and remind your students to be mindful, that our interpretation of what's "feminine" and "masculine" depends on how strictly we adhere to traditional and cultural definitions of gender (Parker, 2009).

Sexual Diversity

Sexuality is another aspect of human diversity. Sexual diversity refers to the full range of human sexual experiences and identities; this range includes lesbians, gay men, bisexuals, transgender people, and heterosexuals. Campuses across the country are increasing their support for these groups and are creating centers and support services to assist them with their adjustment to campus life. These offices also play an important role in helping to reduce homophobia on campus and promote mutual respect for all types of sexual diversity.

As a peer leader, you can help promote awareness and acceptance of sexual diversity. One way to do so is by encouraging your college to invite guest speakers to campus who represent sexually diverse groups. For instance, to promote awareness and tolerance of groups with alternative sexual orientations and lifestyles, you could invite a panel of representatives from a chapter of the Parents and Friends of Lesbians and Gays (PFLAG). This is an international organization with almost 300 chapters in the United States, including at least one in every state. The organization consists of "parents, families and friends of lesbian, gay, bisexual, and transgender persons" and their goal is to "celebrate diversity and envision a society that embraces everyone, including those of diverse sexual orientations and gender identities." Trained panelists from this organization typically speak briefly about their experiences and then field questions from the audience. To increase your students' active involvement with the panel, ask them to bring one or two questions to ask the panelists in advance of their presentation. After the presentation, ask them to reflect on how they felt about the experience, what they learned from it, and what unanswered questions they may still have about it. (To locate a chapter of PFLAG in your geographical area, go to community.pflag.org/page.aspx?pid=803.)

Reflection 9.5

What diverse groups do you see represented on your campus?

Are there groups on campus that you did not expect to see or to see in such large numbers?

Are there groups on your campus that you expected to see but do not see or see in smaller numbers than you expected?

Empirical evidence shows that the actual effects on student development of emphasizing diversity and of student participation in diversity activities are overwhelmingly positive.

—Alexander Astin, *What Matters in College*

The wealth of diversity on college campuses today represents an unprecedented educational opportunity. You may never again be a member of a community that includes so many people from such a rich variety of backgrounds. Seize this opportunity! You're in the right place at the right time to experience the variety of people and programs that will enrich the breadth and depth of your learning, thinking, and preparation for post-college life. Below is a summary of the key benefits of experiencing diversity. Share this information with the students you lead to remind them that appreciating diversity is not just a slogan or the "politically correct" thing to do, but the educationally effective thing to do—for themselves and others.

The Benefits of Experiencing Diversity

Diversity Promotes Self-Awareness

Learning from people with diverse backgrounds and experiences sharpens our self-knowledge and self-insight by allowing us to compare and contrast our life experiences with others whose experiences differ sharply from our own. This comparative perspective gives us a reference point for viewing our own lives, placing us in a better position to see how our cultural backgrounds have influenced the development of our personal beliefs, values, and lifestyle. By viewing our lives in relation to the lives of others, we see more clearly what is distinctive about ourselves and how we may be uniquely advantaged or disadvantaged.

Note well! *The more opportunities you create to learn from others who are different than yourself, the more opportunities you create to learn about yourself.*

Diversity Strengthens Learning and Critical Thinking

Research consistently shows that we learn more deeply and think more critically through interaction with people different from ourselves than with people similar to ourselves (Pascarella, 2001; Pascarella & Terenzini, 2005). When our brains encounter something that's not very familiar or differs from what we're accustomed to, we must stretch beyond our mental comfort zone and work harder to understand it, because we're forced to compare and contrast it to what we are already familiar with (Acredolo & O'Connor, 1991; Nagda, Gurin, & Johnson, 2005). Stretching our minds to understand something that's unfamiliar requires extra psychological effort and energy, which results in a deeper, more powerful learning experience.

When all men think alike, no one thinks very much.

—Walter Lippmann, distinguished journalist and originator of the term *stereotype*

Diversity Promotes Creative Thinking

Experiences with diversity expose us to a wider range of thinking styles, enabling us to think outside the boundaries of our own cultural box. In contrast, limiting our number of cultural vantage points is akin to limiting the variety of mental tools we can use to solve new problems, thereby limiting our creativity. When like-minded people only associate with other like-minded people, they're unlikely to think outside the box and become more likely to engage in *groupthink*—the tendency for tight-knit groups of people to think so much alike that they overlook flaws in their thinking (Baron, 2005; Janis, 1982).

When different cultural perspectives are not sought out or tolerated, the variety of lenses available to us for viewing new problems is reduced, which, in turn, limits or shrinks our capacity for creative thinking. Creativity is more likely to be replaced by conformity or rigidity because ideas don't flow freely and divergently (in different directions); instead, ideas tend to converge and merge into the same cultural channel—the one shared by the culturally homogeneous group doing the thinking.

When the only tool you have is a hammer, you tend to see every problem as a nail.

—Abraham Maslow, psychologist, best known for his theory of human self-actualization

What I look for in musicians is generosity. There is so much to learn from each other and about each other's culture. Great creativity begins with tolerance.

—Yo-Yo Ma, French-born, Chinese-American virtuoso cellist, composer, and winner of multiple Grammy Awards

Diversity Education Is Career Preparation for the 21st Century

Learning about and from diversity has a very practical benefit: it better prepares students for their future work roles. Whatever line of employment college graduates may eventually pursue, they're likely to find themselves working with employers, co-workers, customers, and clients from diverse cultural backgrounds. America's workforce is now more diverse than at any other time in the nation's history, and it will grow ever more diverse throughout the 21st century. Howard Gardner, a renowned psychologist, suggests that to thrive in the economies and societies of the future, students will need to continually develop capabilities in five realms that he calls "minds," one of which is the "respectful mind"—awareness of and appreciation for differences among human beings (Gardner, 2006).

Author's Experience I was once involved in an informal discussion with a small group of engineering students who were bemoaning the accent of one of their professors. A colleague of mine who was also involved in the discussion noted that her husband worked in a multinational company that conducted business transactions with clients from China, India, and many other countries. She explained that if her husband complained about his business associates' accents, it would be viewed as cultural insensitivity and professionally incompetent. She advised the students, with humor but firmness, to get used to accents because work today takes place on a global game board.

— *Greg Metz*

Stereotyping: A Barrier to Diversity

The word *stereotype* derives from a combination of two roots: *stereo* ("to look at in a fixed way") and *type* ("to categorize or group together," as in the word *typical*). Thus, stereotyping is viewing individuals of the same type (group) in the same (fixed) way.

In effect, stereotyping ignores or disregards individuality. Instead, all people sharing the same group characteristic, such as race or gender, are viewed as having the same personal characteristics—as in the expression "You know how they are; they're all the same." Stereotypes involve *bias*, which literally means "slant." A bias can be slanted toward either the positive or negative. Positive bias results in favorable stereotypes (e.g., "Italians are great lovers."); negative bias leads to unfavorable stereotypes (e.g., "Italians are in organized crime."). Here are some other examples of stereotypes:

- Muslims are terrorists.
- Whites can't jump (or dance).
- Blacks are lazy.
- Asians are brilliant in math.
- Irish are alcoholics.
- Gay men are feminine; lesbian women are masculine.
- Jews are cheap.
- Hispanic men are abusive to women.
- Men are strong.
- Women are weak.

While few (if any) people would agree with the crass stereotypes noted above, most people do make subtle assumptions about individuals or groups of individuals. Such assumptions deprive others of their individuality, malign their group identity, and can interfere with their personal potential.

Author's Experience When I was six years old, I was told by another six-year-old from a different racial group that all people of my race could not swim. Since I couldn't swim at that time and she could, I assumed she was correct. When I asked a boy, who happened to be of the same racial group as that little girl, if that statement were true, he responded emphatically, "Yes, it's true!" Since I was from an area where few other African Americans were around to counteract this belief about Blacks, I bought into this stereotype until I finally took swimming lessons as an adult. I am now a lousy swimmer after many lessons because I didn't even attempt to swim until I was an adult. The moral of this story is that group stereotypes can limit the confidence and potential of individual members of the stereotyped group.

— *Aaron Thompson*

Reflection 9.6

Have you ever been stereotyped based on your appearance or group membership? If so, how did it make you feel and how did you react?

Have you ever unintentionally perceived or treated someone else in terms of a group stereotype rather than as an individual? What assumptions did you make about that person? Was that person aware of, or affected by, your stereotyping?

Keep in mind that leadership is the art of empowering people to broaden their possibilities and reach their full potential. Leaders should vigorously oppose stereotypes in all of their manifestations. If you witness stereotyping of any sort, step up and take a public stand against it. Your students may not want or need to hear you "lecture" them on harms of stereotyping. However, they may need to be at least gently reminded that all of us still have some cultural blind spots and that we need to make an intentional effort to interact with and learn from others as individuals—not as members of a stereotyped group. You can do this by periodically asking yourself and your students the following question when you're discussing issues that have diversity implications or consequences: "How may my cultural perspective, personal preferences, or personal biases influence my point of view on this issue?"

Prejudice

If virtually all members of a stereotyped group are judged or evaluated in a negative way, the result is *prejudice*. (The word *prejudice* literally means "to pre-judge.") Technically, prejudice may be either positive or negative; however, the term is most often associated with a negative prejudgment that involves *stigmatizing*—ascribing inferior or unfavorable traits to people who belong to the same group. Thus, *prejudice* may be defined as a negative judgment, attitude, or belief about another person or group of people that's formed before the facts are known. Stereotyping and prejudice often go hand in hand because individuals who are placed in a negatively stereotyped group are commonly prejudged in a negative way.

Those who are prejudiced toward a group typically avoid contact with individuals from that group. This enables the prejudice to continue unchallenged because there's little chance for the prejudiced person to have positive experiences with any member of the stigmatized group that could contradict or disprove the prejudice. Thus, a vicious cycle is established in which the prejudiced person continues to avoid contact with individuals from the stigmatized group, which, in turn, continues to maintain and reinforce the person's prejudice.

> 'See that man over there?'
> 'Yes.'
> 'Well, I hate him.'
> 'But you don't know him.'
> 'That's why I hate him.'
>
> —Gordon Allport, *The Nature of Prejudice* (1954)

Discrimination

Literally translated, the term *discrimination* means "division" or "separation." Whereas prejudice involves a belief or opinion, discrimination involves an *action* taken toward others. Technically, discrimination can be either negative or positive—for example, a discriminating eater may be careful about eating only healthy foods. However, the term is most often associated with a harmful act that results in a prejudiced person treating another person, or group of people, in an unfair way. Thus, it could be said that discrimination is prejudice put into action. Hate crimes are examples of extreme discrimination because they are acts motivated solely by prejudice against members of a stigmatized group.

Reflection 9.7

Prejudice and discrimination can be subtle and only begin to surface when the social or emotional distance among members of different groups grows closer. Honestly rate your level of comfort with the following situations.

Someone from another racial group:

1.	Going to your school	high	moderate	low
2.	Working in your place of employment	high	moderate	low
3.	Living on your street as a neighbor	high	moderate	low
4.	Living with you as a roommate	high	moderate	low
5.	Socializing with you as a personal friend	high	moderate	low

6. Being your most intimate friend or romantic partner   high   moderate   low
7. Being your partner in marriage   high   moderate   low

For any item you rated "low," why did you give it such a low rating?

_____

Box 9.1 contains a summary of biased attitudes, prejudicial beliefs, and discriminatory behaviors that must be overcome if humankind is to experience the full benefits of diversity. As you read through the list, place a checkmark next to any form of prejudice that you have experienced or that a family member or friend has experienced.

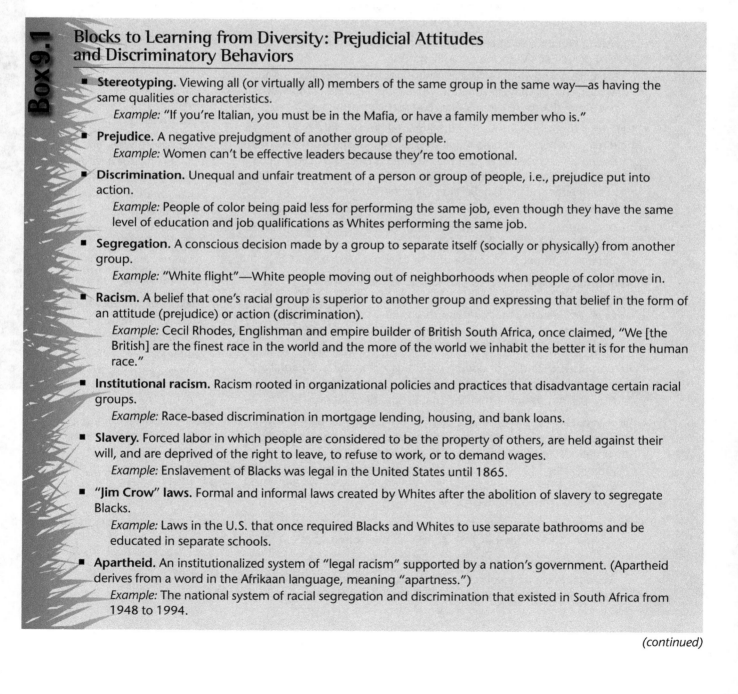

Box 9.1

Blocks to Learning from Diversity: Prejudicial Attitudes and Discriminatory Behaviors

- **Stereotyping.** Viewing all (or virtually all) members of the same group in the same way—as having the same qualities or characteristics.
    Example: "If you're Italian, you must be in the Mafia, or have a family member who is."

- **Prejudice.** A negative prejudgment of another group of people.
    Example: Women can't be effective leaders because they're too emotional.

- **Discrimination.** Unequal and unfair treatment of a person or group of people, i.e., prejudice put into action.
    Example: People of color being paid less for performing the same job, even though they have the same level of education and job qualifications as Whites performing the same job.

- **Segregation.** A conscious decision made by a group to separate itself (socially or physically) from another group.
    Example: "White flight"—White people moving out of neighborhoods when people of color move in.

- **Racism.** A belief that one's racial group is superior to another group and expressing that belief in the form of an attitude (prejudice) or action (discrimination).
    Example: Cecil Rhodes, Englishman and empire builder of British South Africa, once claimed, "We [the British] are the finest race in the world and the more of the world we inhabit the better it is for the human race."

- **Institutional racism.** Racism rooted in organizational policies and practices that disadvantage certain racial groups.
    Example: Race-based discrimination in mortgage lending, housing, and bank loans.

- **Slavery.** Forced labor in which people are considered to be the property of others, are held against their will, and are deprived of the right to leave, to refuse to work, or to demand wages.
    Example: Enslavement of Blacks was legal in the United States until 1865.

- **"Jim Crow" laws.** Formal and informal laws created by Whites after the abolition of slavery to segregate Blacks.
    Example: Laws in the U.S. that once required Blacks and Whites to use separate bathrooms and be educated in separate schools.

- **Apartheid.** An institutionalized system of "legal racism" supported by a nation's government. (Apartheid derives from a word in the Afrikaan language, meaning "apartness.")
    Example: The national system of racial segregation and discrimination that existed in South Africa from 1948 to 1994.

(continued)

- **Hate crimes.** Criminal action motivated solely by prejudice toward the crime victim.

    Example: Acts of vandalism or assault aimed at members of a particular ethnic group or persons with a particular sexual orientation.

- **Hate groups.** Organizations whose primary purpose is to stimulate prejudice, discrimination, or aggression toward certain groups of people based on their ethnicity, race, religion, etc.

    Example: The Ku Klux Klan—an American terrorist group that perpetrates hatred toward all non-White races.

- **Genocide.** Mass murder of a particular ethnic or racial group by another group.

    Example: The Holocaust during World War II, during which millions of Jews were systematically murdered. Other examples include the murder of Cambodians under the Khmer Rouge regime, the murder of Bosnian Muslims in the former country of Yugoslavia, and the slaughter of the Tutsi minority by the Hutu majority in Rwanda.

- **Classism.** Prejudice or discrimination based on social class, particularly toward people of low socioeconomic status.

    Example: Acknowledging the contributions made by politicians and wealthy industrialists to America, while ignoring the contributions of poor immigrants, farmers, slaves, and pioneer women.

- **Religious bigotry.** Denying the fundamental human right of people to hold religious beliefs, or hold religious beliefs that differ from one's own.

    Example: An atheist who forces non-religious (secular) beliefs on others, or a member of a religious group who believes that people who hold different religious beliefs are "sinners" whose souls will not be saved.

- **Anti-Semitism.** Prejudice or discrimination toward Jews or people who practice the religion of Judaism.

    Example: Hating Jews because they're the ones who "killed Christ."

- **Xenophobia.** Extreme fear or hatred of foreigners, outsiders, or strangers.

    Example: Believing that immigrants should be banned from entering the country because they'll undermine our economy and increase our crime rate.

- **Regionalism.** Prejudice or discrimination based on the geographical region in which an individual has been born and raised.

    Example: A northerner thinking that southerners are racists.

- **Jingoism.** Excessive interest and belief in the superiority of one's own nation without acknowledging its mistakes or weaknesses; it's often accompanied by an aggressive foreign policy that neglects the needs of other nations, or the common needs of all nations.

    Example: "Blind patriotism"—not seeing the shortcomings of our own nation and viewing any questioning or criticism of our nation as disloyalty or being "unpatriotic." (As in the slogans "America: right or wrong" or "America: love it or leave it!")

- **Terrorism.** Intentional acts of violence against civilians that are motivated by political or religious prejudice.

    Example: The September 11th attacks on the United States.

- **Sexism.** Prejudice or discrimination based on sex or gender.

    Example: Belief that women should not pursue careers in fields traditionally filled only by men (e.g., engineering) because they lack the natural qualities or skills to do them.

> *Most religions dictate that theirs is the only way, and without believing in it, you cannot enter the mighty kingdom of heaven. Who are we to judge? It makes more sense for God to be the only one mighty enough to make that decision. If other people could understand and see from this perspective, then many religious arguments could be avoided.*
>
> —First-year college student

> *Rivers, ponds, lakes, and streams—they all have different names, but they all contain water. Just as religions do—they all contain truths.*
>
> —Muhammad Ali, three-time world heavyweight boxing champion, member of the International Boxing Hall of Fame, and recipient of the Spirit of America Award as the most recognized American in the world

> *I would like to change the entire world, so that we wouldn't be segregated by continents and territories.*
>
> —College sophomore

- **Heterosexism.** Belief that heterosexuality is the only acceptable sexual orientation.
  - *Example:* Believing that gays should not have the same legal rights and opportunities as heterosexuals.

- **Homophobia.** Extreme fear or hatred of homosexuals.
  - *Example:* Engaging in "gay bashing" (acts of violence toward gays), or creating and contributing to anti-gay websites.

- **Ageism.** Prejudice or discrimination based on age, particularly toward the elderly.
  - *Example:* Believing that "old" people are bad drivers with bad memories who should not be allowed on the road.

- **Ableism.** Prejudice or discrimination toward people who are disabled or handicapped (physically, mentally, or emotionally).
  - *Example:* Avoiding social contact or interaction with people in wheelchairs.

Reflection 9.8

Have you, a family member, or a friend experienced any of the form(s) of prejudice in the above list? Why do you think it occurred?

Strategies for Overcoming Stereotypes and Prejudices

Described below are specific practices that you can model and share with students to help them open up to and appreciate groups toward whom they may hold prejudices, stereotypes, or other subtle biases.

Consciously avoid preoccupation with physical appearances. Go deeper and get beneath the superficial surface; judge people less on how they look and more on how they are and how they act. Remember the old proverb: "It's what's inside that counts." Be ready to judge others by their inner qualities, not by the familiarity or stereotypes associated with their outer features.

Make a conscious effort to perceive individuals of diverse groups as unique human beings. Form your impressions of others on a case-by-case basis, not according to some general rule of thumb. This may seem like an obvious and easy thing to do, but research shows that humans have a natural tendency to perceive individuals from unfamiliar groups as being more alike (or all alike) than members of their own group (Taylor, Peplau, & Sears, 2006). Thus, we need to make a conscious effort to counteract this tendency. While it's important to acknowledge and appreciate one's group identity, it's also important to validate and respect that person's individuality.

Take a stand against prejudice or discrimination by constructively disagreeing with those who make stereotypical statements or prejudicial remarks. By saying nothing, you may avoid conflict, but your silence may be perceived by others to mean that you agree with the person who made the prejudicial remark. Studies show that when members of the same group observe another member of their own group making prejudiced comments, the group's prejudice tends to increase,

Stop judging by mere appearances, and make a right judgment.
—Bible, John 7:24

The common eye sees only the outside of things, and judges by that. But the seeing eye pierces through and reads the heart and the soul.
—Samuel Clemens, a.k.a. Mark Twain, writer, lecturer, and humorist

I realize that I'm black, but I like to be viewed as a person, and this is everybody's wish.
—Michael Jordan, Hall of Fame basketball player

probably due to the pressure of group conformity (Stangor, Sechrist, & Jost, 2001). In contrast, if a person's prejudicial remark is challenged by a member of their own group, particularly a fellow member who is liked and respected, the person's prejudice tends to decrease, as does any similar prejudice held by other members of the group (Baron, Byrne, & Brauscombe, 2006). Thus, by taking a leadership role and not remaining silent when you hear someone make a prejudicial remark, you're likely to reduce that person's prejudice, and you may also reduce the prejudice of others who hear the remark.

Note well! *Appreciating diversity involves more than celebrating ethnic holidays and traditions. It's about being ethical and inclusive and promoting social justice.*

Promoting Interaction and Collaboration among Members of Diverse Groups

Colleges and universities have attempted to promote diversity awareness and appreciation primarily through *access*, i.e., recruiting more diverse students to campus. The assumption underlying this approach is that the mere presence of diverse students on campus will result in positive interaction between minority and majority groups and promote positive inter-group relationships. However, research strongly suggests that simply increasing minority students' access to college and increasing their exposure to majority students doesn't automatically lead to interracial interaction and intercultural appreciation. Something more than mere exposure to minority group members must occur in order to stimulate intercultural contact and multicultural appreciation. As a peer leader, you're in a pivotal position to make this type of intercultural interaction take place by (1) stepping out of your comfort zone and approaching students whose backgrounds are different than your own, and (2) creating opportunities for your students to associate with others from diverse backgrounds. For instance, you can:

- Openly approach, welcome, and engage with students who are different than you.
- Supportively encourage the involvement of student groups who you think may be feeling left out or ostracized.
- Be mindful of whether the groups you form include diverse membership.
- Invite a diversity of students to join your groups or organizations.
- Introduce your students to diversity issues and discussions.
- Encourage all students to welcome others who are "different," particularly if you sense they're uncomfortable about doing so.
- Encourage students to expand their social networks and broaden the range of people with whom they choose to interact.
- Get diverse students working together—e.g., in study groups or on community service projects. (Spending time together working toward a common goal tends to generate a sense of unity and community.)
- Host group celebrations of accomplishments; invite everybody and make a special effort to encourage attendance of students from minority groups.

In addition, you can use the following specific practices to increase interpersonal contact and opportunities to learn with (and from) student diversity.

Make an intentional attempt to interact and collaborate with members of diverse groups. Social contact with diverse students goes beyond simple awareness and tolerance; it moves us up to a higher level of diversity appreciation that involves intercultural interaction. When we take this step across cultural boundaries, we transform diversity appreciation from a personal conviction to an interpersonal commitment.

How comfortable students are with the idea of interacting with people from diverse groups is likely to depend on how much experience they've had with diversity before college. If the students you're leading or mentoring have had little or no prior experience interacting with members of diverse groups, it may be more challenging for them to initiate interactions with diverse students on campus. However, the good news is that those are the students who will benefit the most from interacting and collaborating with members of other ethnic or racial groups. Research consistently shows that when we have new social experiences that differ radically from our prior experiences, we gain the most in terms of learning and cognitive development (Acredolo & O'Connor, 1991; Piaget, 1985). In a national study of peer leaders, it was found that interaction and conversations with others from different cultural backgrounds was the best predictor of leadership development in college (Dugan & Komives, 2007).

> *I've learned that not everyone always agrees with you on everything that you have to say . . . that builds your character. Everyone in the world is not raised like me. There is a whole world out there. I think you need to learn to adapt.*
> —Peer leader, cited in Harmon (2006)

Reflection 9.9

Rate the amount or variety of diversity you have experienced in the following settings:

1. The high school you attended	high	moderate	low
2. The college or university you now attend	high	moderate	low
3. The neighborhood in which you grew up	high	moderate	low
4. Places where you've worked or been employed	high	moderate	low

Which settings had the *most* and the *least* diversity?

What do you think accounts for this difference?

By intentionally placing yourself in situations where individuals from diverse groups are physically nearby, you can create opportunities for social interaction, collaboration, and potential friendships with individuals from diverse groups. Research indicates that meaningful interactions and friendships are more likely to form among people who are in physical proximity to one another (Back, Schmukle, & Egloff, 2008; Latané et al., 1995). You can create this condition in the college classroom by sitting near students from different ethnic and racial groups, or by joining in class discussion groups and group projects. You can also increase your contact with diverse students by visiting resource centers or joining clubs and organizations on campus where these students are likely to congregate (e.g., Multicultural Affairs Center; international student organizations).

Take advantage of the Internet to chat with students from diverse groups. Electronic communication may be a more convenient and comfortable way for students to initially interact with members of diverse groups with whom they've have had little prior experience. After they've communicated successfully online, they may feel more comfortable about interacting in person.

Seek out the views and opinions of classmates from diverse backgrounds. During or after class discussions, ask students from different backgrounds if there was any point made or position taken in class that they would strongly question or challenge. Seeking out divergent (diverse) viewpoints has been found to be one of the best ways to develop critical thinking skills (Inoue, 2005; Kurfiss, 1988). As a peer leader, you can demonstrate academic leadership with respect to diversity during class discussions by ensuring that the ideas of people from minority groups are included, heard, and respected. Encourage and reinforce the contributions of students who may be reluctant to speak up because of their minority status. Having members from different races and cultures on the small-group discussion teams in class has the potential to reduce prejudice and promote intercultural appreciation, but only if each member's cultural identity and perspective is sought and acknowledged as a community member, rather than remaining isolated or ignored (Baron, Byrne, & Brauscombe, 2006).

> *The classroom can provide a 'public place' where community can be practiced.*
>
> —Susanne Morse, author, *Renewing Civic Capacity: Preparing College Students for Service and Citizenship*

If there is little diversity in your discussion group, encourage group members to look at the topic or issue they're discussing from diverse perspectives. For instance: "If there were international students here, what might they be adding to our discussion?" or "If members of certain minority groups were here, would they offer a different viewpoint?"

Intentionally form out-of-class study groups with students from diverse backgrounds. You might begin by forming study groups with students who are different in one way but similar in other ways. For instance, learning teams may be formed among students who have the same major, but who differ in terms of race, ethnicity, or age. This strategy gives the diverse members of the team some common ground for discussion (their major) and can raise the team's awareness that although their group membership may be diverse, they can at the same time have strikingly similar educational plans and life goals.

Serve as a *community builder* by identifying similarities or recurring themes in the different ideas and experiences of students from varied backgrounds. Look for common denominators—themes of unity that underlie diversity. Regardless of their particular group, all humans live in communities, develop relationships, have emotional needs, and undergo life experiences that affect their self-esteem and personal identity. Individuals from different ethnic and racial groups still share many common characteristics as citizens of the same country, persons of the same gender, or members of the same generation. As you look for and learn from diversity, don't overlook the unity that transcends human differences, and use it to build community.

Focusing exclusively on our differences without detecting the underlying similarities may lead to feelings of isolation, separation, or divisiveness among diverse groups. In fact, some studies show that when diversity education focuses on differences alone, minority groups are likely to feel even more isolated (Smith, 1997). To minimize this risk, we need to dig below the surface and unearth the common ground from which our differences grow. One way you can do this is by raising student awareness of the universal themes that unite different groups under the single umbrella of humanity. For instance, before launching students into a discussion of diversity, it may be a good idea to first discuss the common elements of all cultures (language, family, food, fashion, musical and artistic expression, etc.), or the common dimensions of the human self and human development (described in Chapter 7, p. 176). Taking time to initially point out our commonalities can help defuse potential feelings of divisiveness by providing a common ground upon which an open and honest discussion of diversity can be built.

Form collaborative learning teams. A learning team differs from a discussion group or a study group. It moves beyond discussion to collaboration—its members become teammates who "co-labor" (work together) as part of a joint and mutually supportive effort to reach the same team goal. Studies show that when individuals from different ethnic and racial groups work collaboratively toward the attainment of a common goal, racial prejudice is reduced and interracial friendships are promoted (Allport, 1954; Amir, 1976; Brown et al., 2003; Dovidio, Eller, & Hewstone, 2011). These positive developments probably take place because when individuals from diverse groups work on the same team, a social environment is created in which no one is a member of an "out" group ("them"); they're all members of the same "in" group ("us") (Pratto et al., 2000; Sidanius et al., 2000). Research also shows that the most effective leaders are those who enable individuals to see themselves as members of the same group and to see that when they work to advance the group's goals, they're also working to advance their personal goals (Bass & Riggio, 2005). For specific strategies on how to form and lead diverse learning teams, see Box 9.2.

Box 9.2 — Tips for Teamwork: Creating Diverse and Effective Learning Teams

1. **Intentionally form diverse learning teams comprised of students from different cultural backgrounds and life experiences.** Teaming up only with friends or classmates whose lifestyles and experiences are similar to your own can actually impair your team's performance. Your similar experiences can cause your learning team to get off track and onto topics that have nothing to do with the learning task (for example, what you did last weekend or what you're planning to do next weekend).

2. **Have your team identify a clear, common goal.** Your team should create a final product that represents their unified effort and accomplishment (e.g., a completed sheet of answers to questions, a list or chart of specific ideas). A collectively created end product helps individual members function as "we" rather than "me," and helps the team stay on task and moving in the same direction toward their common goal.

3. **All teammates should be given equal opportunity and personal responsibility for contributing to the team's final product.** Each team member should be responsible for making a specific contribution to the team's final product, such as contributing a piece of information to the team's work topic or project (e.g., a specific chapter from the textbook or a particular section of class notes), as if each teammate is bringing a different piece or part that's needed to complete the puzzle.

4. **All teammates should work interdependently—they should depend on or rely upon each other to achieve their common goal.** As on a sports team, each member of a learning team should have a specific role to play. For instance, each teammate could assume one of the following roles:

   ■ Manager, whose role is to assure that the team stays on track and moving toward their goal.
   ■ Moderator, whose role is to ensure that all teammates have equal opportunity to contribute.
   ■ Summarizer, whose role is to monitor the team's progress and identify what's been accomplished and what still needs to be done.
   ■ Recorder, whose role is to keep a written record of the team's ideas.

(continued)

Teammates may also assume roles that involve contributing a particular form of thinking to the learning task (e.g., analysis, synthesis, or application) or bringing a different perspective to the final product (e.g., cultural, national, or international).

5. **Before delving into the work task, teammates should take some social "warm-up" time to interact informally with one another.** Giving team members the opportunity to learn each other's names, backgrounds, and interests will enable them to become comfortable with each other and develop a sense of team solidarity or identity; this is particularly important to do when group members come from diverse (and unfamiliar) cultural backgrounds. Once they get to know each other as individuals, they should feel much more comfortable about sharing their personal thoughts and different viewpoints when they embark on their group task.

6. **Teamwork should take place in a friendly, informal setting.** The context or atmosphere in which group work takes place can influence the nature and quality of interaction among team members. People are more likely to work openly and collaboratively when they are in an environment that is conducive to relationship building. For instance, a living room or a lounge area provides a warmer and friendlier team-learning atmosphere than a sterile classroom.

When contact among people from diverse groups takes place under the above conditions of collaboration and teamwork, group work has the greatest potential for having positive impact on learning and diversity appreciation. A win-win scenario is created; learning is strengthened, and at the same time, prejudice is weakened.

References: Allport (1979); Amir (1969); Aronson, Wilson, & Akert (2009); Brown & Hewstone (2005); Cook (1984); Sherif et al. (1961).

Note well! Working in diverse learning groups not only provides social variety, it also elevates the quality of team learning by allowing group members to tap into the multiple perspectives and life experiences of people from diverse backgrounds.

Summary and Conclusion

Diversity refers to differences among groups of people who, together, comprise humanity. Experiencing diversity increases appreciation of the features unique to different cultures while providing a panoramic perspective on the human experience that's shared by all people, no matter what their particular culture happens to be.

Culture refers to the beliefs and values of a group with the same traditions and social heritage. It helps bind people into supportive, tight-knit communities. However, culture can also lead its members to view the world solely through their own cultural lens—known as *ethnocentrism*—which can blind them to other cultural perspectives. Ethnocentrism can contribute to *stereotyping*—viewing individual members of the same group in the same way and seeing all of them as having the same personal characteristics.

Prejudice is a biased prejudgment about another person or group of people that's formed before the facts are known. Stereotyping and prejudice often go hand in hand because if the stereotype is negative, individual members of the stereotyped group are then prejudged negatively. *Discrimination* takes prejudice one step further by converting the negative prejudgment into action that results in treating others unfairly. Thus, discrimination is prejudice in action. Once stereotyping, prejudice, and discrimination are overcome, students are ready to experience diversity and reap its multiple benefits, which include sharper self-awareness, deeper learning, critical and creative thinking, and career preparation for the 21st century.

As a peer leader, the increasing diversity of students on campus presents you with an unprecedented opportunity to infuse diversity into your college experience and your peer leadership experiences. Seize this opportunity and capitalize on the power of diversity by reaching out to students from diverse groups, facilitating inter-group interaction, and creating diverse learning teams on campus. This chapter contains multiple strategies for helping you do just that; by so doing, you'll enrich the quality of the college experience for your students and magnify the power of your impact as a peer leader.

Internet Resources

For additional information related to the ideas discussed in this chapter, we recommend the following websites:

Combating Stereotypes, Prejudice, and Discrimination
www.tolerance.org

Preservation of Human Rights Worldwide
www.amnesty.org

Cross-Cultural Communication
www.pbs.org/ampu/crosscult.html

Exercise 9.1 *Journal Reflections*

1. Has your life been affected by your race, economic background, gender, or sexual orientation? What other aspects of diversity have contributed to the person you are today?

2. a. Can you think of a time in your life when you were initially uncomfortable with (or just very unfamiliar with) people from a certain type of background, but then became more comfortable with them once you got to know them?

   b. What happened to change your feelings or perceptions?

   c. What can you do as a leader to stimulate similar transformations in others?

3. To what extent do diverse groups mix on your campus (not at all, moderately, frequently, all of the time)? What factors contribute to and detract from their level of interaction?

4. What student group on campus would you say you feel least comfortable or confident leading or mentoring right now? Why?

5. Consider a group that you formally lead or one that you informally influence. What is a practical step you could take to broaden your group members' exposure to diversity? What type of experience or activity could you initiate and how could you get students to "buy in"?

6. Identify a group on campus that you think is most isolated or segregated. What might be one thing you could do as a peer leader to help these students become better connected to the campus community as a whole?

Exercise 9.2 *Gaining Awareness of Multi-Group Identities*

We can be members of multiple groups at the same time, and our membership in these overlapping groups can influence our personal development and self-identity. In the figure that follows, consider the shaded center circle to be yourself and the six non-shaded circles to be six groups you belong to that you think have influenced your personal development or personal identity.

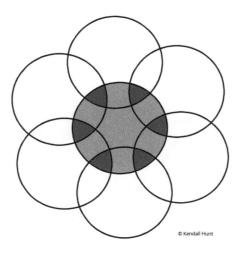

© Kendall Hunt

Fill in the non-shaded circles with the names of groups to which you belong that have had the most influence on your personal development. You can use the diversity spectrum that appears in Figure 9.1 on page 236 of this chapter to help you identify different groups. You don't have to come up with six groups and fill all six circles. What's important is to identify those groups that have had a major influence on your development and identity.

Self-Assessment Questions

1. Which of the groups you identified has had the greatest influence on your personal identity? Why?

2. Have you ever felt limited or disadvantaged by being a member of any particular group(s)?

3. Have you ever felt that you experienced advantages or privileges because of your membership in any group(s)?

E xercise 9.3 *Hidden Bias Test*

Go to www.tolerance.org/activity/test-yourself-hidden-bias and take one or more of the hidden bias tests on the website. These tests assess subtle bias with respect to gender, age, Native Americans, African Americans, Asian Americans, religious denominations, sexual orientations, disabilities, and body weight. The site allows you to assess whether you have a bias toward any of these groups.

Self-Assessment Questions

1. Did the results reveal any bias that you were unaware of?

2. Did you think the assessment results were accurate or valid?

3. What do you think best accounts for or explains your results?

4. If the students you lead or mentor were to take this test, how do you think their results would compare with yours?

Exercise 9.4 *Intercultural Interview*

Identify a student, faculty member, or administrator on campus whose cultural background differs from your own and ask if you could interview that person about his or her culture. Use the following questions in your interview:

1. How is "family" defined in your culture, and what are the traditional roles and responsibilities of different family members?

2. What are the traditional gender (male vs. female) roles associated with your culture? Are they changing?

3. What is your culture's approach to time? Is there an emphasis on punctuality? Is moving quickly and getting things done rapidly valued more than reflection and deliberation?

4. What are your culture's staple foods and favorite beverages?

5. What cultural traditions or rituals are highly valued and commonly practiced?

6. What special holidays are celebrated?

chapter 10

Organizational Leadership
Making Change at a College-Wide Level

Reflection 10.1

What do you think is the most important change that needs to be made on your campus to improve student learning, satisfaction, or enthusiasm for the college experience? As a peer leader, what role (if any) could you play to make this change happen?

An effective student leader goes beyond inspiring and encouraging students to stay in school, get good grades, and graduate. Obviously, all of that matters, but leadership is also demonstrated by producing positive change in the organizations and communities of which you are a member. Leaders can promote positive change not only among individuals, but also in organizations and institutions as well. As a student leader, you may be in a position to see the "big picture" and make a big difference in your student organization and your college as a whole.

What Is Organizational Leadership?

A group of 84 scholars, representing more than 60 countries from all regions of the world, reached consensus on the following definition of *organizational leadership*: "The ability of an individual to influence, motivate, and enable others to contribute toward the effectiveness and success of the organization of which they are members" (House et al., 2004, p. 15).

Compared to group leadership, organizational leadership typically takes place on a wider scale and involves (1) leading a larger number of constituents (e.g., 20 or more), (2) leading a collection of groups rather than a collection of individuals, and (3) interacting with leaders of other student groups and organizations (Komives, Lucas, & McMahon, 2007). In an extensive study of leadership identity development among college students, it was found that peer leaders' view of the student groups to which they belonged and led tended to change over time: at first, they perceived these groups as collections of individuals, but they eventually began to view these groups as integral parts of a larger organizational system (Komives et al., 2005).

Acquiring Organizational Knowledge

Effective organizational leadership requires knowledge and understanding of the larger system in which your particular organization operates. You can begin to

Knowledge is power.
—Francis Bacon, influential English philosopher and advocate for the scientific pursuit of knowledge

acquire this knowledge by learning how your college or university is organized and how "the system" works, so that you can "work the system" to make it work for your leadership cause.

Note well!   *The more you know about how things run, the more likely you are to get things done.*

Here are some specific steps you can take to gain knowledge of how your campus is organized and how it operates:

- Become familiar with your college's table of organization (organizational chart) that lays out who the decision makers are, what positions they occupy, and what the formal chain of command is—from top to bottom. Become aware of the formal positions, rules, and regulations that characterize your campus. Learn about the processes through which individuals on the lower levels of the organizational structure gain access to high-ranking decision makers.

- Learn about the mission and purpose of other student organizations on campus by reviewing your *Student Handbook*. (We encourage you to complete Exercise 10.2 at the end of the chapter.)

- Read the campus newspaper to keep up with current issues, events, and opportunities. Many campuses now send out periodic e-newsletters; if your campus does, make sure you are subscribed and read it regularly.

- Immerse yourself in your campus culture by hanging out in those places on campus where students, faculty, advisors, staff, etc., tend to gather. Keep your "ear to the ground" and listen closely to what members of your campus community are saying. Pay particular attention to discrepancies between student views of the campus and the views of faculty, staff, or administrators.

- You can make connections between your student organization and the larger campus system by:
  a. Researching and reporting back to members of your organization on matters of interest and importance to them (e.g., campus-wide initiatives that affect their life on campus, their activities, or their programs).
  b. Representing your organization in wider forums (e.g., serving as a member of a college committee comprised of leaders from other campus organizations).
  c. Interacting with leaders of other organizations on campus to discuss the possibility of engaging in joint projects and sharing resources.

Organizational Mission

A mission typically consists of a set of statements that spell out (1) what an organization values, (2) organizational goals related to its values, and (3) how the organization attempts to embody and live its values in its day-to-day actions. As a peer leader, your personal actions and the actions of your student organization should be consistent with the mission of your institution. Always keep your organization's mission in sight, do your best to live it in your daily actions, and encourage other members of your organization to do the same.

Reflection 10.2

What is your student organization's stated *mission* or purpose?

What connections do you see between the mission of your college and the mission of the student organization you lead?

Organizational Vision

While *mission* refers to what the organization stands for and the goals it's currently pursuing, *vision* refers to what the organization aspires to be in the future. Like leading groups, leading organizations involves formulating a vision for the members and engaging them in the process of creating an organizational vision. One simple way to get this process started is by asking your constituents, "What would it take to make this organization great?" (Komives, Lucas, & McMahon, 2007, p. 322).

The vision of your organization should reflect the mission of your campus, but it should also reflect your group's unique identity, purpose, and aspirations. Effective organizational leaders enable members to see how their personal aspirations align with the aspirations of their organization. You can do so by asking your members, "What are you hoping to get out of this organization or what would you like this organization to do for you?" Use this input to create a shared vision for your organization, communicate it early and often, and periodically invite open and honest discussion of it to ensure that no one forgets it and everyone continues to live by it.

Leadership, Power, and Decision Making

Since you occupy a formal leadership place in your organization, you are a "positional leader"—i.e., the position you hold supplies you with certain power or decision-making authority (Komives et al., 2007). Make it clear to members of your organization how the decision-making process will work, what legitimate decision-making authority is vested in your leadership position, and how you intend to use it. This is critical because students are likely to have different ideas about how positional leaders should lead and exert their power. Research supports the theory of "implicit leadership" (Lord, Brown, & Frieberg, 1999; Lord & Maher, 1991), which stipulates that the more a leader's self-expectations fit the organizational members' implicit (assumed) expectations of what their leader should be, the more likely it is that the leader will be accepted and effective (Lord & Emrich, 2001).

There are two basic ways or styles in which leaders can use their power to make decisions: (1) *authoritarian* (autocratic) decision making, or (2) *participative* (democratic) decision making. The differences between these decision-making styles are described below.

1. *Authoritarian* (autocratic) decision making. Authoritarian or autocratic leaders make decisions independently, with little or no input from the rest of the group. There are likely to be occasions where you will have to make deci-

sions this way because you may have access to information that other members of your organization don't have, or because time constraints require a decision be made quickly and at a time when your group isn't available to convene. There may also be occasions when you have to take charge and choose a particular course of action because it's simply the right or ethical thing to do (Shankman & Allen, 2008).

That being said, authoritarian decision making should be your last resort. This style of decision making should not be used routinely because it can easily be abused and result in the leader being viewed as controlling, bossy, or dictatorial (Cherry, 2012). As the old saying goes, "Don't let power go to your head." Whenever and wherever possible, consult with members of your organization and include them in the decision-making process by engaging in "participative leadership."

2. *Participative* (democratic) decision-making. In contrast to an authoritarian leader who says, "Here's what we're going to do," a participative leader says, "I offer you this idea for your consideration." As the leader of your organization, you may have the ultimate authority and the final say, but you can exercise your formal authority in an *authoritative* but non-authoritarian manner by:

- Sharing information with your constituents before making a final and binding decision.
- Consulting with your constituents and allowing them to play an advisory role in the decision-making process.
- Carefully considering your constituents' input and factoring it into your final decision.
- If you cannot accept or act on your constituents' input or ideas, providing them with the reasons why (see **Box 10.1** for decision-making criteria you can use to judge the quality of ideas and recommendations presented to you).

Effective peer leaders are facilitators, not dictators. They welcome input from their constituents and use "*referent*" power"—i.e., they harness power through relationships they form with members of their own organization and leaders of other organizations; they exercise power through collaboration rather than command or control (French & Raven, 1959). Some leaders may resist collaborative decision making because they fear losing control or authority (Schroeder, 2005). However, effective leaders are more often those who share decision making by allowing those they lead to have some degree of influence on or input into their decisions. When people affected by a decision are involved in the process of making the decision, the quality of that decision improves because multiple voices are heard, multiple viewpoints are considered, and "multiple partial solutions" are generated (Kelly, 1994). In addition, the decision reached is more likely to be enthusiastically endorsed and implemented by the group because they "own" it (Yukl, 2012).

Box 10.1

Criteria for Evaluating Arguments and Making Decisions

Good leadership decisions are made after different options have been carefully considered, weighed, and evaluated. Here are some criteria you may use to judge the quality of ideas and recommendations offered to you by members of your organization:

- Logical consistency. Does the idea simply make good sense? Does it begin with a premise that's true or reasonable (as opposed to a questionable assumption) and does the conclusion logically follow or flow from the premise?
- Empirical evidence. Is the idea backed by factual information or research findings?
- Feasibility. Is the idea practical to implement and cost-effective?
- Ethicality. Is implementing the idea the right, just, or moral thing to do?
- Impact. Is the idea likely to result in significant change or have an immediate impact?

Another method you can use to reach reasoned decisions is known as a SWOT Analysis, which involves considering the following aspects of an idea or proposal:

- **S**trengths: What are its *advantages* relative to other ideas that have been proposed?
- **W**eaknesses (or Limitations): What are its *disadvantages* compared with other ideas that have been proposed?
- **O**pportunities: What in the external environment may be used to *increase* the decision's probability of implementation or its effectiveness? (For example: Are there opportunities to collaborate with other groups or organizations to make it happen or increase its impact?)
- **T**hreats: What aspects of the external environment may *interfere* with or block the decision's implementation or impact (e.g., lack of support from other student organizations or campus administrators)?

If, after carefully considering all the pros, cons, and consequences of the decision, you still cannot draw a firm conclusion, consider discussing it with a neutral third party (e.g., another peer leader). Sometimes just the process of verbalizing your thoughts with someone else can help you discover the best decision to make.

Reflection 10.3

Would you say that the majority of leaders you've observed are participative (democratic) or authoritarian (autocratic) decision makers?

Which of these two decision-making styles would you feel more comfortable using? Why?

Reaching Decisions through Group Consensus

Participative leadership can be put into practice in two major ways: by voting or by consensus. As you already know, decision making by voting is simply a matter of the "majority rules," i.e., the choice that receives the largest number of votes is the choice that's made.

In contrast to voting—which is a competitive process in which the majority wins and the minority loses—*consensus* is a collaborative decision-making process in which the group strives to reach the best possible decision for all its members. The word *consensus* means "to feel together" and "consent." Giving consent doesn't necessarily mean that the idea being considered is everyone's ideal choice. However, they consent to move forward with the idea because it's the one that the group as a whole agrees is the best possible course of action it can agree to take at this particular time (Saint & Lawson, 1994).

Consensus is reached when all members can say, "This is a group decision I can live with." The consensus-building process involves considerable discussion about the pros and cons of different options, ensures that everyone is heard (including those who oppose the majority's opinion), and requires that everyone agrees to support the decision (Hartnett, 2011). Thus, reaching consensus is a more time-consuming process than simply taking a vote. However, because it's a process that accepts input from all members and generates as much agreement as possible, it has the following major advantages: (1) it promotes buy-in from all members, (2) it's likely to result in greater collaboration among members when the decision is implemented, and (3) it builds stronger group cohesion and a sense of community among members of the organization (Kaner, 2011).

Specific procedures you may use to help members of your organization reach consensus are described in **Box 10.2**.

Box 10.2

Procedures for Reaching Consensus

Nominal Group Process

1. Have the group generate a list of options.
2. Ask each member to pick three top options and rank them in order of priority or desirability (3 = highest; 1 = lowest).
3. Add up the numbers (rankings) for all options and list them on a flip chart or screen.
4. Ask members whether they can accept the highest-ranked option. If some members cannot accept it, ask them to explain why, and then repeat the process for a second round.
5. Ask members if they can live with the top option generated on the second round. If they cannot, ask if them if they can accept the first or second option, and proceed with the option that's more acceptable to them.

Multi-Voting Technique

1. The group generates a list of options.
2. All members vote to accept or reject each option.
3. The options that receive acceptance votes from more than one-half of the members are kept on the list for a second round of voting.
4. On the second round of voting, each member votes to accept no more than half the options listed.
5. The options that receive acceptance votes from more than one-half of the members stay on the list for a third and final round of voting.
6. Each member now votes for only one item. The option receiving the highest number of votes should be acceptable to all members of the group, and thus, consensus is achieved.

Finger Voting

This procedure can be used to reach consensus quickly on a single idea or proposal.

1. Members review the proposed idea and agree that they understand what it involves.
2. Each member raises one to five fingers depending on how strongly they agree with it (5 = I'm enthusiastic about it; 4 = I'm for it; 3 = I'm not sure yet; 2 = I have reservations about it; 1 = I'm strongly opposed to it).
3. If all members raise four or five fingers, consensus is achieved. If not, members who raised one to three fingers are allowed to express their questions, their objections, and what it would take for them to accept the proposal.
4. After everyone's questions and objections have been heard and considered, the process is repeated to see if consensus can be reached in round two.

If your group cannot reach consensus within the time frame you have to reach a decision, as your organization's leader, you will have to step up, thank the group for its effort, and make an authoritative decision that best respects and incorporates the ideas shared during the consensus-seeking process.

Facilitating group decision making can be a challenging process, particularly when leading a large group, which is often the case for leaders of organizations. Although the process can be arduous and may test your patience, remember; research shows that decisions that follow a well-conducted group discussion are almost always more effective and creative than decisions made individually or autocratically (Gunnarsson, 2010; Hall, 1971; Proctor, 2011).

Reflection 10.4

How do members of your organization usually go about making decisions? Do they usually reach decisions that they can live with and are eager to implement?

Delegating and "Dispersing" Leadership

Great leaders know the difference between taking charge and "taking over" or pulling a "power play." Just as an effective small-group leader develops *co-leaders* within the group, an effective organizational leader becomes a "leader of leaders" by *dispersing* leadership throughout the organization (Bryman, 1996; Gordon, 2010). Always ask yourself, "Who else could do this? Who has the drive and determination to do it? Who would welcome and rise to this challenge?"

By dispersing leadership you fulfill one of the key responsibilities of an organizational leader, which is to recruit, prepare, and mentor future leaders (Gardner, 1990). By preparing future leaders, you exhibit an admirable character trait that psychologist Erik Erikson refers to as *generativity*—"concern for establishing and guiding the next generation" (Erikson, 1963, p. 267).

> *A community is like a ship; everyone ought to be prepared to take the helm.*
>
> —Henrik Ibsen, acclaimed 19th-century Norwegian playwright, poet, and "the father of realism"

Note well! *Dispersing leadership and delegating responsibility doesn't mean relegating or simply "dumping" responsibility on others. It's building future leaders not by micromanaging them, but by supporting them, mentoring them, and providing them with feedback that increases the quality of their work and their leadership potential.*

The Advantages of Committees

It's noteworthy that the word *committee* derives from the same root as *commitment*. A committee comprised of committed members can have multiple advantages, which include (1) capitalizing on the power of the collective wisdom of multiple organizational members, (2) creating an inclusive, participative system of shared, team-based decision making, and (3) dispersing leadership across different members of the organization.

Committees also serve to unite members of an organization who otherwise would not have the opportunity to come together and share ideas. Such idea sharing can improve an organization's morale, foster interpersonal interaction and collaboration, and promote critical thinking—particularly if committee members are exposed to others with different approaches to solving problems, exploring

Box 10.3 Strategies for Forming Committees

- Include members who are most likely to be *affected by* the committee's decisions. For example, if commuter students will be heavily affected by the committee's decisions, they should be well represented on the committee.
- Include members who are most likely to be able to *implement* the committee's decisions. Something is more likely to get done if the people making the decision can do it. Try to avoid scenarios in which the decision makers decide what's to be done (the king and queen bees), but others must do all the work to get it done (the worker bees or drones).
- Form "cross-functional teams" comprised of members with different skill sets (e.g., individuals with practical, creative, verbal, and quantitative skills). This will enable committee members to combine their diverse talents to generate *synergy*—a positive multiplicative effect whose collective impact is much more powerful than what members with similar skills could achieve (Krajewski, Ritzman, & Malhotra, 2009).
- Periodically invite non-committee members with special knowledge or skills to committee meetings as consultants or advisors. This practice expands the quantity and quality of information available to the committee, which should result in it making better-informed decisions.

solutions, and making decisions. (See **Box 10.3** for ways in which committees may be formed to maximize their benefits.)

Purposes and Types of Committees

Before a committee begins its work, it should be made clear to all members what its purpose is, what type of decisions it has the power to make, and the nature of its relationship with other committees. Listed below are the major types of committees and the different purposes they serve:

- *Coordinating Committee.* Serves as a vehicle for communicating information to its members and coordinating its members' activities.
- *Advisory Committee.* Generates recommendations that are forwarded to and considered by another person or governing body with the authority to accept or reject its recommendations.
- *Decision-Making Committee.* Has the authority to make final decisions without those decisions having to be approved by another committee or someone in a higher position of authority.
- *Review Committee.* Receives and reviews reports from other committees, and forwards reports to higher-level administration for consideration and action.
- *Ad Hoc Committee* or *Task Force.* Focuses on a specific issue or task (*ad hoc* literally means "for this") and has a short-term deadline date to finish its work, after which it disbands—unlike the typical "standing committee," which occupies a more permanent place in the college's organizational structure and continues to meet from year to year. Ad hoc committees or task forces may be formed within standing committees to divide up the committee's work. For instance, a large committee may be subdivided into three- or four-member task forces, each of which works on a specific issue and then reports its work to the committee at large. After their task is completed, these small task forces disassemble and new subgroups (task forces) may then be assembled to tackle other specific issues or problems. Creating task forces within a committee enables the large group (the committee) to function as a "group of groups." This is particularly advantageous if the committee is large because

task forces can provide more opportunities for personalized face-to-face dialogue among members, thereby increasing each member's sense of personal connection with other organizational members as well as their sense of accountability to each other. Furthermore, when multiple specialized tasks are created to tackle different tasks and assignments, additional members may be needed to complete them. This can be an effective way to attract additional members to your organization (Strange & Banning, 2001).

Reflection 10.5

If you were a new student on campus, would you choose to join the organization you're leading?

1. If yes, what would attract you to and maintain your involvement in the organization?

2. If no, what would prevent or detract new students from becoming involved?

Conducting Meetings

Scheduling and conducting meetings is one of the key responsibilities of an organizational leader. Meetings are one way you can encourage participative decision making and ensure that the voices of your constituents are heard. Members of your organization will want their voices to be heard, but they may also gripe if they feel they're attending too many meetings. Only call special meetings when you think that in-person discussion is needed to solve an important problem and reach a key decision, or if members or your organization believe a special meeting is needed. Time spent at meetings should be devoted to meaningful dialogue among the participants and not on time-consuming announcements or delivery of factual information that could be communicated more efficiently via other formats, such as (1) voice or text messages, or (2) posts on electronic networking sites (e.g., a listserv or Facebook). Face-to face meeting time should be reserved for significant issues and high-impact agenda items that provoke discussion and require action.

Meetings are ways in which an organization holds itself responsible for creating and distributing two major products of its work: (1) an *agenda,* which identifies issues to be addressed at meetings, and (2) *minutes,* which document the decisions, resolutions, and actions taken at the meeting.

Setting an Agenda

The term *agenda* literally means "things to be done." As its Latin root suggests, the ultimate purpose of an agenda is to identify actions to be taken and tasks to be accomplished. To best fulfill this purpose, circulate an agenda in advance of your meetings so that participants can come prepared with ideas for action. Be sure to seek input from committee members about items they'd like to include in the agenda and be sure that the items they propose are not complaints but action-oriented solutions to issues and problems. To further encourage action-oriented thinking prior to meetings, phrase agenda items as problems to be solved or questions to be answered (e.g., "What strategies will we use to _____?" "What position will we take on _____?").

Since an agenda is an action plan, it should include all of the actions to be taken and identify dates by which those actions are to be completed. You can ensure that high-priority actions are taken first by labeling or flagging agenda items in terms of their level of priority: for example, High—must do now, Medium—should do soon, Low—should do eventually. You can address these items at the meeting in order of their priority. (You may also designate the approximate amount of time you will devote to discussion of each item.)

Keeping Minutes

Minutes represent the written record of a meeting, and typically include a summary of the key points made during the discussion of the agenda items, as well as the major decisions made and actions taken with respect to the agenda items. Minutes should include the place, date, and start and end time of the meeting, as well as the names of the participants and facilitator.

One way to evaluate a meeting's effectiveness is to assess whether the outcomes accomplished at the meeting (as captured in the minutes) align with and address the items that appear on the meeting's agenda. In other words: Did the meeting accomplish what it intended to accomplish? Did it solve the problems, resolve the issues, and make the decisions called for by the agenda? Do the minutes reflect a clear action plan that clearly stipulates what is to be done, who will do it, and when it will be done?

Save and post the minutes of all your meetings so that you have a cumulative record of your organization's work and to increase other organizations' awareness of its work. By doing so, you make the work of your organization "transparent"—open and visible to the entire campus community at large—and show the community that your organization is actually getting things done.

Using Parliamentary Procedure

Setting an agenda and recording minutes brings some order or structure to the *content*—what is covered at meetings; in addition, you'll also need to bring structure or order to the *process*—how meetings are conducted. One way to run meetings in an orderly manner is through use of parliamentary procedure—a formal set of operational rules and procedural guidelines for conducting meetings in an effective, efficient, and equitable manner. Parliamentary procedure dates back to the original practices of the United Kingdom's House of Commons of the Parliament (hence the term *parliamentary procedure*). It stipulates that the following sequence of actions be taken at all meetings:

1. Call to order—the presiding officer (person in charge of running the meeting) calls for the attention of all those present,
2. Reading and approval of minutes of the previous meeting,
3. Reports of officers and standing committees,
4. Reports of ad hoc committees,
5. Unfinished business,
6. New business,
7. Announcements, and
8. Adjournment.

Parliamentary procedure also involves rules for debating and reaching group decisions with the least possible friction by voting and majority rule, but ensuring fairness toward the minority by allowing individuals formal opportunities to have their voices heard. Probably the most well known and frequently used form of parliamentary procedure is *Robert's Rules of Order,* originally published in 1876 by Henry Martyn Robert, a U.S. army colonel. Robert observed that people had very different views about how parliamentary rules were to be specifically applied; these differences were interfering with their ability to reach decisions effectively and efficiently. Thus, he constructed a manual of rules to facilitate the decision-making process (modeled loosely after those used in the United States House of Representatives). These rules are still used today, and his manual is in its eleventh edition (Robert, 2011). A brief summary of *Robert's Rules* is contained in Box 10.4.

Box 10.4

- Members must be recognized by the presiding officer before they may make a motion—a proposal of an idea to be discussed and voted on.
- Members must formally state their motions ("I move that . . ."), and only one motion can be stated at a time.
- Another member must second the motion before the original motion is put "on the floor" for discussion by the assembly.
- After the motion is seconded, the presiding officer restates the motion and opens it up to the assembly for discussion.
- All members have the right to agree or disagree with the motion and suggest amendments (modifications) to it; however, any amendment must first be recognized and restated by the presiding officer before the assembly can discuss it.
- No member may speak a second time to a motion (or to an amended motion) until a member who hasn't yet spoken has the opportunity to do so.
- Members must not direct remarks, questions, or criticisms at particular individuals; all comments are addressed to the presiding officer and the group at large.
- Before voting on a motion, members have the right to seek clarification about what the motion specifically states and what an affirmative (yes) or negative (no) vote specifically means.
- The presiding officer takes the vote, and announces the result.

Source: Adapted from *Robert's Rules of Order Newly Revised* (Robert, 2011).

While formal procedures like *Robert's Rules of Order* provide structure, they also have the potential to restrict open discussion and inhibit consensus building. A more informal alternative to *Robert's Rules of Order* are the guidelines developed by Jay Hall (1971), a social psychologist who conducted a classic and extensive study of group decision making in a wide variety of situations and organizations. Hall discovered that the quality of group decisions is superior if the group follows the simple guidelines listed below:

- Members don't argue at length for their own views. Instead, they state their positions as clearly and briefly as possible, then back off, listen to others' reactions, and carefully consider them before pressing their point again.
- When disagreement or debate occurs, members don't automatically assume there will be winners versus losers; instead, they first look for a middle ground that's acceptable to both parties.
- Differences of opinion are viewed as natural and are sought out to ensure that a more balanced decision is reached or more decision-making options are created.
- The group avoids decision-making methods that attempt to minimize discussion and consensus building (e.g., voting, averaging, or bargaining).

■ Members don't change their minds just to avoid conflict and preserve harmony; they yield only to positions they think are reasonable and acceptable. When agreement seems to come too quickly and easily, they make sure that the decision wasn't reached prematurely and everyone truly agrees with it (not just giving in to get along).

Your organization can set whatever ground rules it likes for running meetings. The key is to establish rules that strike the delicate balance between maintaining order, which keeps the meeting focused on its agenda, and maintaining flexibility, which allows opportunity for some spontaneity and creativity. As the presiding officer, you'll often have to play the role of "traffic cop" or "court judge," deciding whether the meeting is veering off track and needs to be reeled in, or whether you should "go with the flow" and allow discussion not directly related to the current agenda item to continue, particularly if it's thought-provoking and productive. If a discussion happens to emerge that's exhilarating and meaningful, but doesn't align with the meeting's formal agenda or motion, a middle-ground strategy you could take is to "table" (postpone) the discussion for the moment and come back to it at the end of the meeting (e.g., under "new business"), or make it a high-priority item at your next meeting.

Another key role you play as the meeting's presiding officer is to ensure that all voices are heard, whether those voices are expressed in speech or in writing. One way to do so is by setting aside some time at the end of each meeting for participants to write down any ideas they didn't express at the meeting, either because time ran out or because they were reluctant to compete with others for "air time." For instance, before the meeting is brought to a close, you could ask members to provide a written response to the question, "What would you have said at today's meeting if you had more time or opportunity to do so?"

Handling Conflict at Meetings

Organizations are systems within which differences of viewpoints are inevitable and invaluable, particularly if you can ensure that they are aired openly and courteously. A heated discussion often is a sign that members are intensely interested in and passionate about reaching the best possible decision about the topic being discussed. Such vigorous dialogue often results in a stronger decision and a stronger organization in the long run. Thus, it's important not to squelch controversy, but to ensure that it takes place in a civil and respectful manner (Higher Education Research Institute, 1996).

When disagreements emerge at meetings, here are three key things you can do (1) remind the disputants to keep the discussion positive and constructive, (2) listen objectively to the arguments of both parties and carefully weigh their pros and cons, and (3) look for areas of agreement that may serve as bridges between the differing positions. When disputants are involved in an intense disagreement, they often overlook alternative courses of action that are agreeable to both parties. Often, they get locked into opposing (win-lose) positions, constructing an artificial barrier that blocks creativity and discovery of win-win solutions. To help the disagreeing parties break through this win-lose barrier, you may need to remind them to think beyond the competitive boundaries of their opposing positions and look for common ground. As the presiding officer, you can be the objective third party and see win-win alternatives that the disputants cannot. When you use your leadership position to help disagreeing parties explore and identify

> *Leadership has a harder job to do than just choose sides. It must bring sides together.*
> —Jesse Jackson, American civil rights activist and recipient of the Presidential Medal of Freedom

bipartisan (two-party) solutions, you not only help resolve the disagreement, you also model effective problem-solving and consensus-building skills that students can use throughout life.

Promoting Organizational Change

Organizational change may be defined as the process of improving an organization's policies, programs, practices, or procedures to enable it to better achieve its mission and serve its members. As an organizational leader, you are positioned to move beyond promoting change individually ("I can make it happen") to promoting it collectively ("we can make it happen together"). Furthermore, organizational leaders are positioned to advocate and agitate for campus-wide changes that may benefit not only currently enrolled students, but also future generations of students who come to your campus—especially if the changes become incorporated into your college's organizational structure and are "institutionalized."

Reflection 10.6

If you were to choose a *campaign* for change on your campus, what would it be?

Who would the change campaign help?

What positive change(s) would take place on campus as a result of the campaign?

Assessing Where Campus Change Is Needed

Peer leaders are in a position to hear about student experiences on campus and how well the campus is meeting student needs. You can learn about student experiences and needs by simply asking questions and listening attentively to detect common themes of concern, satisfaction, or dissatisfaction. Studies show that dissatisfaction among members of an organization (including colleges and universities) reduces their enthusiasm and morale, and increases the likelihood they will leave the organization (Noel & Levitz, 1995; Strange & Banning, 2001). In addition to asking questions and listening actively, you can identify sources of student dissatisfaction and potential targets for campus-change efforts by using more formal methods, such as the following:

Surveys and questionnaires. You can create instruments that ask students to rate their level of satisfaction with various campus programs and experiences, which can yield a large amount of quantitative information that can be quickly analyzed and summarized. Here are a few quick tips on how to improve the quality of any surveys you may decide to construct.

- Use a rating scale that includes the following five options:

1	2	0	3	4
strongly agree	agree	not sure	disagree	strongly disagree

The "not sure" option will allow students who have had little or no experience with the campus program or service to choose a neutral option rather than forcing them to rate an experience they've never had or know little about.

- Beneath each item (statement) to be rated, leave a space for written comments that allow the respondent to provide a reason or explanation for the rating, as illustrated below.

1	2	0	3	4
strongly agree	agree	not sure	disagree	strongly disagree

Reason/explanation for rating. Written responses that accompany a quantitative rating can provide a window into *why* the rating was given and help you understand the reasoning behind the rating.

- In addition to asking students to provide a satisfaction rating, ask them to rate how *important* that experience or program is to them. Thus, students give two ratings for each item on the instrument: (1) a rating of how *satisfied* they are with that experience/program characteristic, and (2) how *important* that experience or program is to them. The instrument could be structured to efficiently obtain both sets of ratings by centering the item statements in the middle of the page; a "satisfaction" scale could then be positioned to the left of the items and an "importance" scale to the right of the same item, as illustrated below.

The variety of student activities offered on campus.

Satisfaction

1	2	0	3	4
strongly agree	agree	not sure	disagree	strongly disagree

Importance

1	2	0	3	4
strongly agree	agree	not sure	disagree	strongly disagree

Items on the survey that students rate high in importance but low in satisfaction represent highest-priority student needs that are not being met and can serve as key target areas for campus-change efforts.

- At the end of the instrument, include a section that asks for demographic information, such as the student's (1) gender, (2) race/ethnicity, (3) age (traditional vs. re-entry), (4) residential status (campus resident vs. commuter), (5) national citizenship (domestic vs. international), (6) enrollment status (full time vs. part time), (7) academic-decision status (declared major, undecided, or in transition), and (8) work status (not working, working part time or full time, working on or off campus). Collecting this information will enable you to analyze how student satisfaction may vary across different student groups. Studies show that different groups of students are likely to vary in terms of their perceptions and levels of satisfaction with campus programs and services (Schuh & Upcraft, 2001).
- Before officially distributing the survey, have students review it and get their feedback on how to improve it. You can do this by asking a sample of students to complete the instrument and comment on its strengths and ways in which it could be improved. Soliciting student feedback on the assessment instrument serves two valuable purposes (1) it helps identify student perspectives and concerns that the assessment instrument may have failed to ad-

dress, and (2) it demonstrates participative leadership by allowing students to actively participate in the process.

Focus group interviews. A focus group consists of a relatively small group (e.g., six to eight people) that meets with a moderator in a relaxed environment to explore the group's perceptions, attitudes, and ideas about a particular topic. In contrast to surveys or questionnaires, which generate data in the form of numerical ratings and written comments, focus group interviews collect verbal (oral) information. Students' verbal responses to questions posed "live" (in person) can often be richer and more detailed than responses obtained through surveys.

Focus group interviews may also be used in conjunction with surveys. For instance, group interviews may be used as a follow-up to student surveys by asking the groups for their interpretation or explanation of the survey's results. The sequence may also be reversed, whereby focus groups are conducted first to identify student needs and issues that are later included as items on a survey or questionnaire.

Focus groups can be formed in either of two ways:

1. *Heterogeneous* groups, where members of different student populations comprise the focus group (e.g., minority and majority students are included in the same group). The advantage of this procedure is that a cross-section of different subgroups is present at the same time, which can enrich the diversity of the focus group dialogue.
2. *Homogeneous* groups, where members of different student populations comprise separate focus groups (e.g., minority and majority students are placed in different focus groups). The primary advantage of this grouping procedure is that it allows students to discuss their perceptions and concerns with peers who may have common experiences and with whom they may feel more comfortable expressing their views.

Open forums. These are meetings with no set agenda; instead, the agenda emerges spontaneously from questions and issues raised by the participants. Some ground rules should be established for such sessions to keep them orderly and civil. For example, participants should comment on issues that involve college processes, practices, or policies rather than citing and criticizing particular individuals, and complaints cited should be followed by suggested solutions or remedies before another complaint is raised. When students are encouraged to openly express their concerns and discuss potential strategies for dealing with them, it can unearth target areas for organizational change. If numerous students cite a particular experience as frustrating or dissatisfying, this might be viewed as a "critical incident" and used as a focal point for campus-wide discussion with college administrators.

Suggestion boxes. Students can write down change-related ideas or concerns that may come to them at any time and deposit them in a conveniently located box. Students can do this anonymously, which may allow them to express ideas that they are not willing to share publicly.

Higher education research. In addition to identifying targets for organizational change by collecting data from students on campus, you can also use research that has been conducted by higher education scholars. In a nutshell, this research suggests that higher education organizations should strive to make changes that enable them to operate less like "complex organizations" and more like "developmental environments" (Strange & Banning, 2001). The differences between these two modes of operation are described in **Box 10.5**. You may use this chart to identify areas where change is needed on your campus and initiate change efforts designed to move your campus closer to becoming a true developmental environment.

Box 10.5

Characteristics of Complex Organizations	Characteristics of Developmental Environments
Emphasis on formality and rigid procedural routines	Emphasis on procedural flexibility and openness to innovation and creativity
Minimize risk taking to maximize	Encourage risk taking to maximize educational organizational efficiency effectiveness
Minimize discussion of differing viewpoints to avoid conflict or controversy	Diverse viewpoints and multiple perspectives are welcomed to encourage critical thinking
Decision making is centralized by restricting power to a few high-ranking authorities	Decision making is decentralized and power is distributed throughout the organization
Personal status is stratified by one's position (level) in the organizational hierarchy	Positional status is minimized and members at all levels of the organization are valued
Human interactions are based on members' formal roles and functions in the organization	Human interactions are based on personal relationships and mentoring

Powerful developmental environments are those that exhibit characteristics of dynamic organizations, where individual differences are appreciated, participation is expected, interactions are personal rather than functional, and risk-taking is encouraged.
—Carney Strange & James Banning, *Education by Design: Creating Campus Learning Environments That Work*

Source: Adapted from Strange (1983) and Strange & Banning (2001).

Strategies for Catalyzing Organizational Change

As a peer leader, you have the potential to use your organizational position to promote positive change on campus, particularly if you have a strategic plan that allows you to capitalize on all the change tools and tactics available to you. Described below is a systematic set of tactical strategies for promoting organizational change that includes how to do it, whom to do it with, and when to do it.

The HOW of Change: The Art, Science, and Politics of Persuasion

To ensure that your message for change reaches all members of the campus community, be sure to use all *communication modalities* available to you, including social media (e.g., Facebook and Twitter) and campus ecology (e.g., making your change-campaign slogan visible on campus via stickers, placards, and postings on bulletin boards and kiosks).

Reflection 10.7

What would you say are the most persuasive forms of *media* for stimulating change on your campus?

To increase the likelihood that people buy into your change message, use *multiple methods of persuasion*. Listed below are the major persuasive appeals you can use to get buy-in from others to support your change initiatives:

- Appeal to Reason (the Rational Approach). Show how the proposed change "makes sense"—i.e., is logically sound. For example, point out how the change being sought is logically consistent with the college mission, program goals, strategic plans, or accreditation reports.
- Appeal to Evidence (the Empirical Approach). Show how the proposed change is supported by research, data, and facts. For example, cite student-satisfaction research on your campus and/or national research findings that support the change you're seeking to make.
- Appeal to Personal Conscience and Ethical Principles (the Moral Approach). Show how the change being proposed is the right, just, or fair thing to do.
- Appeal to Self-Interest (the What's-in-It-for-Me Approach). Show how the change will benefit the people you're trying to persuade (e.g., make their jobs easier, more secure, or more fulfilling). Studies of organizational change show that when members of the organization see how the change aligns with their personal interests, they are much more likely to support it (Jenkins, 2011).
- Appeal to Feasibility (the Practical and Manageable Approach). Show how the change is doable, i.e., not cost-prohibitive, time-consuming, or labor-intensive. Don't forget the "law of least effort": the probability that people will be persuaded to accept change is negatively (inversely) related to the amount of time, effort, or energy required to make the change.

The WHO of Change: Finding Partners and Enlisting Allies

Organizational change rarely happens through the efforts of a single individual: it typically takes place through collective and collaborative effort. Think about members of your campus community who can help you advocate and agitate for change. Build coalitions with these people and other groups on campus that are sympathetic to your cause and willing to support your efforts. In particular, try to build coalitions comprised of people who bring different change-promoting qualities to the table (e.g., "idea" people and "action" people).

Since making organizational change happen often requires buy-in from individuals at different levels in the organizational hierarchy, enlist allies that can support your change campaign from three key levels or directions:

1. Top→Down (support from high-ranking administrators),
2. Bottom→Up (support from faculty, staff, and students) and
3. Side→In (support from middle managers).

Each of the key three vectors for catalyzing organizational change is described in **Box 10.6.**

Key Vectors or Forces for Catalyzing Organizational Change

1. Top→Down (trickle-down). Change catalyzed by high-level administrators. Research on change agents who successfully made campus changes that benefited first-year college students indicates that that the factor most responsible for their ability to promote change was the support they received from the president or other high-level administrators (Anttonen & Chaskes, 2002). High-ranking campus leaders can support your change efforts by virtue of their decision-making power and their ability to supply you with needed resources. You can also enlist their support by requesting high-level administrators to call attention to your change effort in formal addresses and written communications to the campus community (e.g., at kickoff events that inaugurate a new academic year or state-of-the-college reports), and by asking if they would be willing to make a brief appearance at your meetings or rallies (e.g., to provide a welcoming or closing message).

2. Bottom→Up (bubble-up). Change catalyzed by faculty, staff, students, and leaders of other student organizations. There are likely to be people on your campus who are not high-ranking administrators. They are the "foot soldiers" on the "front line" who, because of their closeness to the action, may be well-positioned to promote "grassroots" change from the ground up—particularly if they are held in high esteem by their peers. These members of the organization have informal power and can serve as effective catalysts for change. They include seemingly powerless students whom high-level administrators will often listen to, because they are the organization's tuition-paying customers and primary constituents. You can rally these student troops into a sizable force for change, particularly by collaborating with leaders of other student organizations to coordinate efforts and pool your resources to form a united front that's broad-based and campus-wide.

3. Side→In (across-the-center). Change catalyzed by department chairs and program directors. Colleges and universities are typically characterized by a high degree of decentralization because they are organizations that are subdivided into specialized academic departments and educational services (Strange & Banning, 2001). Considerable decision-making authority resides within these different departments or divisions, and the "middle managers" who lead them often wield considerable power. Whenever possible, try to collaborate and coordinate your change efforts with these mid-level leaders.

The WHEN of Change: Timing Matters

Promoting change depends not only on what you do, how you do it, and whom you do it with; it also depends on *when* you do it. Timing may not be everything, but it's a very important thing. Introduce change at a time when people are most likely to be receptive to it. At the very least, avoid introducing change initiatives at crunch times and stressful junctures during the term when people are likely to be stressed out or pooped out.

Try to initiate change at times when people are likely to be more energized and easily mobilized. In particular, "strike when the iron is hot"—when the campus community is most likely to see a need for change. Campus crises (e.g., a disturbing incident on campus), or when the campus has received some negative results (e.g., a drop in student enrollment, low student satisfaction results, or a poor accreditation report) are times when administrators are most likely to be more receptive to change. You may have heard of the old expression, "Necessity is the mother of invention." It could also be said that necessity is the mother of change.

Reflection 10.8

Is there a current crisis or serious issue on campus that could serve as a rallying point for change?

If yes, what is it and how could you begin rallying people to make this change?

Summary and Conclusion

Leaders can promote positive change not only among individuals, but also in organizations and institutions as well. As a student leader, you may be in a position to see the "big picture" and make a big difference in your student organization and your college as a whole. Effective organizational leadership requires knowledge and understanding of the larger system in which your particular organization operates. You can begin to acquire this knowledge by learning how your college or university is organized and how "the system" works, so that you can "work the system" to make it work for your leadership cause.

There are two basic ways or styles in which leaders can use their power to make decisions:

1. *Authoritarian* (autocratic) decision making, and
2. *Participative* (democratic) decision making.

Authoritarian or autocratic leaders make decisions independently, with little or no input from the rest of the group. There are likely to be occasions where you will have to make decisions this way because you may have access to information that other members of your organization don't have, or because time constraints require a decision be made quickly and at a time when your group isn't available to convene. However, authoritarian decision making should be your last resort. Whenever and wherever possible, consult with members of your organization and include them in the decision-making process by engaging in participative leadership. Participative leadership can be put into practice in two major ways: by voting (majority rules), or by consensus. In contrast to *voting*, which is a competitive process in which the majority wins and the minority loses, *consensus* is a collaborative decision-making process in which the group strives to reach the best possible decision for all its members.

Committees also serve to unite members of an organization who otherwise would not have the opportunity to come together and share ideas. Such idea sharing can improve an organization's morale, foster interpersonal interaction and collaboration, and promote critical thinking—particularly if committee members are exposed to others with different approaches to solving problems, exploring solutions, and making decisions.

Scheduling and conducting meetings is one of the key responsibilities of an organizational leader. Meetings are one way you can encourage participative decision making and ensure that the voices of your constituents are heard. Meetings are ways in which an organization holds itself responsible for creating and distributing two major products of its work (1) an *agenda,* which identifies issues to be addressed at meetings, and (2) *minutes,* which document the decisions, resolutions, and actions taken at the meeting. Setting an agenda and recording minutes brings some order or structure to the *content*—what is covered at meetings; in addition, you'll also need to bring structure or order to the *process*—how meetings are conducted. One way to run meetings in an orderly manner is through the use of *parliamentary procedure*–a formal set of operational rules and procedural guidelines for conducting meetings in an effective, efficient, and equitable manner. Your organization can set whatever ground rules it likes for running meetings. The key is to establish rules that strike the delicate balance between maintaining order, which keeps the meeting focused on its agenda, and maintaining flexibility, which allows opportunity for some spontaneity and creativity.

Peer leaders are in a position to hear about student experiences on campus and how well the campus is meeting student needs. You can learn about student experiences and needs by simply asking questions and listening attentively to detect common themes of concern, satisfaction, or dissatisfaction. In addition to asking questions and listening actively, you can identify sources of student dissatisfaction and potential targets for campus-change efforts by using more formal methods, such as surveys and questionnaires, focus group interviews, open forums, and suggestion boxes.

Organizational change may be defined as the process of improving an organization's policies, programs, practices, or procedures to enable it to better achieve its mission and serve its members. As an organizational leader, you are positioned to advocate and agitate for campus-wide changes that benefit the entire student body. Furthermore, if the changes you help to make become incorporated into your college's organizational structure and are "institutionalized," they will not only benefit currently enrolled students, but also future generations of students who come to your campus for years to come.

Internet Resources

For additional information related to the ideas discussed in this chapter, we recommend the following websites:

Leadership and Decision-Making Power
www.uthscsa.edu/gme/documents/LspasaFunctionofPower.pdf
www.ccl.org/leadership/pdf/research/roleOfPower.pdf

Conducting Meetings
Strategies for Conducting Meetings
treegroup.info/topics/facilitation_primer.pdf

Summary of Robert's Rules of Order
www.robertsrules.org

Organizational Change Strategies
www.organizational-change-management.com/organizational-change
www.ncbi.nlm.nih.gov/pubmed/18090518

Exercise 10.1 *Journal Reflections*

1. What topic or issue do you think would be the most difficult for members of your organization to reach consensus on? What would be the easiest?

2. If you were to construct a survey of students to assess their needs and sources of campus satisfaction/dissatisfaction, what questions would you include on the instrument?

3. If you were to conduct focus group interviews with students, what do you think would emerge as their greatest sources of campus satisfaction and dissatisfaction?

4. Based on your prior experience with meetings, what do you think are the most important ground rules to establish to ensure that meetings run in an orderly and productive manner?

Exercise 10.2 *Organizational Structure and Communication*

Locate the table of organization or organizational chart for your campus that outlines offices and positions, levels of authority, and how communication flows from top to bottom.

1. To what person or position does your student organization report?

2. Where does that person or position fall in the organizational hierarchy?

3. If you want to communicate an idea or concern to the highest authorities on your campus, can you go directly to them, or are you expected to first express that idea or concern to someone at a lower or intermediate level?

Exercise 10.3 *SWOT Analysis*

Engage in a reflective analysis of the student organization you lead, or in which you play a leadership role, and answer the following questions as honestly as possible:

1. **S**trengths: What are your organization's strong points? What's working really well?

2. **W**eaknesses: What are your organization's limitations or areas in which it needs to improve the most?

3. **O**pportunities: What possibilities exist on campus that your organization could take advantage of to increase its effectiveness?

4. **T**hreats: What aspects of your campus environment, or how it operates, tend to interfere with or weaken your organization's effectiveness?

Exercise 10.4 *Forming Committees and Task Forces*

Reflect on the purpose, goals, and functions of your organization.

1. What standing committees do you think should be formed and meet regularly to ensure that your organization fulfills its purpose and reaches its goals?

2. What temporary task forces should be periodically created to tackle specific tasks or functions?

3. What members of your organization do you think would work well together on the above committees and task forces?

chapter 11

Civic Leadership
Making Change at Local, National, and Global Levels

A leader's influence can extend beyond an individual, a group, or an organization to the larger society. (See **Figure 11.1**.) The mission of most colleges and universities is not only to help students better themselves, but also to help them better their local communities and society as a whole. As a peer leader, you can help fulfill this mission by exhibiting leadership that improves the quality of life for people beyond the immediate boundaries of your campus.

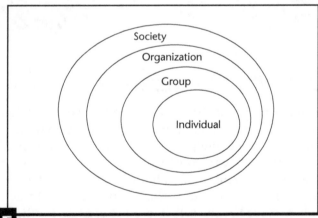

Figure 11.1 Peer Leadership: Circles of Influence

Civic Engagement

The word *civic* derives from the same root as *citizen*—a member of a city or community. *Civic engagement* refers to actions that citizens make, either individually or collectively, to promote the welfare of their community (American Psychological Association, 2012). Responsible citizens are *civically engaged*—i.e., they actively participate in their community to make it the best it can be (Komives, Lucas, & McMahon, 2007). They understand that members of their community are not merely a collection of independent entities, but are interdependent parts of a

To be a good citizen is to work for positive change on behalf of others and the community.

—Higher Education Research Institute, University of California at Los Angeles

larger whole—a part of something bigger than themselves—whose collective well-being depends on its members supporting each other and working together for a common cause (Higher Education Research Institute, 1996; Wagner, 2006).

Civility

> *The right to do something does not mean that doing it is right.*
> —William Safire, American author, journalist, and presidential speechwriter

At the very least, civic engagement involves exhibiting *civility*—respect for and sensitivity to the rights of other community members. Civility could be defined as "responsible freedom," whereby individuals exercise their personal rights and freedoms without stepping or stomping on the rights and freedoms of others (Forni, 2002).

 *Freedom isn't synonymous with anarchy; it includes social responsibility and a commitment to the common good.*

> *Injustice anywhere is a threat to justice everywhere.*
> —Martin Luther King, Jr., civil rights leader and winner of the Nobel Peace Prize

Civility also involves taking action (not looking away) when the rights or dignity of other community members are being violated. The quality of a community is threatened when any of its members' sense of security or belonging is threatened (Strange & Banning, 2001). At a national level, when the personal rights and freedom of fellow citizens in a democratic country are threatened by prejudice and discrimination, the political stability and viability of democracy itself is threatened. Thus, diversity and democracy go hand in hand; by appreciating the former, you safeguard the latter.

Note well! *When you take an active role by confronting prejudice and discrimination, you demonstrate both civic leadership and civic character by protecting human rights and promoting social justice.*

Community Leadership

> *Skill in the building and rebuilding of community is one of the highest and most essential skills a leader can command.*
> —J. W. Gardner, former secretary of health, education, and welfare, U.S. Marine Corps captain, and recipient of the Presidential Medal of Freedom

> *Effective communities realize they are not insular but are in a constant, dynamic interaction with the broader environment.*
> —Komives, Lucas, & McMahon, *Exploring Leadership: For College Students Who Want to Make a Difference*

The word *community* derives from Latin roots meaning "with/together" and "gift." Sociologists define a community as a societal group whose members share an identity, plus a sense of interpersonal connection and commitment (Bruhn, 2005). Thus, a community can consist of people that are not necessarily connected in the same geographical place, but who are connected by a commitment to each other or to a common cause. What distinguishes all true communities is that their members move beyond self-interest to concern for the common good.

As illustrated in **Figure 11.2**, each of us as an individual is embedded in a subset of progressively larger communities, ranging from our local community to the global community. Communities involve linkages to the larger society (Strange & Banning, 2001); when people view themselves as nested in a web of interconnections, they become aware of the common bonds that unite all humans and unite humans with their shared environment (the earth). This common bond increases their sense of connection to the world around them, and reduces their feelings of isolation and alienation (Bellah et al., 1985).

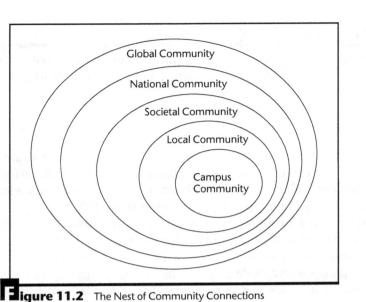

Figure 11.2 The Nest of Community Connections

> *Humankind has not woven the web of life. We are but one thread within it. Whatever we do to the web, we do to ourselves. All things are bound together. All things connect.*
>
> —Chief Seattle, prominent Native American after whom the city of Seattle was named

The Campus Community

It's noteworthy that the term *university* derives from the Latin root meaning "the whole," and the term *college* derives from the Latin root meaning "community." Thus, colleges and universities are places where the ideals of a community can be put into practice.

You can start this process by advising students, particularly college students, on how civility is displayed in the college classroom. Behavior that interferes with the rights of others to learn or teach in the college classroom represents a violation of civility. **Box 11.1** identifies two common forms of classroom incivility that involve student use of personal technology. These behaviors are increasing in college, as is the anger of college instructors and college students who witness them. As a peer leader, you can increase student awareness of them and intercede when you observe them.

> *For some students, college represents their first opportunity to experience what it is like to live in a real community where we assume responsibility for each other.*
>
> —David Boren, president of the University of Oklahoma

Box 11.1

Campus Incivility: Insensitive Use of Personal Technology in the Classroom

Cell Phones

Keeping a cell phone on in class is a form of classroom incivility because if it rings, it will interfere with the right of others to learn. In a study of college students who were exposed to a cell phone ringing during a class session and were later tested for their recall of information presented in class, they scored approximately 25% worse when attempting to recall information that was presented at the time a cell phone rang. This attention loss occurred even if the material was covered by the professor prior to the cell phone ringing and if it was projected on a slide during the call. The study also showed that classmates are further distracted when classmates frantically search through handbags or pockets to find and silence a ringing (or vibrating) phone (Shelton et al., 2009). These findings clearly suggest that the civil thing to do is for students to turn off their cell phones before entering the classroom, or keep them out of the classroom altogether.

Text Messaging

Although it doesn't involve interfering sounds, text messaging can interfere with learning by distracting classmates from listening to and learning from the educational message being delivered in the classroom. It's also discourteous or disrespectful to the instructors when students have their heads down (reading or delivering a text message) while the instructor is trying to engage them in the learning process.

Reflection 11.2

Have you observed examples of incivility on campus that you thought were particularly despicable? Where did it take place and what uncivil behavior was displayed?

In addition to combating incivility on campus, you can promote campus community by involving students in campus traditions and rituals (or help create them if they don't already exist). Such practices serve to unite students by connecting them to the campus and to each other (Kuh, 1997).

Stronger campus communities are also created through the sharing of common space (Strange & Banning, 2001). You can take a leadership role in strengthening the sense of community on your campus by creating or advocating for spaces and places where students can come together and engage with others who share common interests and experiences. For example, you can arrange for a common place or space where open forums can be held on campus, during which student "citizens" come together to discuss collective concerns and ideas for community improvement. By so doing, you create opportunities for students to practice the civic skills that prepare them for active citizenship in a democratic society.

You can also encourage students' civic engagement in the campus community by encouraging them to participate in college governance, campus elections, and political organizations on campus, such as Young Democrat and Republican clubs (Bok, 2006). Studies show that students' engagement in student government and other campus organizations while in college is a powerful predictor of whether they will become engaged citizens at the larger societal or national level (Verba, Schlozman, & Brady, 1995). As a peer leader, you can also foster active citizenship by using democratic processes to run student organizations, such as the participative decision-making practices described in Chapter 10 (pp. 269–273).

The Local Community

In addition to being members of a campus community, students are members of the *local community*—the neighborhood in which they live and go to school. If you want to improve the human condition and take a first step to make the world a better place, this is a good place to start. You can begin to practice civic leadership by encouraging and organizing students to serve the local community surrounding your campus. Specific strategies for doing so are provided on pp. 302–304.

The Societal Community

Moving beyond their local communities, students are also members of a larger *society*—a group of people organized under the same social system. Societies include subgroups that are divided into different regions (e.g., north, south, east, west), states, population densities (e.g., urban, suburban, rural), and socioeconomic classes (levels of income, education, and job status). Society is stratified into groups of people with unequal levels of social and economic capital. In the United States, the wealthiest 20 percent of the population controls approximately

50 percent of the total income, while the 20 percent of Americans with the lowest level of income controls only 4 percent of the nation's wealth (U.S. Census Bureau, 2000). Groups occupying lower socioeconomic strata also have poorer educational and social-networking opportunities (Feagin & Feagin, 2003).

One way in which you can serve as a civic leader is by engaging students in volunteer experiences that are specially intended to help members of society who have fewer educational opportunities and socioeconomic privileges.

Reflection 11.3

Why do you think poverty continues to exist in our society? Do you think it will ever be eliminated? If no, why not? If yes, what will it take?

> *For I was hungry and you gave me food, I was thirsty and you gave me something to drink, I was a stranger and you welcomed me.*
>
> —Jesus of Nazareth, Matthew 25:34–36

The National Community

In addition to being members of society, students are also citizens of a nation. Rather than being governed by dictators or autocrats, people in a democratic nation govern themselves by selecting (electing) their own leaders. The term *democracy* derives from the Greek *demos* (people) and *kratos* (rule); thus, literally translated, *democracy* means "people rule." The right to vote is the distinctive privilege of living in a democratic nation. This privilege of living in a free nation brings with it the responsibility of participating in the nation's governance through the voting process. In a democracy, voting is not just a political thing to do; it's the patriotic thing to do.

For a democratic nation to succeed and for political freedom to be preserved, its voting citizens must be well educated, ask intelligent questions of their potential political leaders, and make wise choices about whom they elect as their leaders and lawmakers (Bishop, 1986; Cheney, 1989). In fact, this was a primary reason why American colleges (the colonial colleges) were established in the first place—to educate young adults broadly and deeply so that they could use their knowledge to vote wisely, choose their political leaders in a well-informed and well-reasoned manner, and become future leaders of our new nation (Association of American Colleges & Universities, 2007).

> *Knowledge will forever govern ignorance; and a people who mean to be their own governors must arm themselves with the power which knowledge gives.*
>
> —James Madison, fourth president of the United States and signer of the American Constitution and Bill of Rights

The quality of a democracy depends on citizens who learn deeply and think critically, and who can apply these skills to the voting process by making wise, well-informed decisions about whom they elect. As a peer leader, you can serve as a learning coach to help students learn deeply and think critically (see Chapter 6), and you can help them apply these skills to the voting process by encouraging them to vote in national, state, and local elections.

Disappointingly, American citizens between the ages of 18 and 24 continue to display the lowest voter turnout rate of any age group that is eligible to vote (Center for Information & Research on Civic Learning and Engagement, 2010). Surveys also show that beginning college students rank preparation for citizenship and civic engagement as among the least important reasons for attending college (Schneider, 2005).

As a peer leader, you are in a position to change student attitudes and behavior, and encourage students to become engaged citizens who participate actively and knowledgeably in the voting process. **Box 11.2** supplies you with specific strategies for doing so.

> *It is such good fortune for people in power that people do not think.*
>
> —Adolf Hitler, German dictator

> *Most people today think of college primarily as a stepping-stone to well-paid careers but not as a vital means for achieving getter government or stronger communities.*
>
> —Derek Bok, president emeritus and research professor, Harvard University

Box 11.2

Strategies for Encouraging Students to Become Active and Knowledgeable Participants in the Voting Process

- Encourage students on campus (and in local high schools) to register to vote, and collect pledges to vote.
- Work with the technology department on campus to place the "Rock the Vote" registration tool on campus websites (see www.rockthevote.com).
- Work with the local board of elections to create an on-campus polling location.
- Plan parades to polls and absentee ballot mailing parties (see www.longdistancevoter.org).
- Serve as a poll watcher on Election Day and encourage other students to join you.
- Steer students to resources where they can access candidates' stands on key issues (e.g., www.votesmart.org).
- Help students question misleading campaign ads by encouraging them to visit such websites as FactCheck.org, FlackCheck.org, and PolitiFact.com.
- Invite candidates or candidates' advocates to campus for debates, discussion forums, or town hall meetings. A "town hall meeting" is a type of informal public meeting that was originally held in the towns of colonial America. Everybody in the community is invited to attend, voice their opinions, and hear the responses from public figures and elected officials. By getting students involved in town hall meetings and similar public debates, you not only facilitate civic engagement, you help develop two of the primary skills associated with a college education: reasoning skills and appreciation for alternative points of view (Bok, 2006).

Source: Adapted from Loeb (2012).

> *Get involved. Don't gripe about things unless you are making an effort to change them. You can make a difference if you dare.*
>
> —Richard C. Holbrooke, former director of the Peace Corps and American ambassador to the United Nations

> *Too many people have developed into observers instead of activists . . . they act as if they are spectators instead of citizens. Instead of complaining or doing nothing, we need to become engaged in the process of improving our shared experience.*
>
> —Komives, Lucas, & McMahon, *Exploring Leadership: For College Students Who Want to Make a Difference*

You can also help students become politically engaged by involving them in efforts to raise public awareness about important national issues (e.g., poverty and homelessness). You can help them partake in this form of civic engagement by encouraging and involving them in any of the following activities:

- Letter writing campaigns to political representatives;
- Volunteering for a political party or candidate they are passionate about;
- Attending meetings on local government or school affairs;
- Signing petitions;
- Attending political rallies; and
- Fundraising—gathering money or resources for a local, regional, national, or international need.

Studies show that the above forms of political engagement are dwindling in America (Bok, 2006; Putnam, 2000). As a civic leader, you can help restore them.

Reflection 11.4

How would you respond to students who don't vote and aren't politically active because they claim that "all politicians are the same" or "the system is corrupt and can't be changed"?

Community organizing and protest are other ways to promote political change. A recent example of this approach involved a group of people (most of them young) who rallied in various public places around the country to call attention to income inequality. They organized sit-ins and protests aimed at financial institutions they considered responsible for widening the income gap in favor of the very wealthy. Their protest movement influenced the governor of New York to reverse his initial opposition to renewing the state's "millionaire's tax" and the Los Angeles City Council to pass a "responsible banking" ordinance that requires banks to disclose details about their lending practices (Loeb, Astin, & Plamer, 2012). Also, at the time when this book was being written, a new community-organizing group called "Can Kicks Back" had just formed to give young Americans a voice in the debate over tax hikes and budget cuts. Part of their plan is to send a giant mascot in the shape of a can to at least 500 college campuses, where they hope to launch chapters in 2013, with the goal of attracting the attention of Congress to their concerns (Puzzanghera, 2012).

The Global Community

Beyond being citizens of a national community, students are also members of an international community that includes close to 200 nations (Rosenberg, 2009). The lives of citizens in every nation today are affected by events that take place in other nations. Traditional boundaries between countries are blurring and disappearing due to increased international travel, international trading, and multinational corporations; direct communication among citizens of different nations is greater today than at any other time in world history due to the explosion of information technology (Dryden & Vos, 1999; Friedman, 2005; Smith, 1994). The World Wide Web has made today's world a "small world after all," and success in it requires an international perspective.

Encourage students to take courses in international relations and to engage in experiential learning that enables them to view the world from an international perspective (e.g., study abroad). Research on students who study abroad indicates that this experience changes their perspective on the world; for example, study abroad promotes greater appreciation of international and cross-cultural differences, greater interest in world affairs, and greater commitment to peace and international cooperation (Bok, 2006; Kauffmann, Martin, & Weaver, 1992). Furthermore, research shows that study abroad also benefits students on a personal level; for example, they develop greater self-confidence, independence, and ability to function in complex environments (Bok, 2006; Carlson et al., 1990). When students learn from and about different nations, they become more than citizens of their own country—they become cosmopolitan citizens of the world, and step beyond the narrowness of national borders to become members of the global community.

The global community consists of all humanity (almost seven billion humans and still growing) from all cultures and nations. A global perspective also includes concern for other forms of life inhabiting planet earth and the earth's natural resources. We must remain mindful that we share the earth and its natural resources with approximately ten million animal species (Myers, 1997) and more than 300,000 forms of vegetative life (Knoll, 2003). Global citizenship includes being good stewards of our planet by preserving the earth's resources and guarding against human practices that threaten the earth's well-being (e.g., practices that increase global warming and decrease environmental sustainability).

As a peer leader, one way you can demonstrate civic leadership is by elevating students' global awareness and encouraging them to become engaged in causes that serve to preserve our shared humanity and our shared ecology.

The well-being of all the communities to which we belong (local, societal, national, and global) is a byproduct of the commitments and contributions of mem-

Treat the Earth well. It was not given to you by your parents. It was loaned to you by your children.
—Kenyan proverb

bers who comprise them. We have received much from our communities, and it is our obligation—our civic responsibility—to give back to them. According to Howard Gardner, internationally acclaimed psychologist, for today's students to thrive in the communities of the future, they will need to demonstrate ethical commitment—an understanding of the needs of others and a willingness to go beyond narrow self-interest and take action on broader societal and global issues (Gardner, 2008).

Serving the Community

> *We make a living by what we get; we make a life by what we give.*
>
> —Winston Churchill, English prime minister and Nobel Prize-winning author

One of the most powerful forms of civic engagement involves people stepping beyond narrow self-interest to volunteer their time and energy to help other members of their community. Community volunteers measure their success as much by what they do for others as by what they do for themselves. They are *humane*—they have compassion for humans less fortunate than themselves—and they are *humanitarian*—they have passion for helping humans in need, such as the sick and the poor, the weak and the handicapped, the very young and the very old.

Reflection 11.5

Have you engaged in a volunteer (community service) effort that you thought was especially meaningful, gratifying, or rewarding? If you have, what made it such a powerful experience?

What or who motivated you to get involved in the first place?

Students can engage in community service through such volunteer activities as tutoring, working in a soup kitchen, or engaging in community cleanup. Additional target areas for community service activities are summarized in Box 11.3.

Box 11.3   Target Areas for Community Service

Community renewal. Helping people who have lost their jobs or their homes by supplying food and donating clothing.

Disaster preparedness. Helping communities prepare for natural disasters (e.g., hurricanes, floods, and earthquakes).

Education. Helping to close the learning gap for educationally underprivileged children by tutoring, reading with children, or organizing book drives.

Energy and environment. Helping members of the community reduce energy costs and preserve their environmental resources.

Health. Helping members of the community make healthy lifestyle choices to prevent costly disease and improve their quality of life.

Hunger. Feeding hungry families in the community and organizing food drives.

Veterans and military families. Supporting military families and injured veterans who have served our country.

Source: Corporation for National & Community Service (2010).

Author's Experience I've been amazed, delighted, and at times even awestruck by the service projects that teams of students have created and implemented. I admire the capacities of student leaders to inspire and mobilize fellow students and the spirit and generosity of the countless students who participate. I've seen students gather clothing and other resources for a local needy family of seven children, construct and deliver hundreds of Halloween cards for sick children at a local hospital, assemble and mail "goody bags" for troops overseas, assemble Relay for Life teams, put together dodgeball tournaments to raise money for local charities, and create a video for *Extreme Home Makeover* to rehabilitate a community center in Haiti ravaged by an earthquake.

Students enjoy participating and making a difference. So much is possible. It just requires some imaginative thinking, some inspiration, some organization, and some follow-through. As leaders, you can help turn these possibilities into realities.

— *Greg Metz*

As a peer leader, you can enable students to engage in community service by keeping them informed about opportunities that are available and how they can take advantage of them. It's likely that your campus has a centralized office or person that organizes volunteer opportunities and works with various local, regional, and national organizations (for example, see a description of the University of Cincinnati's Community Service Office at www.uc.edu/sas/cce/default.html).

You can also seek leads for volunteer opportunities from campus advisors, student development professionals, and faculty members. Consider creating a website or bulletin board that alerts and updates students about community service opportunities, and make it as easy as possible for students to capitalize on these opportunities by including the specific steps and contact information they need to make it happen.

Another way you can help engage students in community service is by encouraging them to enroll in service learning courses that integrate community service into their course work, and to choose research projects that allow them to help with current social problems or issues in the local community. In particular, encourage students to consider options outside of their normal zones of familiarity and comfort. Studies show that students benefit most from community service experiences that enable them to interact with people from diverse groups with whom they've had little or no prior experience (Astin et al., 2000; Gurin et al., 2002; Vogelgesang & Astin, 2000).

You can also model the way by engaging in community service yourself, or doing it together with your students and creating opportunities for everyone to come together and share their experiences. If and when students do volunteer, be sure to acknowledge their contributions.

Be prepared to encounter resistance from students about volunteering. You're likely to hear the following explanations or excuses (1) "I'm too busy with schoolwork.", (2) "I have a job.", (3) "That's not my thing." You certainly don't want to dismiss students' particular concerns and unique circumstances, but you can still encourage their involvement by helping them identify the amount or type of service appropriate to their circumstances. Don't come across as preachy or sanctimonious, but do supportively encourage and sensitively challenge students to become involved by being a role model for volunteerism and by pointing out the many ways in which community service benefits them, such as those described below.

Reflection 11.6

Where, or from whom, can you learn about the variety of volunteer or service opportunities available on your campus and in the surrounding community?

Advantages of Community Service

> *It is one of the beautiful compensations of this life that no one can sincerely try to help another without helping himself.*
>
> —Ralph Waldo Emerson, 19th-century American essayist, poet, and leader of the Transcendentalist movement

Research indicates that participation in community service promotes deep learning and intellectual development (Gurin et al., 2002; Zlotkowsky, 2002). Community service is often referred to as service learning or community-based learning, particularly if students reflect and connect their service experiences to what they're learning in class and to other "hands-on" learning experiences they're having outside the classroom. In addition, when students volunteer their services to others and contribute to the welfare of their community, they experience gains in self-esteem and self-satisfaction (Astin et al., 2000; Vogelgesang et al., 2002). Doing something to improve the lives of others makes the people doing it feel like they're doing something meaningful with their own lives. Studies show that individuals who go beyond themselves to focus on the needs of others are more likely to report feeling personally fulfilled and happy (Myers, 1993).

Furthermore, students who engage in community service benefit themselves by engaging in a form of experiential learning that promotes their career-success skills, such as teamwork, problem solving, decision making, intercultural communication skills, and leadership (Astin et al., 2000; National Association of Colleges & Employers, 2007). The consensus building that often takes place when students collaborate on community service projects also prepares students for the type of balanced thinking and participative decision making they are expected to use when performing other civic responsibilities, such as jury duty and bipartisan leadership.

Community service also supplies students with opportunities to learn about careers related to their areas of service and equips them with resume-building experiences that may be directly relevant to their future careers or professions—as illustrated by the following story:

Author's Experience A few years ago, members of a Communication Sciences and Speech Disorders Learning Community at the University of Cincinnati made Valentine's Day cards for the residents of a local nursing home. The students subsequently arranged a visit to the home to present the cards to the residents and mingle with them. Not only did this make the day of the residents, it also provided students in the field of speech and hearing with the opportunity to gain career-relevant experience with the population of people with whom they will eventually work: the elderly.

— *Greg Metz*

Community service can also provide students with real-world experience that helps them determine what careers best fit their interests, needs, and talents—as reflected by the experiences of the two students in the following story:

Author's Experience I was once advising two first-year students, Kim and Christopher. Kim was thinking about becoming a physical therapist and Chris was considering a career as an elementary school teacher. I suggested to Kim that she visit the hospital near our college to see whether she could volunteer in the physical therapy unit. As it turned out, the hospital needed help, so she volunteered in the physical therapy unit—and just loved it. That volunteer experience confirmed for her that physical therapy was the career she wanted to pursue. She completed a degree in physical therapy and is now a professional physical therapist.

I suggested to Chris, the student who was thinking about becoming an elementary school teacher, that he visit some local schools to see whether they could use a volunteer teacher's aide. One of the schools did need his services, so Chris volunteered as a teacher's aide for about ten weeks. At the halfway point during his volunteer experience, he came into my office to tell me that the kids were just about driving him crazy and he no longer had any interest at all in becoming a teacher! He ended up majoring in communications.

Kim and Chris were the first two students I advised to get involved in volunteer work to test their career interests. Their volunteer experiences turned out to be so valuable for helping them clarify their future career paths that I've continued to encourage all students I advise to get volunteer experience in the fields they're considering as possible careers.

— *Joe Cuseo*

Reflection 11.7

Are you optimistic about your capacity to get other students involved in volunteer or service efforts? Why?

Summary and Conclusion

A leader's influence can extend beyond an individual, a group, or an organization to the larger society. Colleges and universities are places where the ideals of a community can be put into practice. You can start this process by advising students, particularly college students, on how civility is displayed in the college classroom. In addition to combating incivility on campus, you can promote campus community by involving students in campus traditions and rituals (or help create them if they don't already exist). Such practices serve to unite students by connecting them to the campus and to each other. Stronger campus communities are also created through the sharing of common space. You can take a leadership role in strengthening the sense of community on your campus by creating or advocating for spaces and places where students can come together and engage with others who share common interests and experiences. You can also encourage students' civic engagement by encouraging them to participate in college governance, campus elections, and political organizations on campus. Lastly, as a peer leader, you can foster active citizenship by using democratic processes to run student organizations, such as participative decision-making practices.

In addition to being members of their campus community, students are members of the *local community*—the neighborhood in which they live or go to school.

You can begin to practice civic leadership by encouraging and organizing students to serve the local community surrounding your campus.

Moving beyond local communities, students are also members of a larger *society*—a group of people organized under the same social system. Society is stratified into groups of people with unequal levels of social and economic capital. Groups occupying lower socioeconomic strata have poorer educational and social-networking opportunities. One way in which you can serve as a civic leader is by engaging students in volunteer experiences that are specially intended to help members of society who have fewer educational opportunities and socioeconomic privileges.

In addition to being members of society, students are also citizens of a nation. The privilege of living in a free nation brings with it the responsibility of participating in the nation's governance through the voting process. In a democracy, voting is not just a political thing to do; it's the patriotic thing to do. The quality of a democracy depends on citizens who learn deeply and think critically, and who can apply these skills to the voting process by making wise, well-informed decisions about whom they elect. As a peer leader, you can serve as a learning coach to help students learn deeply and think critically, and you can help them apply these skills to the voting process by encouraging them to vote in national, state, and local elections.

Beyond being citizens of a national community, students are also members of an international community that includes close to 200 nations. The lives of citizens in every nation today are affected by events that take place in other nations. The World Wide Web has made today's world a "small world after all," and success in it requires an international perspective. Encourage students to take courses in international relations and to engage in experiential learning that enables them to view the world from an international perspective (e.g., study abroad). When students learn from and about different nations, they become more than citizens of their own country—they become cosmopolitan citizens of the world and step beyond the narrowness of national borders to become members of the global community.

A global perspective also includes concern for other forms of life inhabiting planet earth and the earth's natural resources. We must remain mindful that we share the earth and its natural resources with approximately ten million animal species and more than 300,000 forms of vegetative life. Global citizenship includes being good stewards of our planet by preserving the earth's resources and guarding against human practices that threaten the earth's well-being. As a peer leader, one way you can demonstrate civic leadership is by elevating students' global awareness and encouraging them to become engaged in causes that serve to preserve our shared humanity and our shared ecology.

One of the most powerful forms of civic engagement involves people stepping beyond narrow self-interest to volunteer their time and energy to help other members of their community. As a peer leader, you can enable students to engage in community service by keeping them informed about opportunities that are available and how they can take advantage of them. In particular, encourage students to consider volunteer opportunities that take them outside of their normal zones of familiarity and comfort.

Supportively encourage and sensitively challenge students to become involved by being a role model for volunteerism and by pointing out the many ways in which community service benefits them, including deep learning and intellectual development, increased self-esteem, and personal fulfillment. Community service also supplies students with opportunities to learn about careers related to their areas of service and equips them with resume-building experiences that are directly relevant to their future careers or professions, such as teamwork, problem solving, decision making, intercultural communication, and leadership. Remind students that by helping others, they're also helping themselves.

Internet Resources

For additional information related to the ideas discussed in this chapter, we recommend the following websites:

Community Service

www.nationalservice.gov

This is a nationwide online resource for locating volunteer opportunities in your community and for creating your own; it is the website for the Corporation for National and Community Service, a federal agency that leads President Obama's national call to service initiative, "United We Serve."

www.payitforwardfoundation.org

Website for the Pay It Forward Foundation, an organization started by a small group of University of Minnesota students who wanted to find a way for students to do things to improve their world, both locally and internationally. They created a group called "Students Today, Leaders Forever" (STLF). Their main event each year is the "Pay It Forward" tour, during which college students spend their spring break on a bus trip to several cities and engaging in community service projects, with the idea that those they serve will, in turn, "pay it forward" and do the same for other members of their community.

www.ysa.org/servicevote

Home page for Youth Service America, an organization that improves communities by increasing the number and diversity of young people ages five to 25 who become engaged in community service, service learning, and leadership.

www.americorps.gov

Home page for AmeriCorps, a governmental organization that addresses critical needs in communities all across America. AmeriCorps is made up of three main programs:

1. AmeriCorps State and National supports a broad range of local service programs that engage thousands of Americans in intensive service to meet critical community needs.
2. AmeriCorps Volunteers in Service to America (VISTA) is a national service program designed specifically to fight poverty.
3. AmeriCorps National Civilian Community Corps (NCCC) is a full-time residential program for 18- to 24-year-olds that's designed to strengthen communities while developing leaders through their involvement in direct, team-based national and community service projects.

www.peacecorps.gov

The Peace Corps originated in 1960, when then Senator John F. Kennedy challenged students at the University of Michigan to serve their country in the cause of peace by living and working in developing countries. Since then, Peace Corps volunteers from the U.S. have served in close to 140 countries to help their citizens with issues such as AIDS education, information technology, and environmental preservation.

Voting and Political Engagement

www.aascu.org/programs/ADP

Website of the American Democracy Project (ADP), a multi-campus initiative focused on higher education's role in preparing the next generation of informed, engaged citizens for our democracy. The project began in 2003 as an initiative of the American Association of State Colleges and Universities (AASCU), in partnership with *The New York Times*.

www.compact.org/initiatives/campus-vote-home

Home page for Campus Compact's election engagement resources and the Campus Election Engagement Project, a related effort led by Paul Loeb, author of *Soul of a Citizen*, who works with Campus Compact to help get students involved in elections.

www.rockthevote.com

Website for Rock the Vote, an organization that uses music, popular culture, new technologies, and grassroots organizing strategies to motivate and mobilize young people across the country to participate in every election and use their right to vote to foster political and social change.

Community Organizing

www.communitychange.org

Website for the Center for Community Change, a national organization whose mission is to build the power and capacity of low-income citizens to improve their communities to change the political policies that adversely affect their lives.

www.npa-us.org

Home page for the National People's Action (NPA), a direct-action community organizing group devoted to issues relating to economic and racial justice. It has over 200 organizers working to unite everyday people in cities, towns, and rural communities.

Exercise 11.1 *Journal Reflections*

1. When you hear the word *political*, what thoughts or images come to your mind?

2. When you hear the word *community*, what thoughts or images come to your mind?

3. On a scale of 1–5 (5 = high; 1 = low), how would you rate your campus in terms of how it embodies the following six principles of a campus community?

   - An educationally purposeful community. The campus is a place where faculty and students share academic goals and work together to strengthen teaching and learning.

     Rating:

     Reason for rating:

   - An open community. The campus is a place where freedom of expression and differences of opinion are accepted and protected, and where civility is affirmed.

     Rating:

     Reason for rating:

   - A just community. The campus is a place where the sacredness of each person is honored and where diversity is aggressively pursued.

     Rating:

     Reason for rating:

- A disciplined community. The campus is a place where individuals accept their obligations to the group and where well-defined governance procedures guide behavior for the common good.

  Rating:

  Reason for rating:

- A caring community. The campus is a place where the well-being of each member is sensitively supported and where service to others is encouraged. (This is the glue that makes the first four principles work; caring is the key to establishing a place where every individual's feelings are affirmed.)

  Rating:

  Reason for rating:

- A celebrative community. A place where the heritage of the institution is remembered and where rituals affirming both tradition and change are widely shared.

  Rating:

  Reason for rating:

Exercise 11.2 *Getting Students Involved in the Voting Process*

1. Go to www.compact.org/initiatives/campus-vote-home. This is the home page for the Campus Election Engagement Project, a nationwide effort to help get students involved in elections.

2. Click on the link titled "Checklist of Things to Do" and print out the checklist.

3. Share the checklist with your students and ask for volunteers to take responsibility for implementing different items on the checklist.

Exercise 11.3 *Promoting Political Knowledge and Engagement*

1. Go to www.aascu.org/programs/ADP. This is the site of the American Democracy Project (ADP), an initiative of the American Association of State Colleges and Universities (AASCU), in partnership with *The New York Times*, whose mission is to prepare the next generation of informed, engaged citizens for our democracy.

2. Click the link titled "Civic Engagement in Action Series" and print out each of the topics in this series (listed in the side margin).

3. Share this list with your students and discuss whether any of these action items could and should be pursued by members of your student organization, or the student body at large.

Exercise 11.4 *Identifying and Organizing Local Community Service Opportunities*

1. Go to www.nationalservice.gov. This is a nationwide online resource for locating volunteer opportunities in your community.

2. In the "Find an Opportunity" window, type in a category of service that would interest you and the students you lead (e.g., poverty, education, veterans).

3. From the list of possibilities that comes up, choose three that you think would be most interesting to you and your students.

4. Ask the students you work with to reach consensus on what their first choice would be and contact that organization to discuss ways in which your student group could help advance its cause.

Exercise 11.5 *Creating Service Opportunities at Local, National, and International Levels*

1. Go to www.payitforwardfoundation.org. This is the Pay It Forward Foundation, an organization started by a small group of University of Minnesota students who wanted to find a way for students to do things to improve their world, both locally and internationally.

2. Click on the "How to Get Involved Video" and show it to your students.

3. If any of your students show interest or excitement about getting involved in this organization, ask them to follow up by contacting the person whose contact information is listed at the end of the video.

4. Have those students report back to your group about what they learned and whether this is an organization that your group should join.

Exercise 11.6 *Identifying and Publicizing Service-Learning Courses*

Check your catalog or bulletin to see what courses on campus integrate community service into students' course work and compile a list of these courses that you can share with students. (If such courses are not designated in the catalog, check with the Academic Dean or Vice President for Academic Affairs.)

Leadership Self-Assessment
Assessing Your Leadership Skills and Leadership Development

Effective leaders engage in an ongoing process of assessing how they're doing and what they need to do better. This self-assessment instrument is designed to support you in this process of continuous leadership improvement. Be honest with yourself. This isn't a test of your leadership competence or potential: it's an opportunity for you to recognize your strengths and identify areas that you can target for future growth.

The leadership self-assessment questions comprising this instrument correspond to each of the 11 chapters of the book. You may encounter some questions that are difficult to answer because you haven't yet had much formal leadership experience in college. If you do, that's fine; just answer these questions on the basis of any leadership-like experiences you've had in high school or in other contexts (e.g., work or athletics). If a question asks you about something that you've had no experience with in any setting, answer on the basis of how you think you would respond.

You can answer these questions at any time during your leadership experience, either to assess you current reality (where you are right now), or to assess how you've changed and improved by answering the questions twice—before and after you've had more leadership training or experience.

When assessing yourself on the questions that comprise this instrument, use the following rating scale:

5 = Strongly Agree; 4 = Agree; 3 = Not Sure; 2 = Disagree; 1 = Strongly Disagree

Chapter 1
The Purpose and Power of Peer Leadership

_____ 1. I have a clear understanding of what *leadership* means.

_____ 2. I'm aware of the multiple ways in which peer leaders can have a positive influence on students' success in college.

_____ 3. I'm aware of the variety of roles and positions available to peer leaders on college campuses.

_____ 4. My decision to become a peer leader took place after thoughtful reflection and consideration.

_____ 5. My interest in becoming a peer leader stems from a genuine concern for helping others, not just a desire to receive social recognition or pad my resume.

_____ 6. I have learned about the personal attributes of effective leaders and attempt to embody these attributes in my work as a peer leader.

_____ 7. I take time to self-examine my leadership strengths and weaknesses.

_____ 8. I seek feedback from others on my leadership effectiveness.

_____ 9. I'm able to successfully balance the roles of being a "friend" and "mentor" to the students I lead.

_____ 10. I consult with other peer leaders and campus professionals to learn from their experiences.

Chapter 2
The Essence of Leadership

_____ 1. I have learned about leadership research and theories, and I've used that knowledge to help guide my leadership practices.

_____ 2. I have reflected on whether my personal leadership interests and talents are a good match for the leadership position I hold.

_____ 3. I'm a leader who is reliable and accountable (who can be counted on).

_____ 4. Students see me as a leader who is "real" (authentic); not phony or hypocritical.

_____ 5. I'm an honest and ethical leader.

_____ 6. I'm very aware of remaining humble; not coming across as power-hungry or boastful.

_____ 7. I model what I tell students to do.

_____ 8. I am an enthusiastic and optimistic leader.

_____ 9. I have high expectations for students and recognize their personal accomplishments and achievements.

_____ 10. I am a reflective leader who regularly reviews what I do to continually improve what I do.

_____ 11. I maintain a portfolio to track and document my leadership development.

Chapter 3
The College Experience

_____ 1. I can clearly articulate to students how college will benefit them.

_____ 2. I encourage students to invest the same amount of time and effort in their college education as they would in a full-time job.

_____ 3. I'm aware of the different types of student support services and resources on my campus.

_____ 4. I convey to students that the student support professionals on our campus care about them and can play an important role in helping them succeed.

_____ 5. I suggest to students ways in which students can become actively involved in the college experience, both inside and outside the classroom.

I promote students' social integration into the campus community by connecting them with:

_____ 6. Academic advisors.

_____ 7. Faculty.

_____ 8. Student development (student support) professionals.

_____ 9. Peers.

_____ 10. I help students see how they can take advantage of their college experience to find meaning, purpose, and direction in life.

Chapter 4
Social and Emotional Intelligence

_____ 1. Students know that I care about them and want to see them succeed.

_____ 2. I reach out to students and initiate relationships with them.

_____ 3. I get to know students on an individual basis by collecting personal information about them (e.g., their interests, talents, needs, and values).

_____ 4. I show interest in students by asking open-ended questions that encourage them to give more than one-word or one-sentence answers.

_____ 5. I ask students what they expect of me as a peer leader and mentor.

_____ 6. I'm an effective referral agent who regularly connects students to student support services and campus resources.

_____ 7. I'm good at "breaking the ice" with new students so they initially feel comfortable with me.

_____ 8. I make an intentional attempt to listen attentively and actively to students during my conversations with them.

_____ 9. I make students aware that I'm available to them if and when they need me.

_____ 10. I share my experiences with students to encourage them to share their experiences with me.

_____ 11. I remain optimistic when my students continue to make mistakes or engage in counterproductive behaviors.

_____ 12. I encourage students to remain resilient when they encounter setbacks or disappointments.

Chapter 5
Setting Goals, Managing Time, and Maintaining Motivation

_____ 1. I encourage students to set goals that will bring them closer to becoming the types of people they would like to be.

_____ 2. I stress to students the importance of setting long-range, mid-range, and short-range goals.

_____ 3. I remind students that self-awareness is the first and most important step in the goal-setting process and that meaningful goals are built on a deep understanding of oneself.

_____ 4. I help students set SMART goals—i.e., goals that are specific, meaningful, actionable, realistic, and time-framed.

_____ 5. I establish SMART goals for myself as a peer leader.

_____ 6. I continually monitor the progress I'm making toward the leadership goals I've set for myself.

_____ 7. I help students prioritize tasks they must complete to reach their goals.

_____ 8. I encourage students to plan their time and use effective time-management tools (e.g., a daily planner).

_____ 9. I follow up with students to see if they're making steady progress toward their goals.

_____ 10. I help students maintain their motivation by providing them with supportive (yet realistic) feedback and personal encouragement.

Chapter 6
Becoming a Learning Coach

_____ 1. I've taken the time to familiarize myself with research and theory on effective learning.

_____ 2. I help students understand the difference between "deep" and "shallow" learning.

_____ 3. I share effective learning strategies with students.

_____ 4. I model effective learning strategies for students to observe and emulate.

_____ 5. I provide students with feedback on their learning habits and strategies.

I encourage students to:

_____ 6. Complete assignments prior to class.

_____ 7. Take thorough notes in their classes.

_____ 8. Review their notes and reflect on them between class sessions.

_____ 9. Participate in study groups.

_____ 10. Use the results of tests and assignments as feedback to improve their future performance.

_____ 11. I can articulate to students what critical thinking is and how they can demonstrate it.

_____ 12. I remind students that learning effectively is not just a "school thing," but a process that will benefit them throughout life.

Chapter 7
Holistic Leadership

_____ 1. I'm aware of the key elements or components that comprise the "self."

_____ 2. I encourage students to set goals for developing different dimensions of self (social, emotional, physical, spiritual, etc.).

_____ 3. I take interest in each student as a "whole person" and support them in ways that go beyond just academics.

_____ 4. I can articulate the concept of "wellness" to students and why it's important.

_____ 5. I help students maintain awareness of how their eating and sleeping habits can affect their academic performance and general well-being.

_____ 6. I'm familiar with common eating disorders among college students and am able to recognize them if I see them.

_____ 7. I can recognize and explain to students what constitutes sexual abuse, sexual assault, and sexual harassment.

_____ 8. I can detect the telltale signs of substance abuse and am aware of effective strategies for helping students who may be experiencing it.

_____ 9. I'm aware of the telltale signs of anxiety and can provide students with stress-management strategies for reducing it.

_____ 10. I'm aware of the telltale signs of depression and can provide students with self-help strategies for coping with mild or moderate depression.

Chapter 8
Leading Groups

_____ 1. I am knowledgeable about group dynamics and patterns of group interaction.

_____ 2. I engage groups I lead in setting goals and monitoring their progress toward these goals.

_____ 3. I use team-building activities in the groups I lead to create a sense of interdependence and camaraderie among group members.

_____ 4. I collaborate with group members to establish ground rules (norms) for how we should interact with and treat each other.

_____ 5. I encourage the groups I lead to periodically revisit the ground rules they've established to assess whether they're working effectively.

_____ 6. I strive to improve my public speaking and presentation skills so I can communicate effectively with groups I lead.

_____ 7. I use a variety of group-interaction formats to keep group work interesting and engaging.

_____ 8. I strive to develop co-leaders for the groups I lead.

_____ 9. I request feedback from the groups I lead about the effectiveness of my group-facilitation skills.

_____ 10. I engage group members to reflect, assess, and discuss how well they're performing as a team.

_____ 11. I organize recognition and celebration events for group accomplishments.

Chapter 9
Leadership for Diversity

_____ 1. I can articulate to students the meaning and value of diversity.

_____ 2. I remind students to consider how their background (ethnicity, socioeconomic status, gender, etc.) can influence their beliefs and behaviors, and how it may have affected their access to certain opportunities and privileges.

_____ 3. I initiate discussions of diversity among students I lead.

_____ 4. I make an intentional attempt to welcome students from diverse backgrounds onto campus and into groups I lead.

_____ 5. I make a point of interacting with people from diverse backgrounds.

_____ 6. I reach out to students who appear to be isolated, segregated, or marginalized.

_____ 7. I encourage students to learn from and about different cultures.

_____ 8. I urge students to step beyond their comfort zones to interact with students who are different than themselves.

_____ 9. I intentionally form groups or teams comprised of students from diverse backgrounds.

_____ 10. I confront students who engage in stereotyping, prejudice, or discrimination.

Chapter 10
Organizational Leadership

_____ 1. I'm aware of the mission of my college or university, and I clearly and persuasively articulate the mission of my campus to others.

_____ 2. I can articulate the mission and vision of my student organization to others and how it relates to the campus mission.

_____ 3. I periodically review the mission and vision of my organization with its members to ensure that we are faithfully implementing it and modeling it.

_____ 4. I understand the difference between authoritative and authoritarian decision making, and I engage members of my organization in participative decision making.

_____ 5. I disperse leadership across my organization by delegating responsibility to different groups and committees.

_____ 6. I'm aware of the purpose of committees and task forces, and I use them effectively to help my organization accomplish its mission and goals.

_____ 7. I establish procedural rules to ensure that meetings of my organization run in an orderly and equitable manner.

_____ 8. At all organizational meetings I facilitate, an agenda is set and minutes are kept.

_____ 9. I read the campus newspaper regularly to learn about sources of student interest, concern, and dissatisfaction that I may help address as a peer leader.

_____ 10. I question and supportively challenge campus processes, policies, and practices that appear to be unfair or are interfering with the quality of education experienced by students.

Chapter 11
Civic Leadership

_____ 1. I can articulate to students the meaning and value of community and the different types of communities to which they belong.

_____ 2. I challenge students to display civility as members of their campus community (both inside and outside the classroom) and confront students who do not.

_____ 3. I can articulate to students the meaning and importance of civic engagement.

_____ 4. I engage in community service activities.

_____ 5. I alert students to community service opportunities.

_____ 6. I can articulate to students the variety of benefits they experience by engaging in community service.

_____ 7. I help organize community service projects.

_____ 8. I encourage students to take on leadership roles in community service projects.

_____ 9. I urge students to vote in national, local, and campus elections.

_____ 10. I encourage students to become engaged in political efforts to help solve current and recurrent social problems (e.g., poverty and homelessness).

Leadership
A Matter of Character

The Meaning and Value of Character

Throughout this book, you have acquired knowledge about effective leadership strategies and tactics. However, successful leadership ultimately emerges from the inside out; it's grounded in and grows from a collection of positive qualities and attributes found within you, known as your *character*.

Leaders become powerful change agents when their strategies and actions are a natural extension of who we are and how we live. The observable leadership behaviors they display reflect inner virtues—qualities that are valued as good, admirable, and worthy of emulation by others. A person who possesses an integrated collection of virtues is said to be a person of character (Peterson & Seligman, 2004). The character of an effective and committed leader comprises a constellation of five core virtues:

1. Wisdom,
2. Integrity,
3. Drive,
4. Discipline, and
5. Determination.

> *If you do not find it within yourself, where will you go to get it?*
>
> —Zen saying (Zen is a branch of Buddhism that emphasizes seeing deeply into the nature of things and ongoing self-awareness)

> *If you don't live it, it won't come out of your horn.*
>
> —Charlie "Bird" Parker, famous jazz saxophonist, composer, and originator of Bebop

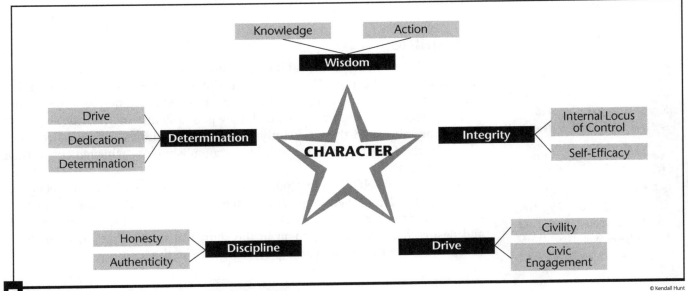

Figure E.1 Five Virtues Possessed by People of Character

© Kendall Hunt

Wisdom

We demonstrate wisdom when we use the knowledge we acquire to guide our actions toward doing what's best and what's right (Staudinger & Baltes, 1994). By applying the knowledge you've acquired in this book to guide yourself toward the most influential and most ethical leadership behavior, you're exhibiting wisdom.

Leaders with character do not pursue success and influence at any ethical cost. They have a strong set of personal values that serves as a rudder to steer them in the right moral direction. Besides doing the most effective thing, they do the right thing.

Integrity

The word *integrity* comes from the same root as the word *integrate*. The fact that these two words stem from a single source captures the key characteristic of people with integrity: their outer selves are integrated and in harmony with their inner selves. They've "got it together" in the sense that their inner character and outer behavior are in sync—what they think and feel match what they say and do. The actions of leaders with integrity are grounded in and driven by an internal conscience; not by a need to seek external recognition, status, or power. They do it to be part of something rather than the center of everything; they do it for the cause, not the applause.

Drive

Drive is the force within us that supplies us with the energy and passion to initiate action. People with drive are not just dreamers; they're also doers. Influential leaders are initiators who take the action needed to convert their dreams into reality; they hustle—they go all out and give it their all, all of the time, to achieve their goals. They don't hold back and work halfheartedly; they put their whole heart and soul into it. Studies show that individuals who are deeply committed to what they do are not only more successful, they're also healthier and happier (Csikszentmihalyi, 1990; Maddi, 2002; Myers, 1993).

Discipline

Discipline is a character trait that includes such positive qualities as commitment, devotion, and dedication. These are the attributes that enable us to keep going and moving toward our long-range goals over an extended period of time. Successful leaders think big but start small; they patiently take all the little steps that need to be taken and they diligently do all the tiny things that must be done, which, in the long run, add up to a big accomplishment—achievement of their leadership goals.

Leaders with self-discipline put in the day-to-day sweat, toil, and perspiration needed to attain their long-term leadership goals. They're willing to tolerate short-term strain or pain for long-term gain. They sacrifice the immediate needs and desires that may satisfy them in the short run to do what's needed to get them, and those they lead, where they want to be in the long run.

Determination

People with determination pursue their goals with relentless intensity and tenacity. They have the fortitude to persist in the face of frustration and the resiliency to bounce back after setbacks. If they run into something along the road to their goal that's hard to do, they work harder at doing it. When they bump into a barrier, they don't let it stand in their way by giving up or giving in; instead, they dig deeper and keep going. Studies of highly successful people in all fields, including leadership, show that their success was achieved not solely by the grace of natural talent, but required very high levels of effort, determination, and dedicated practice (Gladwell, 2008; Levitin, 2006).

People with determination also seek challenges, such as the challenge of leadership. Research shows that those who continually seek challenges and opportunities for personal growth and self-development throughout life are more likely to report higher levels of health and happiness (Maddi, 2002; Myers, 1993). Rather than remaining stagnant and simply doing what's safe, secure, or easy, they stay hungry and display an ongoing commitment to self-improvement; they keep striving and driving to be the best they can possibly be in all aspects of life. Similarly, successful leaders are those who continuously challenge themselves to be the best leaders they can be by assessing where they are, identifying what they need to know or do to get better, and monitoring whether they're actually getting better. The extensive self-assessment instrument found in the Appendix to this book (pp. 321–327) is designed to help you engage in this process of continuous leadership improvement.

> *Give the world the best you have, and it may never be enough; give the world the best you've got anyway.*
>
> —Mother Teresa, Catholic missionary nun and recipient of the Nobel Peace Prize

> *SUCCESS is peace of mind which is a direct result of self-satisfaction in knowing you made the effort to become the best that you are capable of becoming.*
>
> —John Wooden, college basketball coach and creator of the "Pyramid of Success"

Conclusion and Farewell

We hope that the ideas presented in this book will propel you to a fast start as a peer leader and will continue to contribute to your leadership success throughout college and beyond. Remember that it takes time for any effective skill to take hold and take effect; the same is true for leadership. At first, developing the habits associated with outstanding leadership requires focused concentration and intentional effort because these behaviors may be new to you. However, when you engage in these actions consistently, they are eventually transformed into natural habits.

When we repeatedly engage in good habits regularly, they become integral elements of who we are; they become part of our character. If you remain patient and continue to use the effective strategies and exhibit the virtuous traits described in this book, the impact of your leadership efforts will accumulate and eventuate in your making a real difference in the lives of those you lead.

> *We are what we repeatedly do. Excellence, then, is not an act, but a habit.*
>
> —Aristotle, ancient Greek philosopher

> *Sow an act and you reap a habit; sow a habit and you reap a character; sow a character and you reap a destiny.*
>
> —Frances E. Willard, 19th-century American educator and women's rights activist

Sincerely,

Greg Metz, Joe Cuseo, & Aaron Thompson

P.S.: We'd love to receive any feedback you can provide us about this book. Let us know what you tried and how it worked. Your comments will be read carefully and seriously considered.

We're also interested in your ideas about how we can improve our work; we'll make every effort to incorporate your suggestions into the next edition of this book.

Send your feedback to:

Paul Carty
Director of Publishing Partnerships
Kendall Hunt Publishing Company
4050 Westmark Drive
Dubuque, IA 52002
pcarty@kendallhunt.com

We'll be sure to write back to you.

index